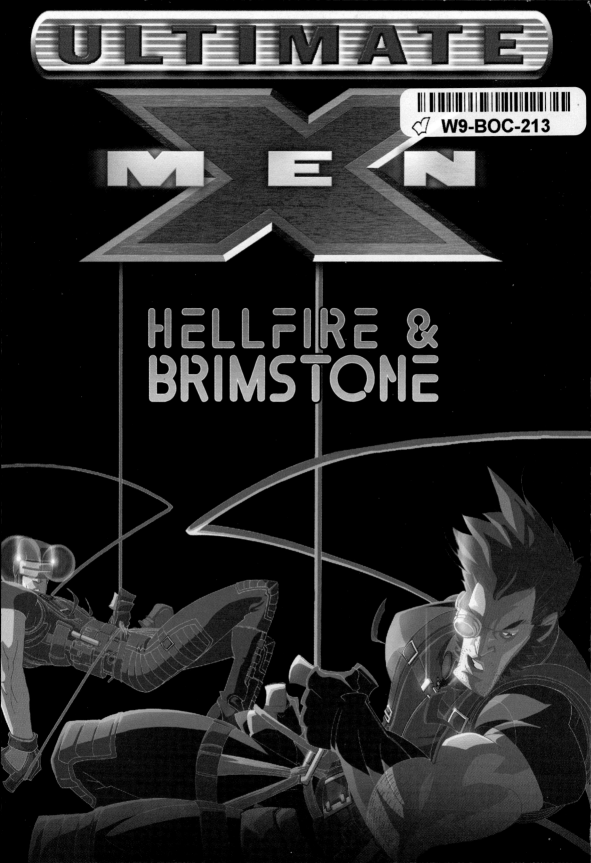

# ULTIMATE X-MEN

## HELLFIRE & BRIMSTONE

**ULTIMATE X-MEN VOL. 4: HELLFIRE & BRIMSTONE.** Contains material originally published in magazine form as ULTIMATE X-MEN #21-25. First printing 2003. ISBN# 0-7851-1089-5. Published by MARVEL COMICS, a division of MARVEL ENTERTAINMENT GROUP, INC. OFFICE OF PUBLICATION: 10 East 40th Street, New York, NY 10016. Copyright © 2002 and 2003 Marvel Characters, Inc. All rights reserved. $12.99 per copy in the U.S. and $21.00 in Canada (GST #R127032852); Canadian Agreement #40668537. All charac-ters featured in this issue and the distinctive names and likenesses thereof, and all related indicia are trademarks of Marvel Characters, Inc. No similarity between any of the names, characters, persons, and/or institutions in this magazine with those of any living or dead person or institution is intended, and any such similarity which may exist is purely coincidental. **Printed in Canada.** STAN LEE, Chairman Emeritus. For information regarding advertising in Marvel Comics or on Marvel.com, please contact Russell Brown, Executive Vice President, Consumer Products, Promotions and Media Sales at 212-576-8561 or rbrown@marvel.com

10 9 8 7 6 5 4 3 2 1

## Story
### Mark Millar

## Art
### Issues #21-22 & #25: Adam Kubert & Danny Miki
### Issues #23-24: Kaare Andrews

**Colors**
Issues #21-22: Dave Stewart
Issue #25: Chris Sotomayor

**Digital Paints**
Issues #23-24: Dave McCaig
with Chris Sotomayor

**Letters**
Chris Eliopoulos

**Cover**
Adam Kubert & Richard Isanove

**Associate Editors**
C.B.Cebulski
Brian Smith

**Editor**
Ralph Macchio

**Editor in chief**
Joe Quesada

**President**
Bill Jemas

# PREVIOUSLY IN ULTIMATE X-MEN:

Professor Charles Xavier brought them together to bridge the gap between man and mutant: Cyclops. Marvel Girl. Storm. Iceman. Beast. Colossus. Wolverine. They are The X-Men, soldiers for Xavier's dream of peaceful coexistence.

But now this dream may be dead!

After a madcap chase across Europe, The X-Men were finally able to catch up with and confront Xavier's mutant son, Proteus. They were able to end his deadly rampage, but not without paying a heavy toll themselves; left with no choice, they were forced to abandon their peaceful directives and kill Proteus; psychic mutant Betsy Braddock sacrificed her own life; and Iceman sustained life-threatening injuries in the battle. All the death and destruction is more than Xavier had ever bargained for and he decides to disband The X-Men!

Xavier concludes that he has been much too idealistic in his hopes of bringing man and mutants together in peaceful co-existence. In order to put everything right, Xavier makes the decision that he must also remove the psychic blocks he placed in the mind of the deadly mutant Magneto. However, when he finally confronts Erik Lensherr, the civilian persona he created for the brainwashed Magneto, Xavier is quite shocked. He learns that Erik has embraced his dream and romantic ideals of his own free will. This revelation proves to Xavier that the cause is still worth fighting for and he reinstates The X-Men!

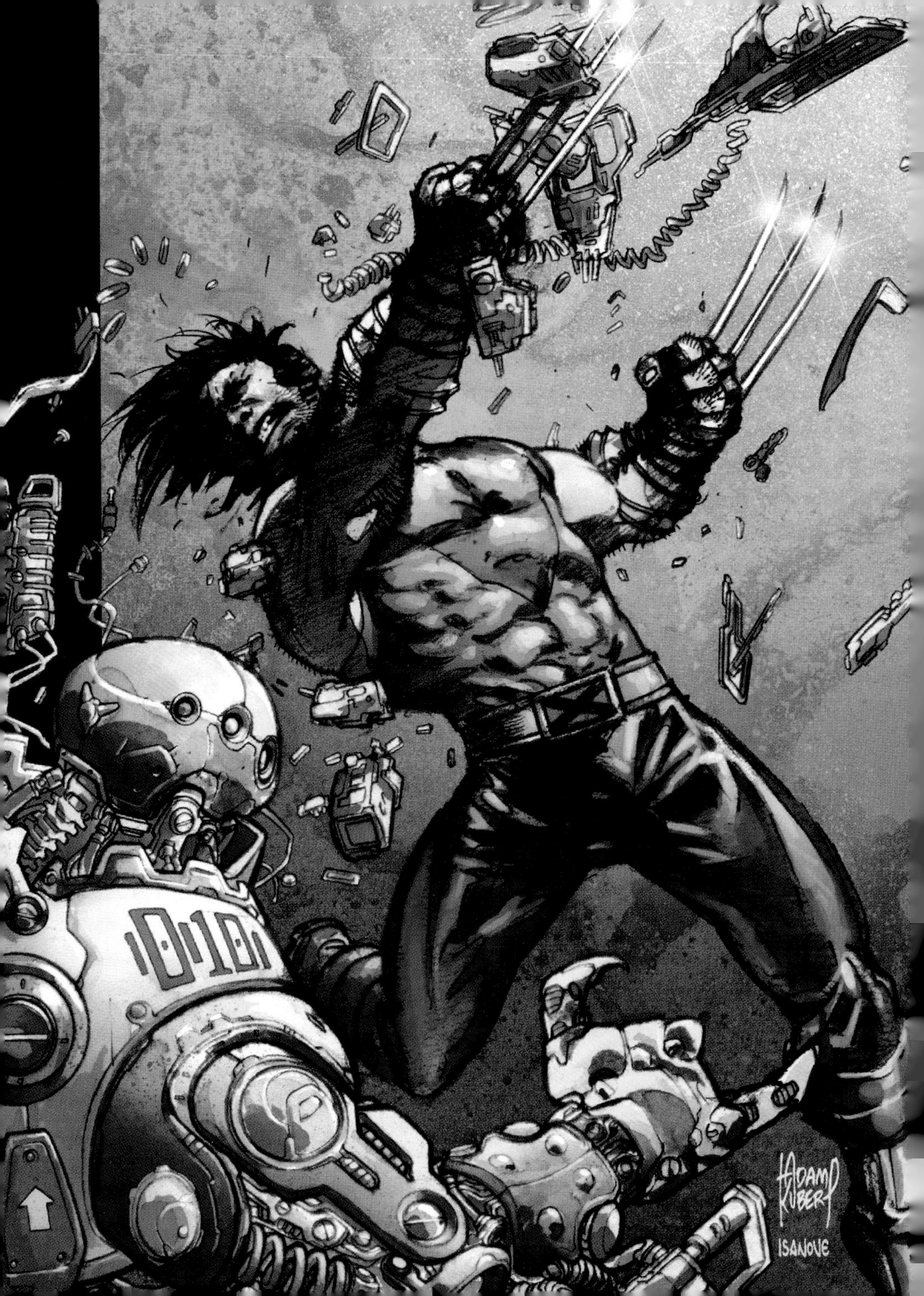
ADAM KUBERT
ISANOVE

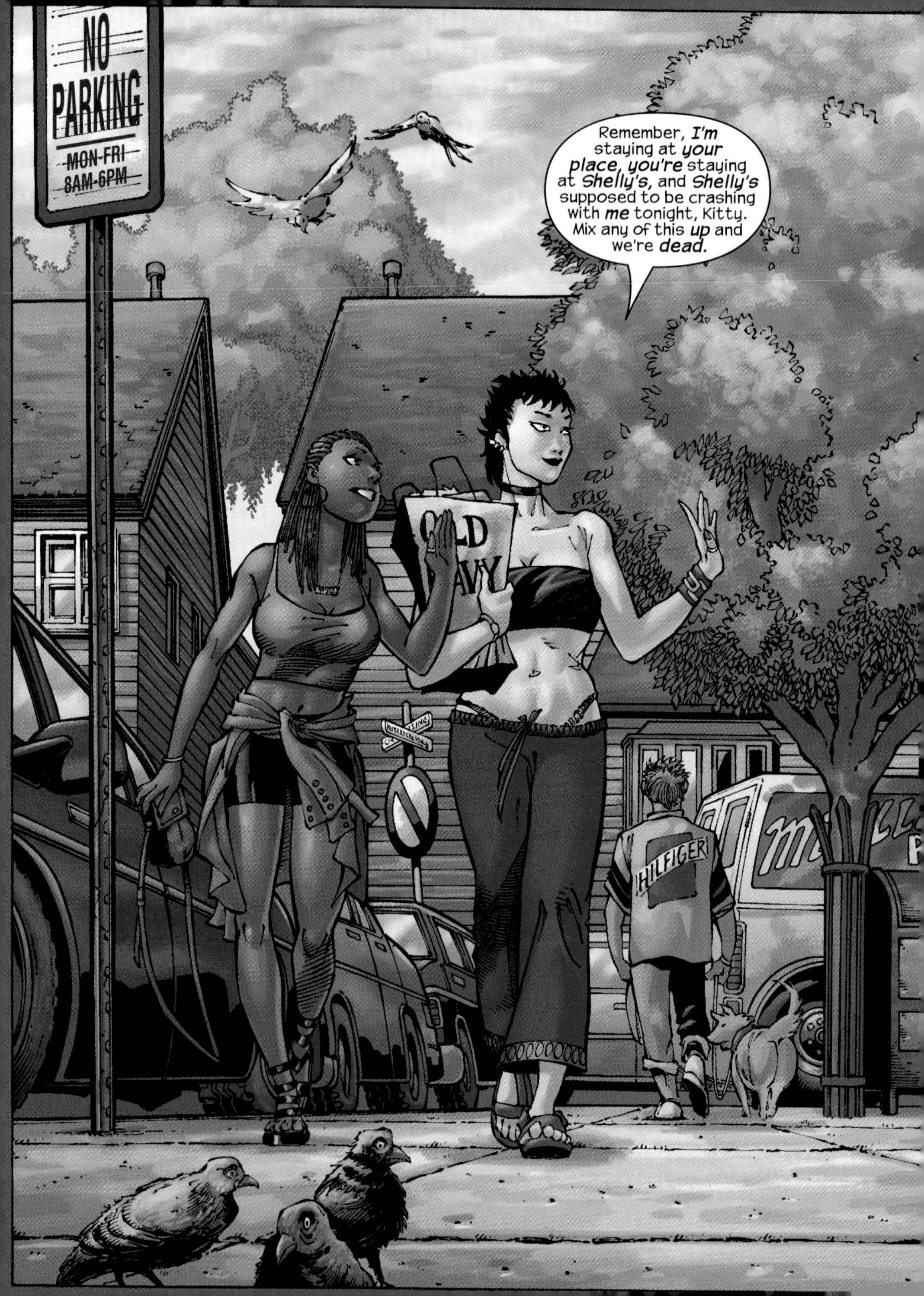
NO PARKING
MON-FRI
8AM-6PM
Remember, I'm staying at your place, you're staying at Shelly's, and Shelly's supposed to be crashing with me tonight, Kitty. Mix any of this up and we're dead.
OLD NAVY
HILFIGER

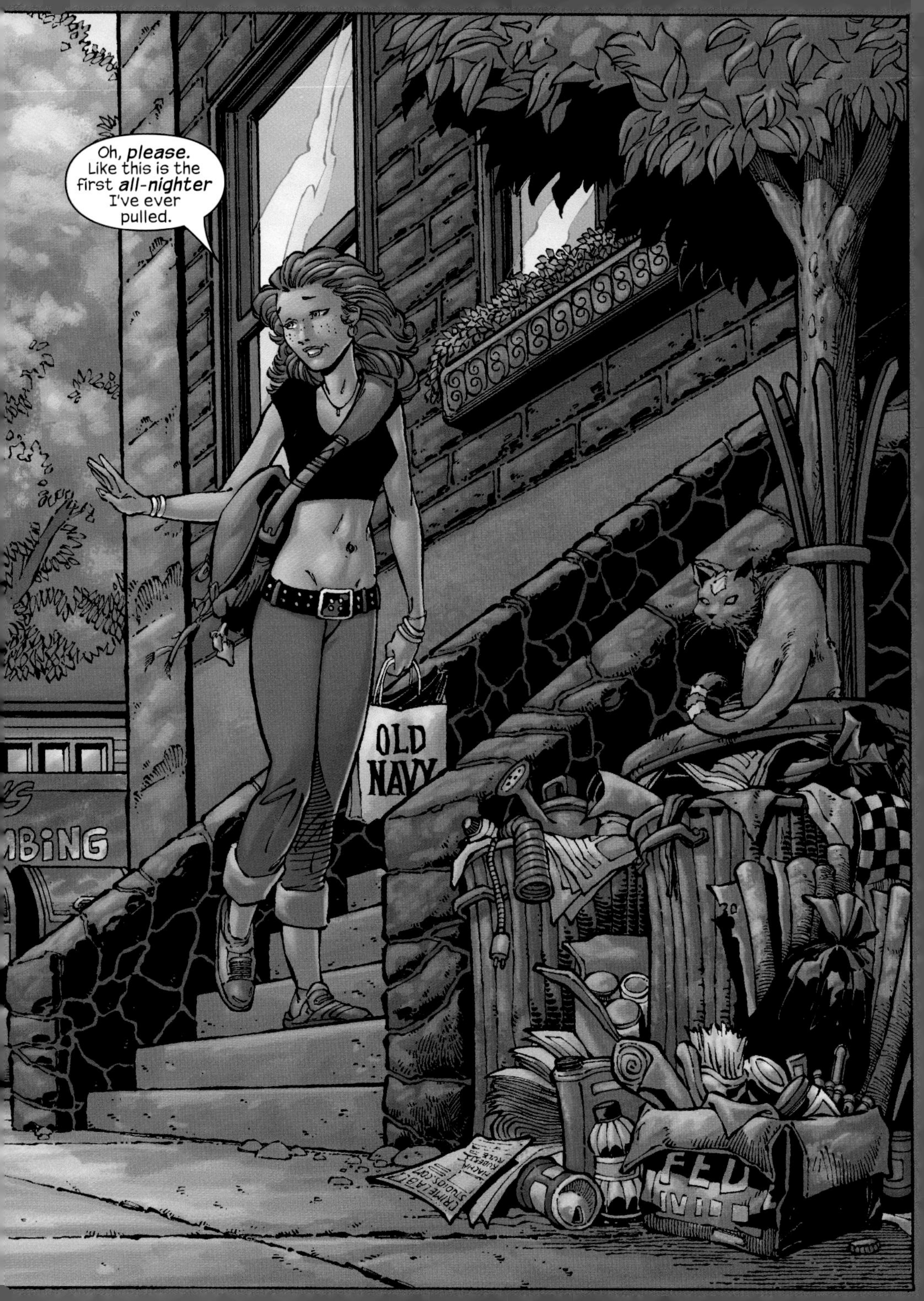
Oh, *please.* Like this is the first ***all-nighter*** I've ever pulled.
OLD NAVY

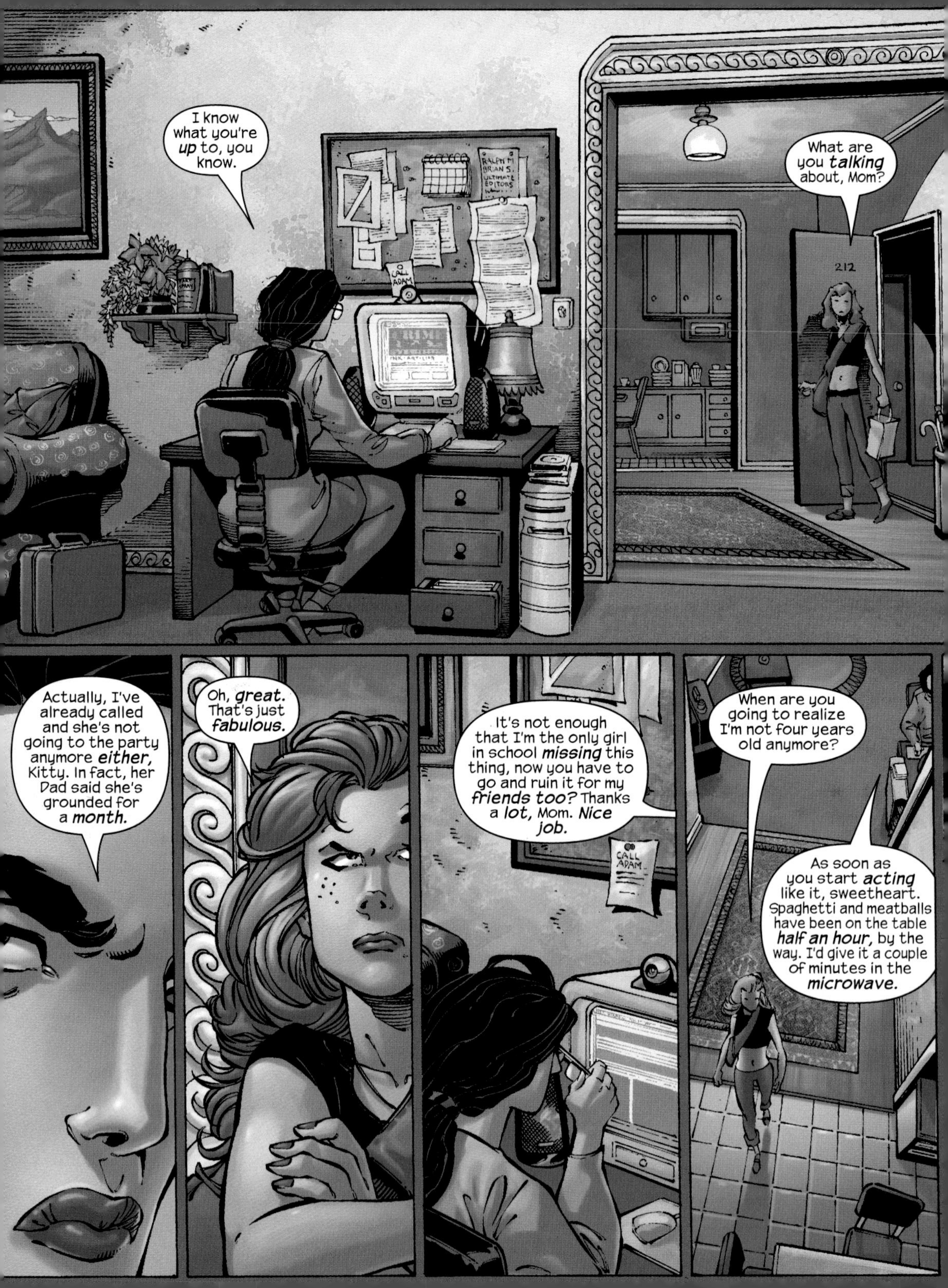
I know what you're up to, you know.
What are you talking about, Mom?
Actually, I've already called and she's not going to the party anymore either, Kitty. In fact, her Dad said she's grounded for a month.
Oh, great. That's just fabulous.
It's not enough that I'm the only girl in school missing this thing, now you have to go and ruin it for my friends too? Thanks a lot, Mom. Nice job.
When are you going to realize I'm not four years old anymore?
As soon as you start acting like it, sweetheart. Spaghetti and meatballs have been on the table half an hour, by the way. I'd give it a couple of minutes in the microwave.
CALL ADAM
212

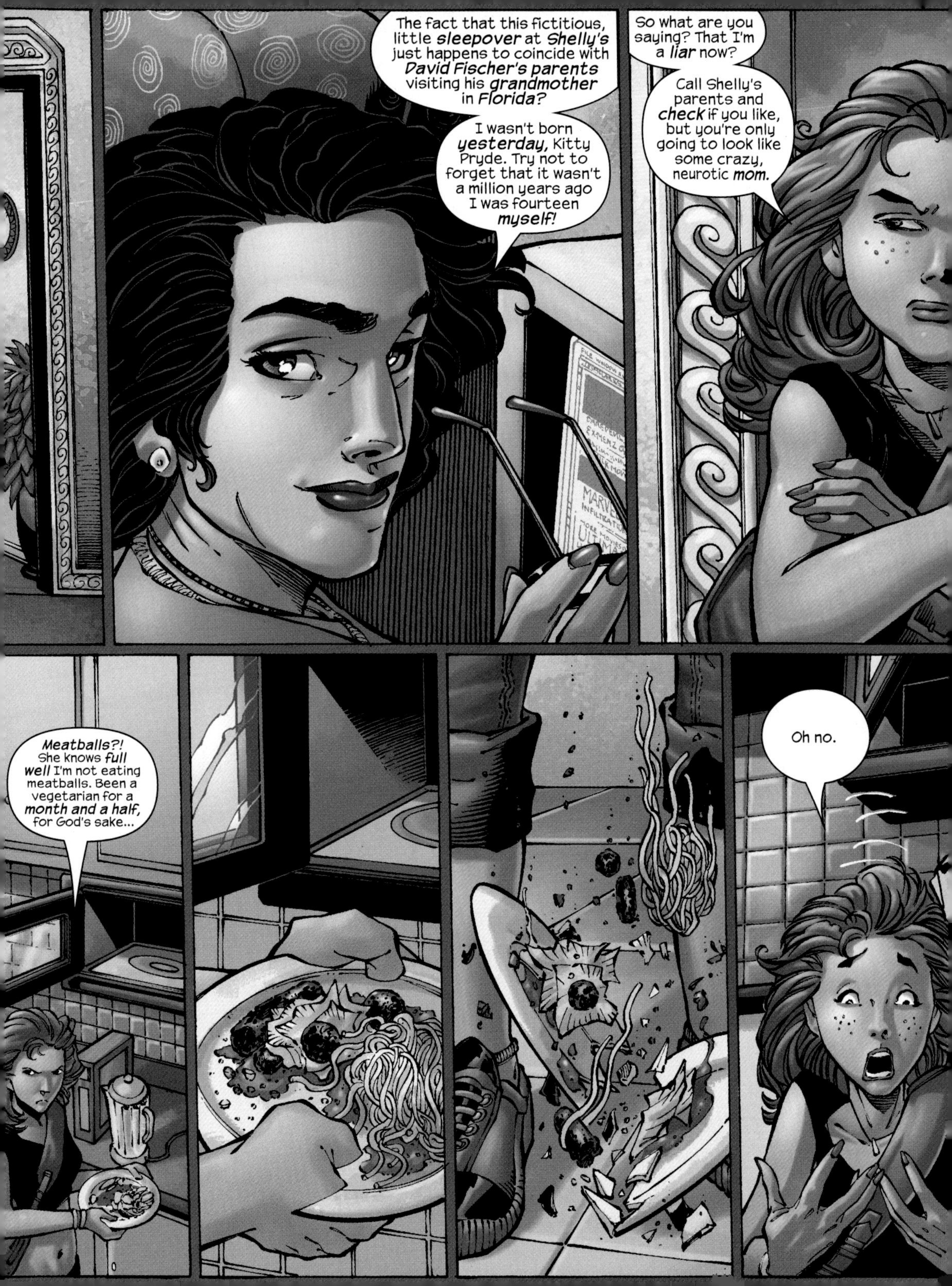
The fact that this fictitious, little sleepover at Shelly's just happens to coincide with David Fischer's parents visiting his grandmother in Florida?
I wasn't born yesterday, Kitty Pryde. Try not to forget that it wasn't a million years ago I was fourteen myself!
So what are you saying? That I'm a liar now?
Call Shelly's parents and check if you like, but you're only going to look like some crazy, neurotic mom.
Meatballs?! She knows full well I'm not eating meatballs. Been a vegetarian for a month and a half, for God's sake...
Oh no.

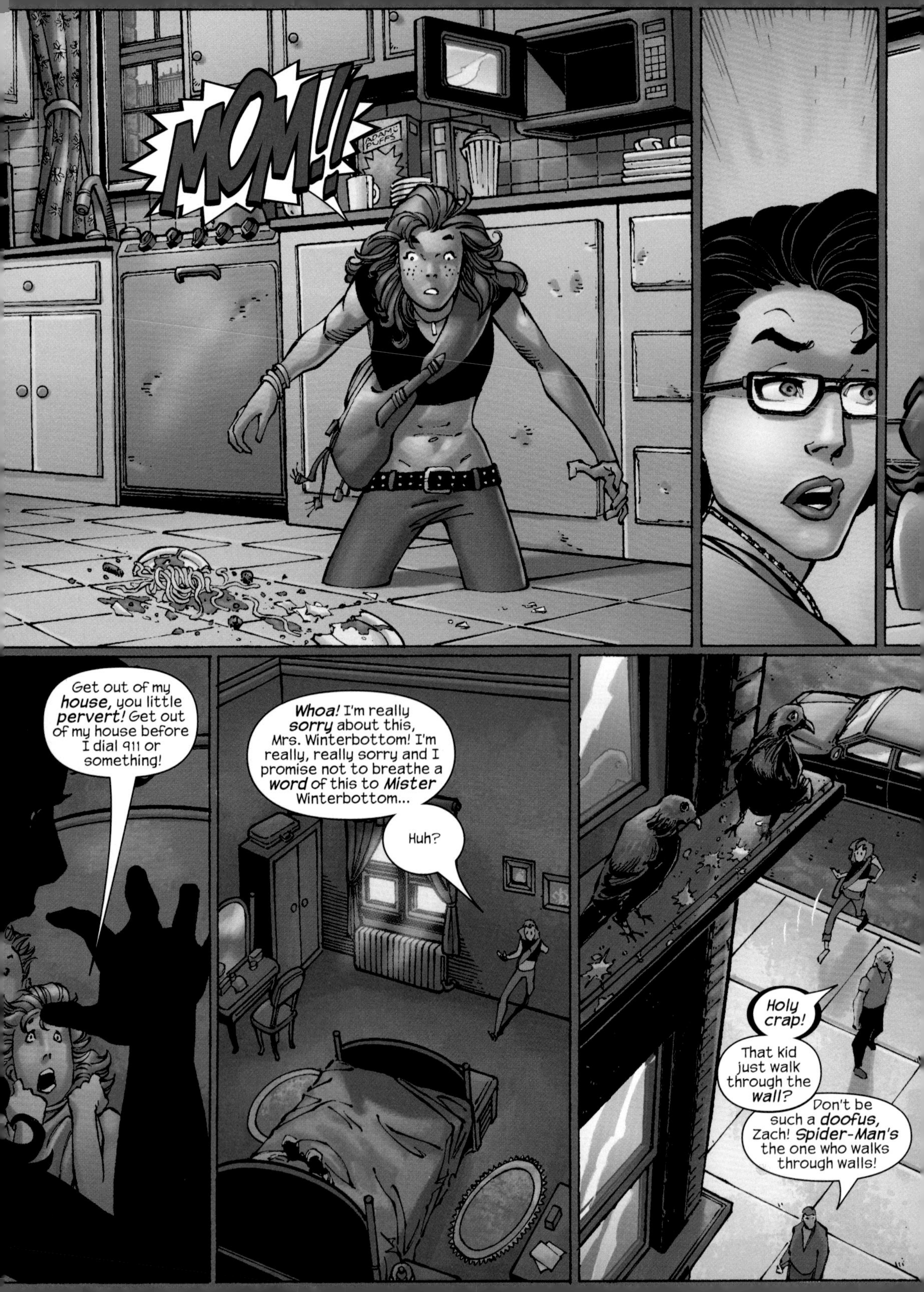

MOM!!
Get out of my house, you little pervert! Get out of my house before I dial 911 or something!
Whoa! I'm really sorry about this, Mrs. Winterbottom! I'm really, really sorry and I promise not to breathe a word of this to Mister Winterbottom...
Huh?
Holy crap!
That kid just walk through the wall?
Don't be such a doofus, Zach! Spider-Man's the one who walks through walls!

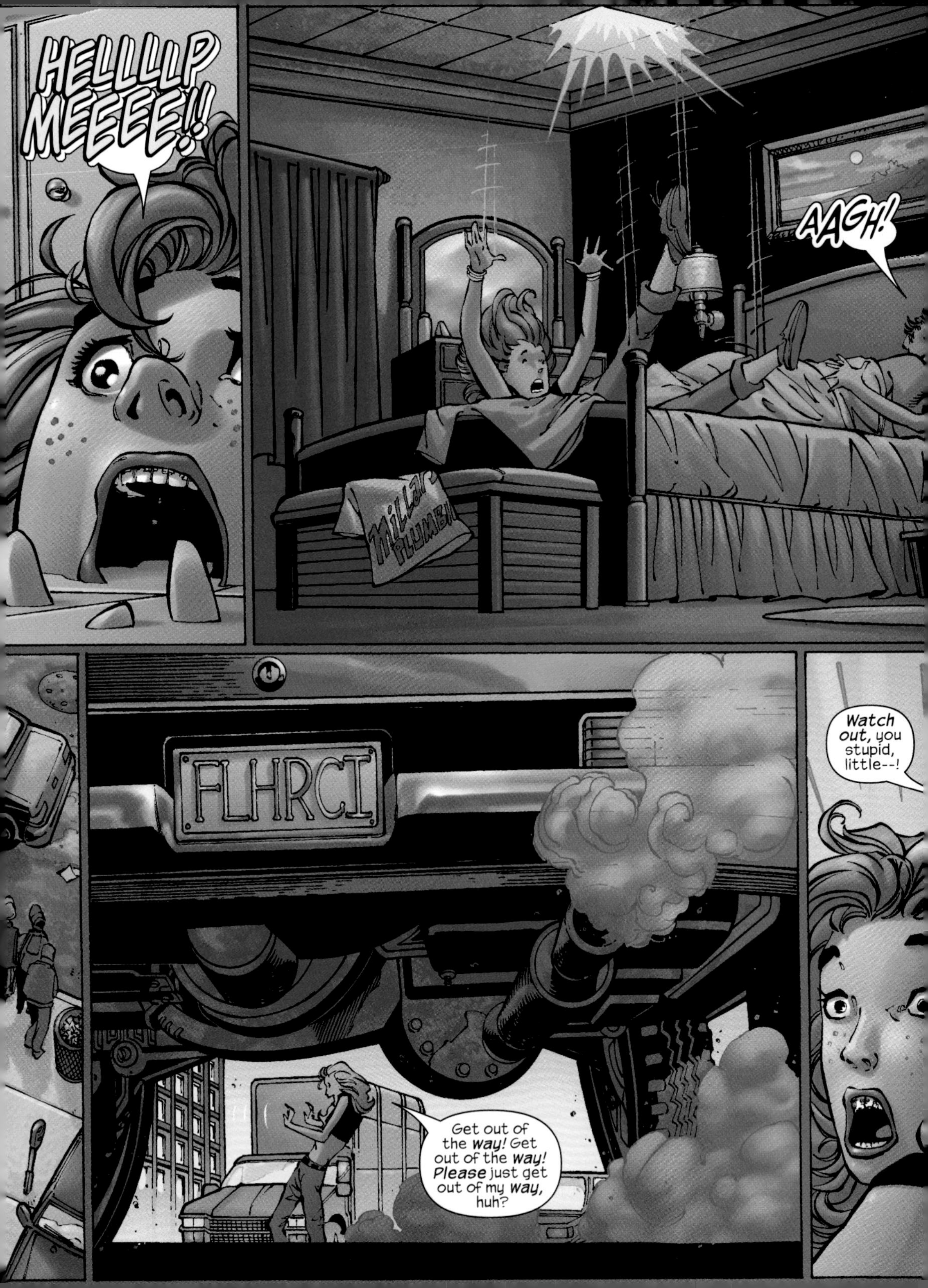
HELLLLP MEEEE!!
AAGH!
MILLAR PLUMBI
FLHRCI
Get out of the way! Get out of the way! Please just get out of my way, huh?
Watch out, you stupid, little--!

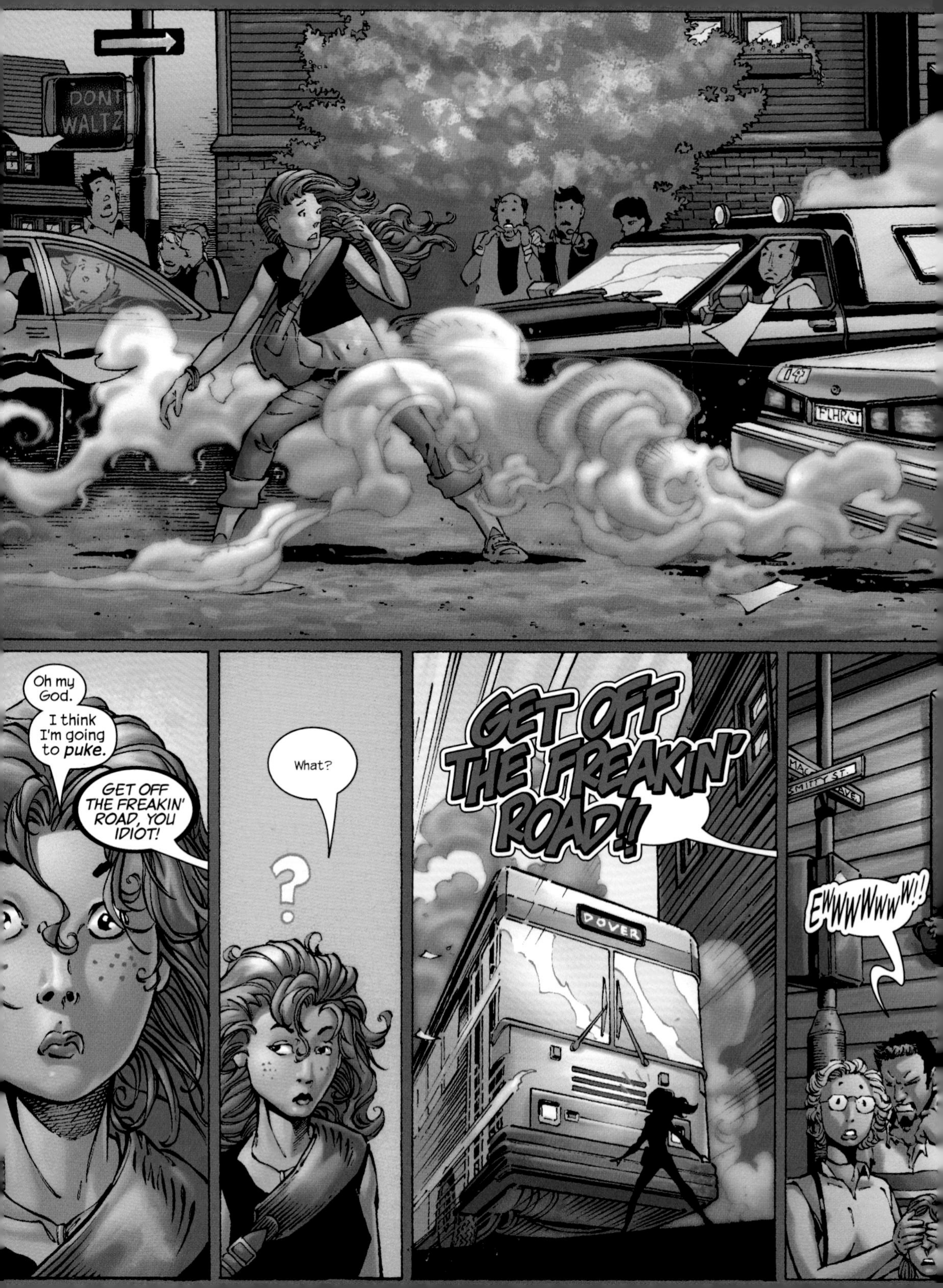
DONT WALTZ
Oh my God.
I think I'm going to puke.
GET OFF THE FREAKIN' ROAD, YOU IDIOT!
What?
?
GET OFF THE FREAKIN' ROAD!!
DOVER
SMITTY ST.
EWWWWWWW!!

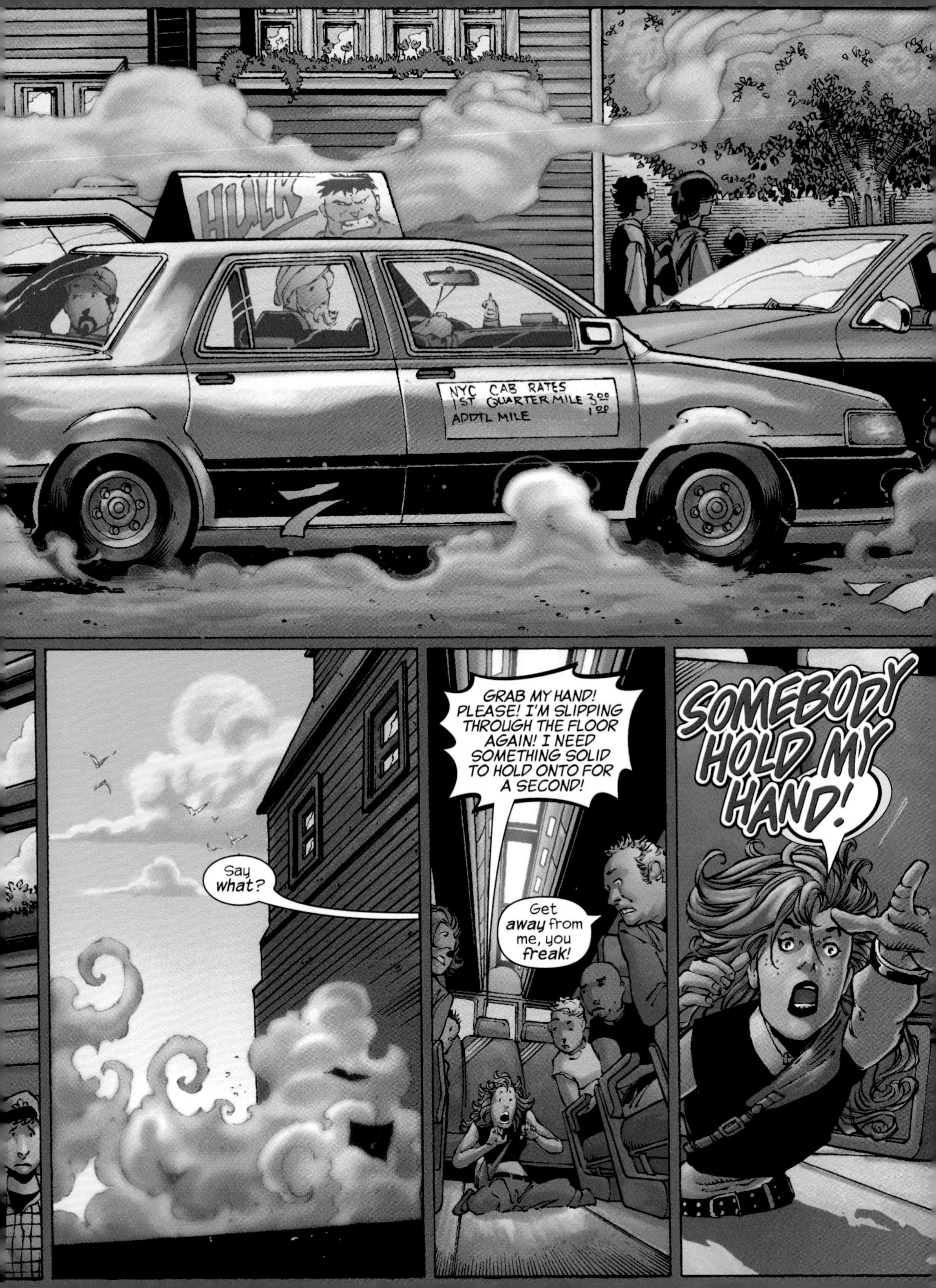
HULK
NYC CAB RATES
1ST QUARTER MILE 3.00
ADDTL MILE 1.00
Say what?
GRAB MY HAND! PLEASE! I'M SLIPPING THROUGH THE FLOOR AGAIN! I NEED SOMETHING SOLID TO HOLD ONTO FOR A SECOND!
Get away from me, you freak!
SOMEBODY HOLD MY HAND!

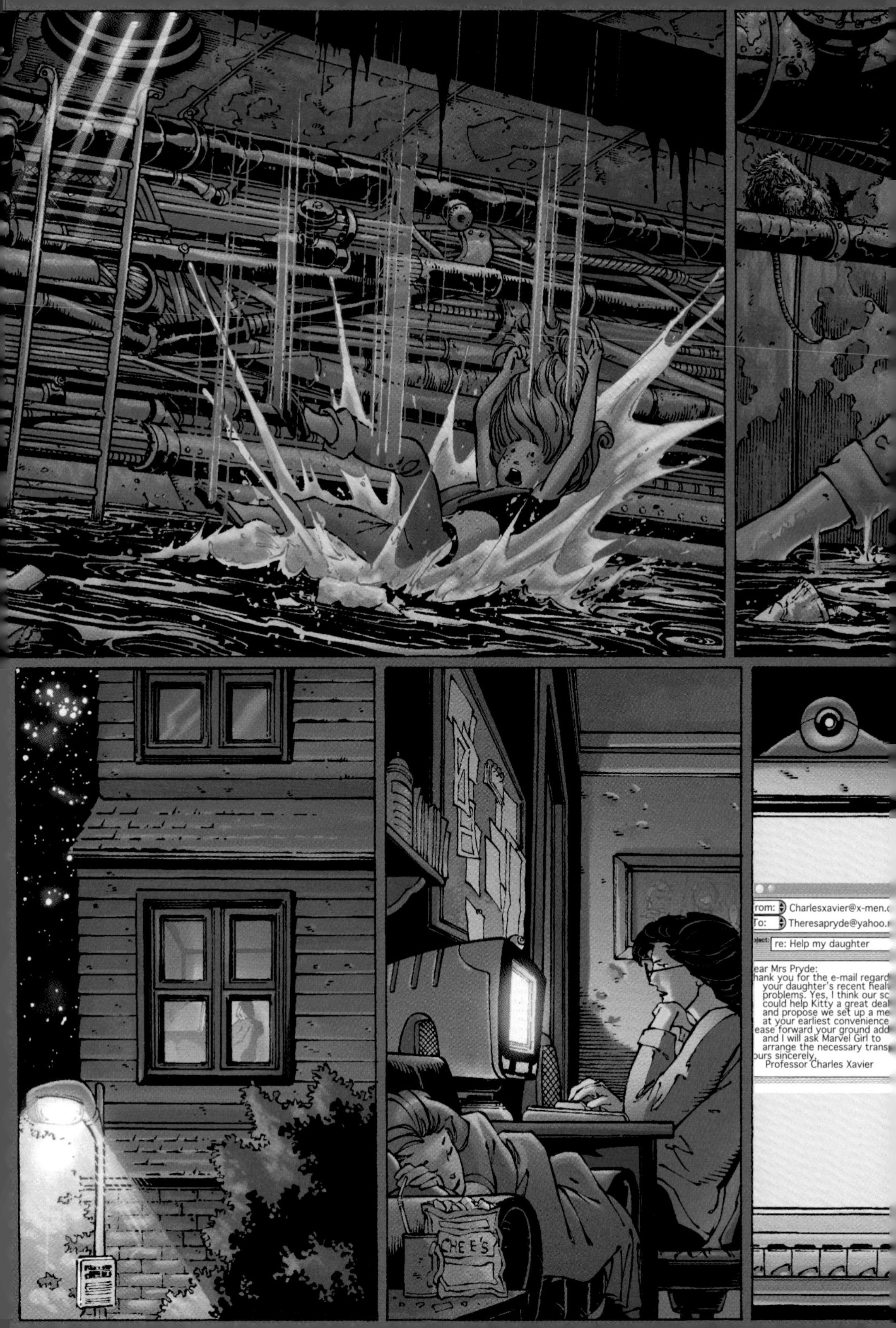
rom: Charlesxavier@x-men.c
To: Theresapryde@yahoo.
re: Help my daughter
ear Mrs Pryde:
hank you for the e-mail regard
your daughter's recent heal
problems. Yes, I think our sc
could help Kitty a great deal
and propose we set up a me
at your earliest convenience
ease forward your ground add
and I will ask Marvel Girl to
arrange the necessary trans
ours sincerely,
Professor Charles Xavier
CHEE'S

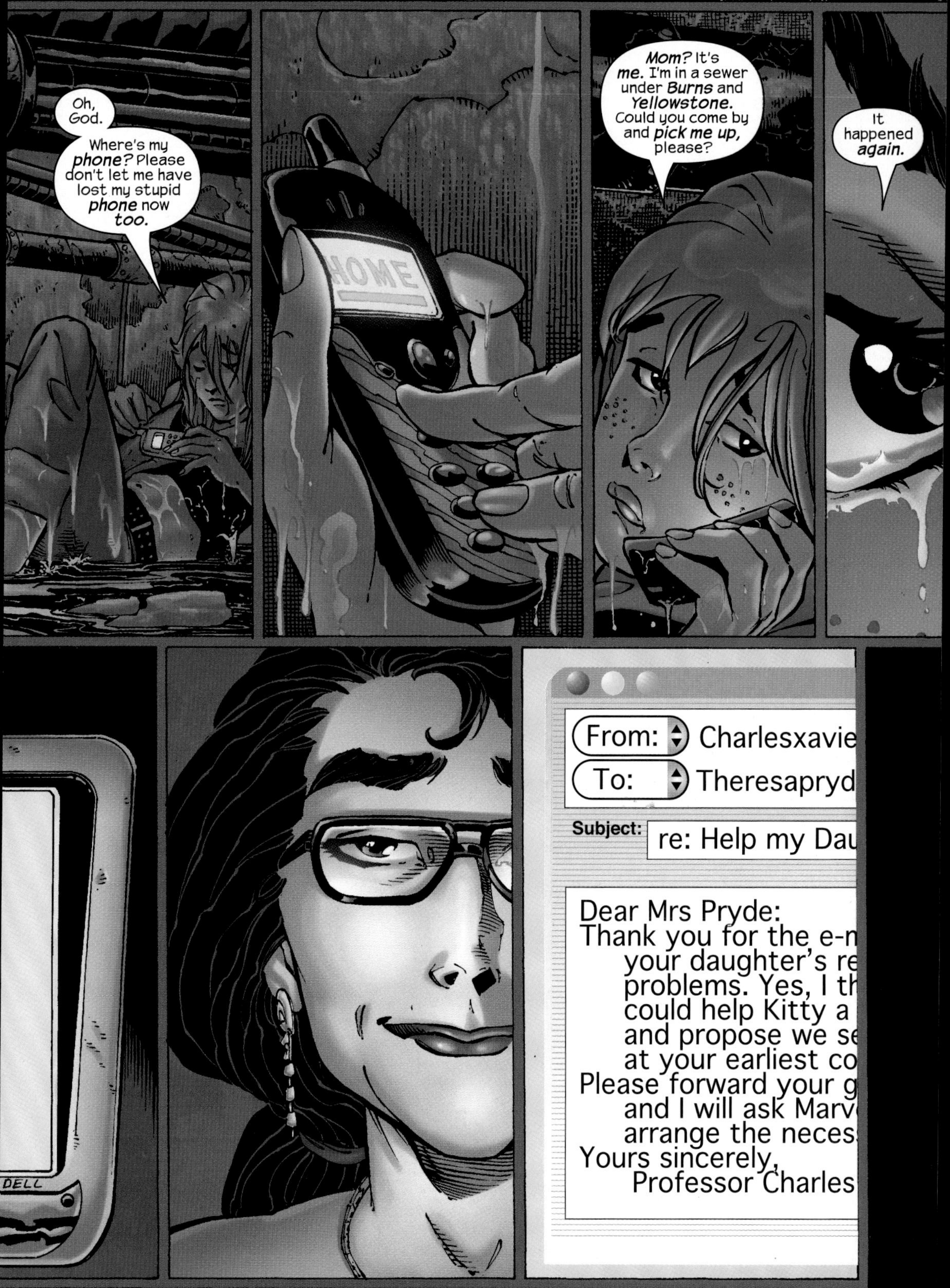

Oh, God.
Where's my phone? Please don't let me have lost my stupid phone now too.
HOME
Mom? It's me. I'm in a sewer under Burns and Yellowstone. Could you come by and pick me up, please?
It happened again.
DELL
From: Charlesxavie
To: Theresapryd
Subject: re: Help my Dau
Dear Mrs Pryde:
Thank you for the e-m
your daughter's re
problems. Yes, I th
could help Kitty a
and propose we se
at your earliest co
Please forward your g
and I will ask Marv
arrange the neces
Yours sincerely,
Professor Charles

Dear Mrs. Pryde:

Thank you for the e-mail regarding your daughter's recent health problems. Yes, I think our school could help Kitty a great deal and propose we set up a meeting at your earliest convenience.

Please forward your ground address and I will ask Marvel Girl to arrange the necessary transport.

Yours sincerely,

Professor Charles Xavier

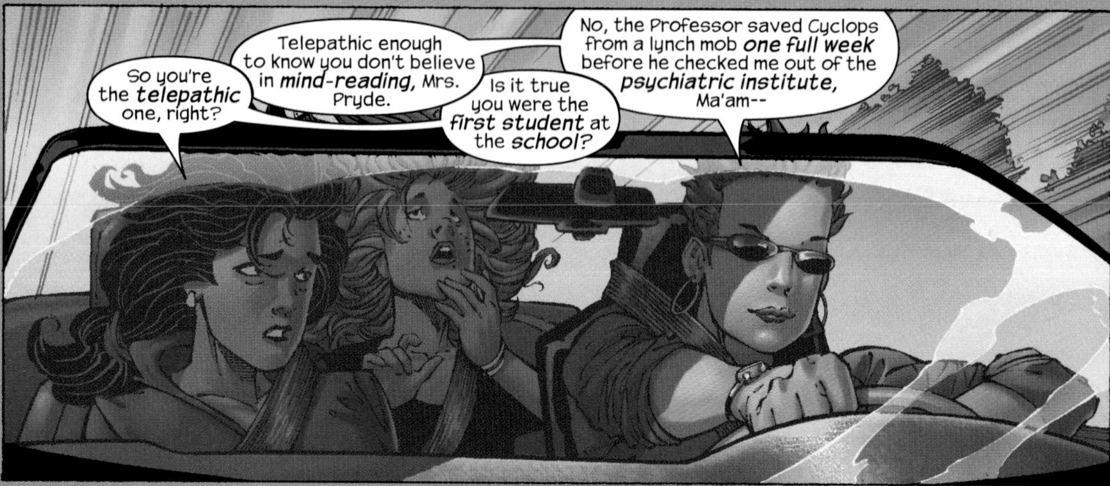

So you're the *telepathic* one, right?
Telepathic enough to know you don't believe in *mind-reading,* Mrs. Pryde.
Is it true you were the *first student* at the *school*?
No, the Professor saved Cyclops from a lynch mob *one full week* before he checked me out of the *psychiatric institute,* Ma'am--


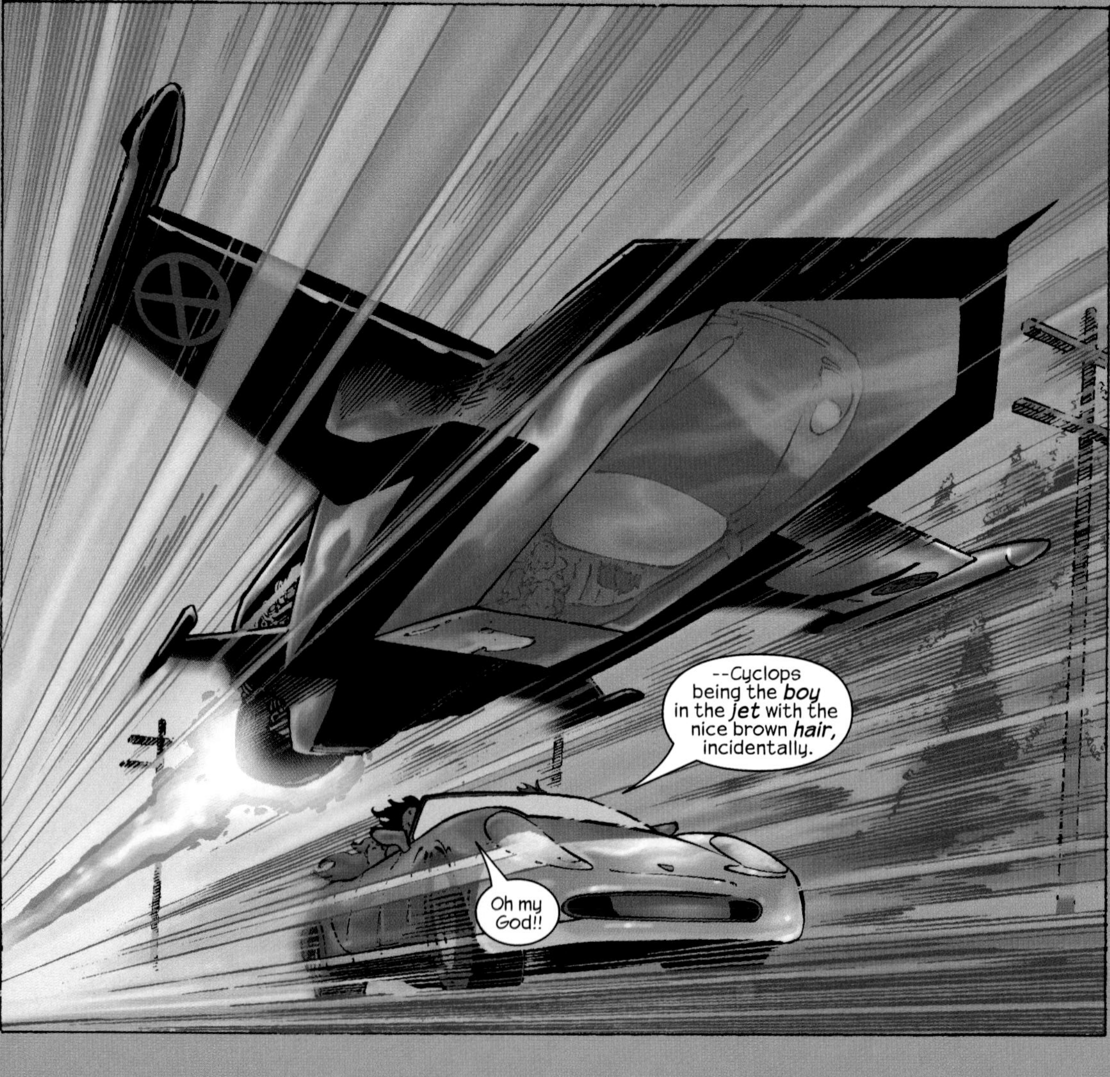

--Cyclops being the *boy* in the *jet* with the nice brown *hair,* incidentally.
Oh my God!!

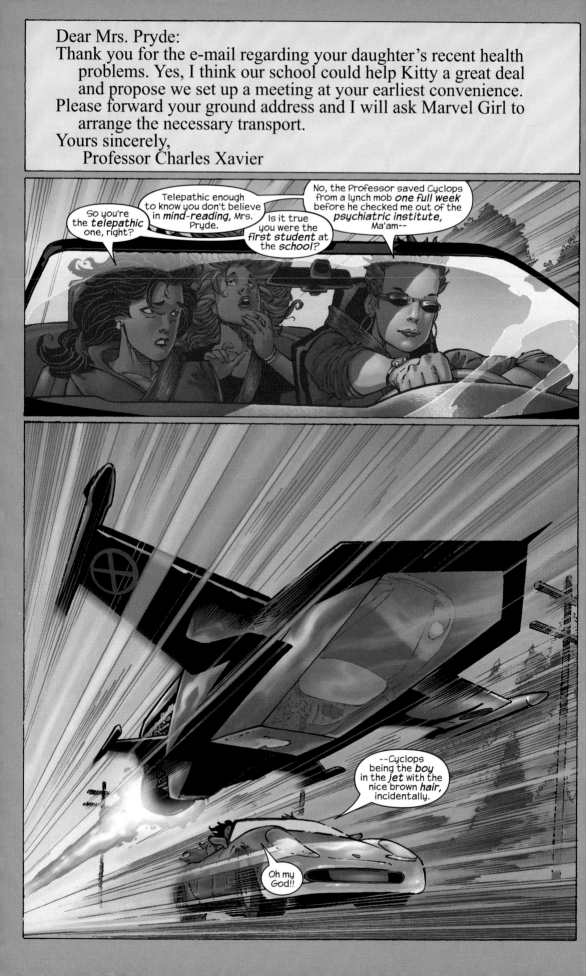

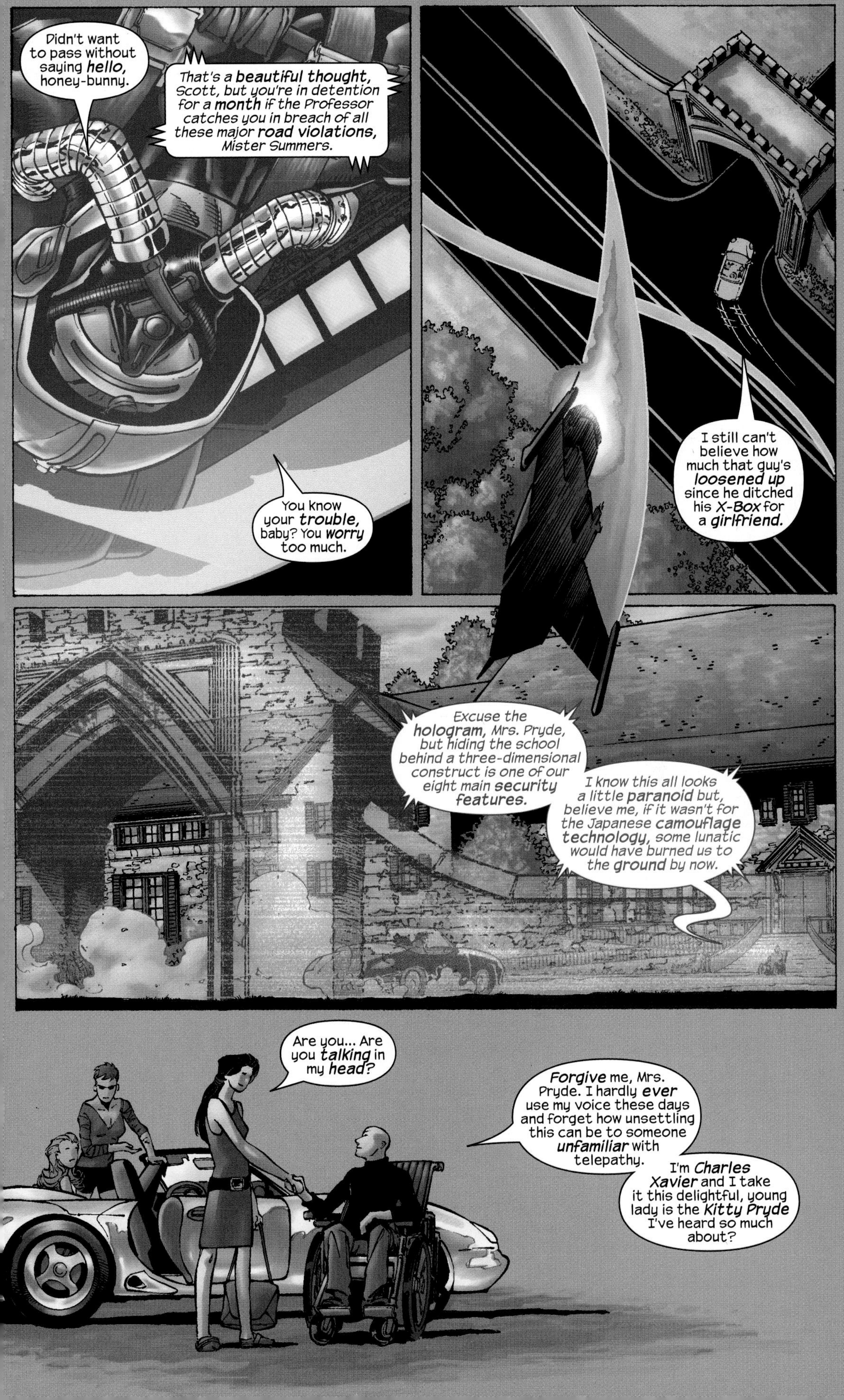

Didn't want to pass without saying hello, honey-bunny.
That's a beautiful thought, Scott, but you're in detention for a month if the Professor catches you in breach of all these major road violations, Mister Summers.
You know your trouble, baby? You worry too much.
I still can't believe how much that guy's loosened up since he ditched his X-Box for a girlfriend.
Excuse the hologram, Mrs. Pryde, but hiding the school behind a three-dimensional construct is one of our eight main security features.
I know this all looks a little paranoid but, believe me, if it wasn't for the Japanese camouflage technology, some lunatic would have burned us to the ground by now.
Are you... Are you talking in my head?
Forgive me, Mrs. Pryde. I hardly ever use my voice these days and forget how unsettling this can be to someone unfamiliar with telepathy.
I'm Charles Xavier and I take it this delightful, young lady is the Kitty Pryde I've heard so much about?

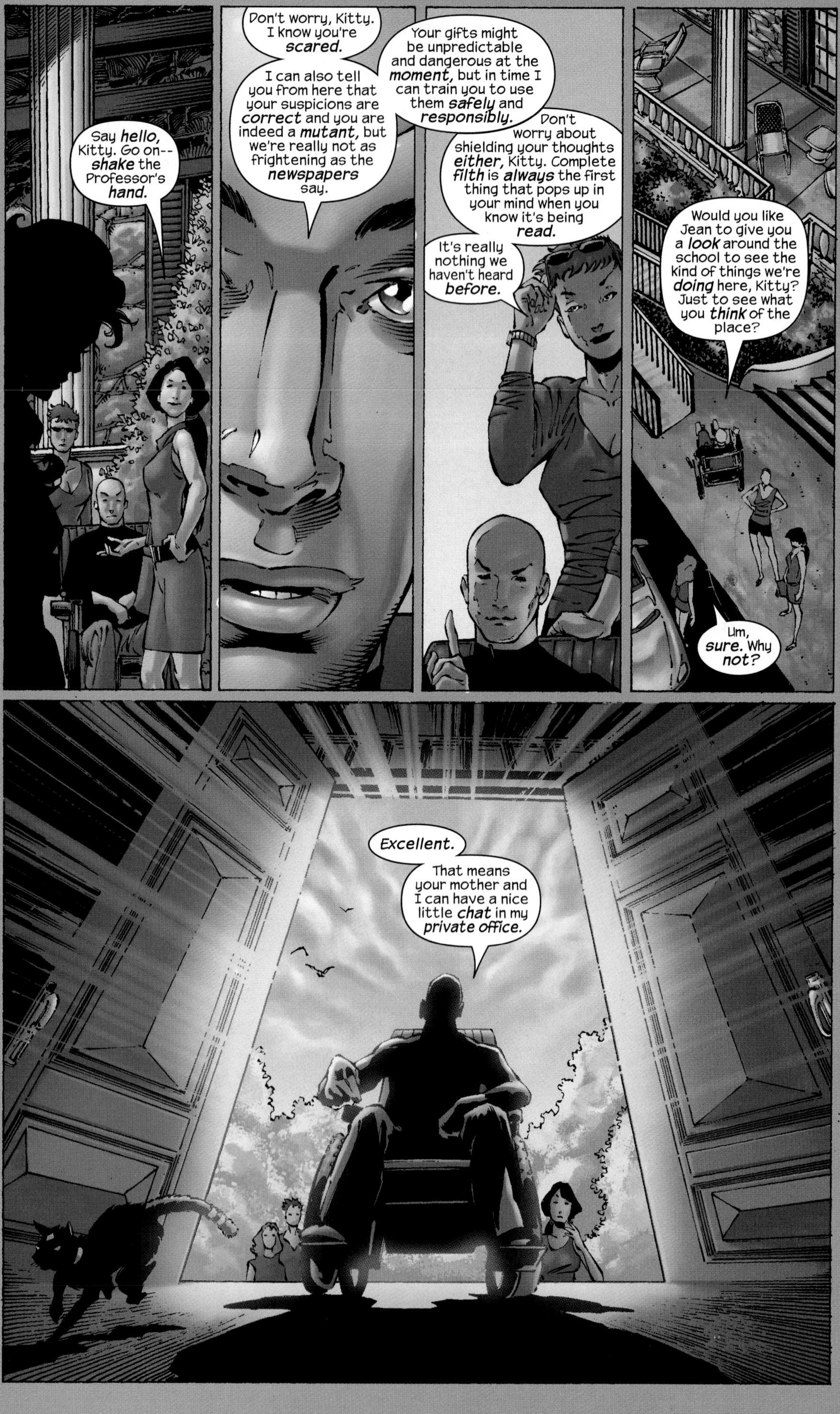
Say **hello,** Kitty. Go on-- **shake** the Professor's **hand.**
Don't worry, Kitty. I know you're **scared.**
I can also tell you from here that your suspicions are **correct** and you are indeed a **mutant,** but we're really not as frightening as the **newspapers** say.
Your gifts might be unpredictable and dangerous at the **moment,** but in time I can train you to use them **safely** and **responsibly.**
Don't worry about shielding your thoughts **either,** Kitty. Complete **filth** is **always** the first thing that pops up in your mind when you know it's being **read.**
It's really nothing we haven't heard **before.**
Would you like Jean to give you a **look** around the school to see the kind of things we're **doing** here, Kitty? Just to see what you **think** of the place?
Um, **sure.** Why **not?**
*Excellent.*
That means your mother and I can have a nice little **chat** in my *private office.*

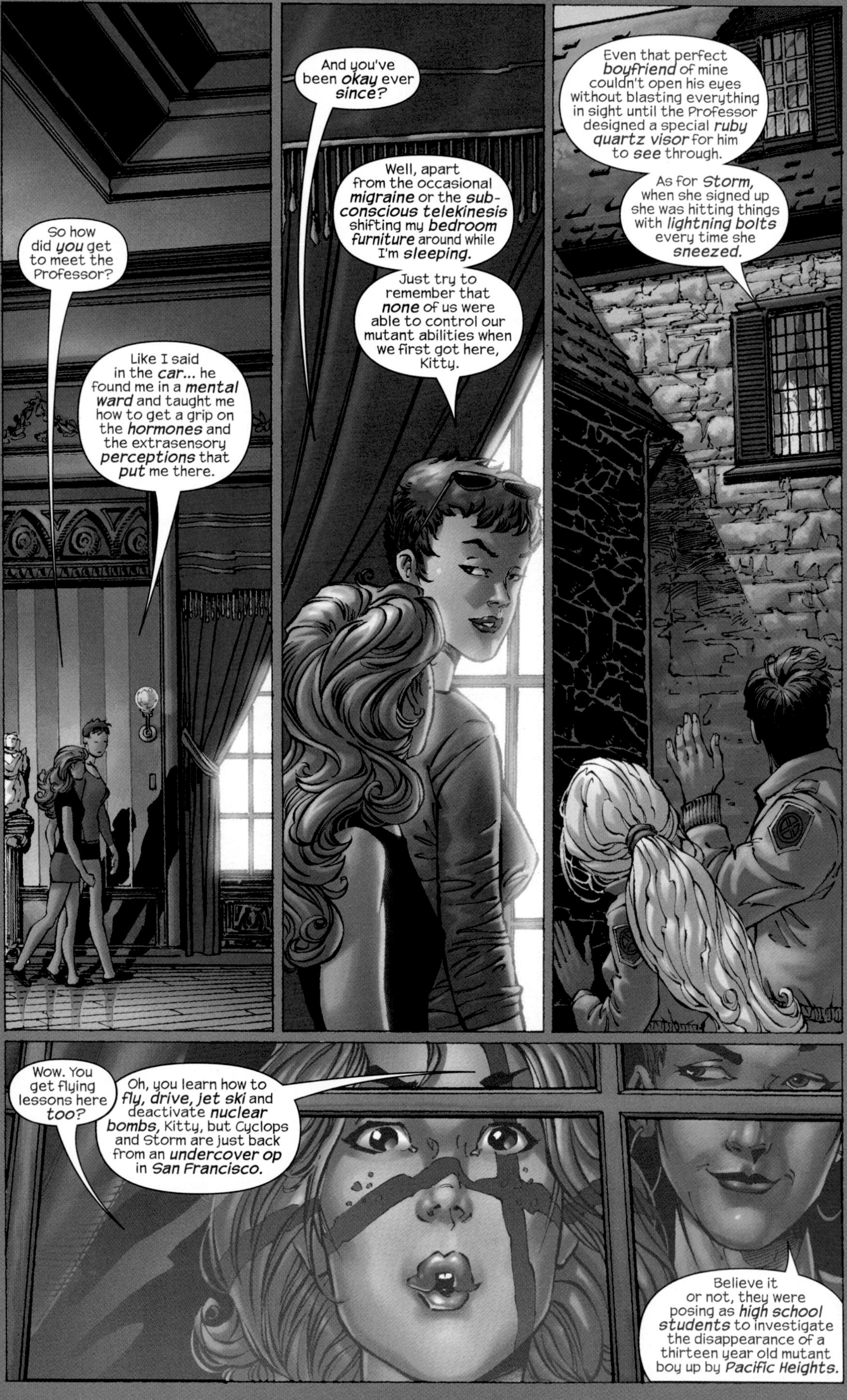

So how did you get to meet the Professor?
Like I said in the car... he found me in a mental ward and taught me how to get a grip on the hormones and the extrasensory perceptions that put me there.
And you've been okay ever since?
Well, apart from the occasional migraine or the sub-conscious telekinesis shifting my bedroom furniture around while I'm sleeping.
Just try to remember that none of us were able to control our mutant abilities when we first got here, Kitty.
Even that perfect boyfriend of mine couldn't open his eyes without blasting everything in sight until the Professor designed a special ruby quartz visor for him to see through.
As for Storm, when she signed up she was hitting things with lightning bolts every time she sneezed.
Wow. You get flying lessons here too?
Oh, you learn how to fly, drive, jet ski and deactivate nuclear bombs, Kitty, but Cyclops and Storm are just back from an undercover op in San Francisco.
Believe it or not, they were posing as high school students to investigate the disappearance of a thirteen year old mutant boy up by Pacific Heights.

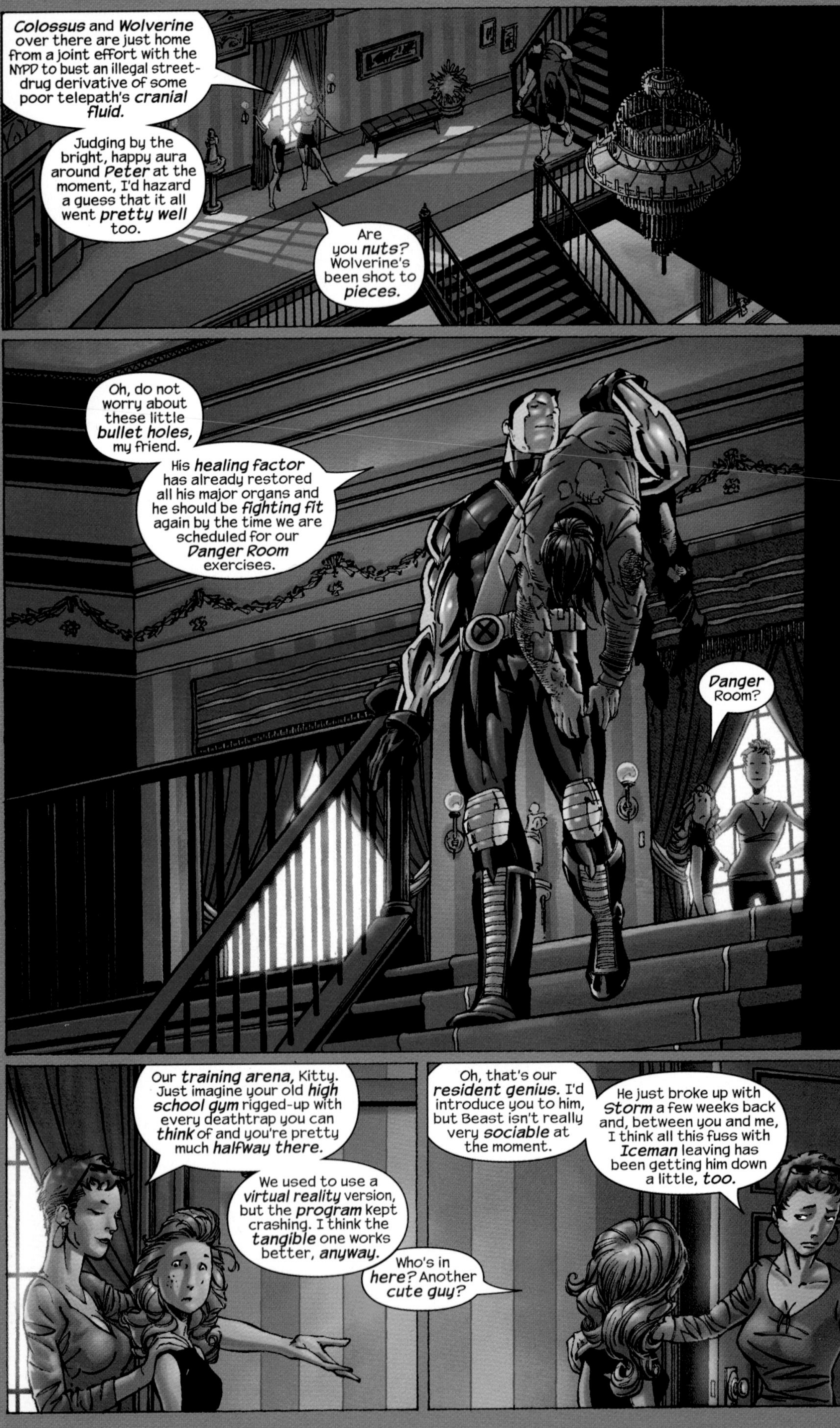
Colossus and Wolverine over there are just home from a joint effort with the NYPD to bust an illegal street-drug derivative of some poor telepath's cranial fluid.
Judging by the bright, happy aura around Peter at the moment, I'd hazard a guess that it all went pretty well too.
Are you nuts? Wolverine's been shot to pieces.
Oh, do not worry about these little bullet holes, my friend.
His healing factor has already restored all his major organs and he should be fighting fit again by the time we are scheduled for our Danger Room exercises.
Danger Room?
Our training arena, Kitty. Just imagine your old high school gym rigged-up with every deathtrap you can think of and you're pretty much halfway there.
We used to use a virtual reality version, but the program kept crashing. I think the tangible one works better, anyway.
Who's in here? Another cute guy?
Oh, that's our resident genius. I'd introduce you to him, but Beast isn't really very sociable at the moment.
He just broke up with Storm a few weeks back and, between you and me, I think all this fuss with Iceman leaving has been getting him down a little, too.

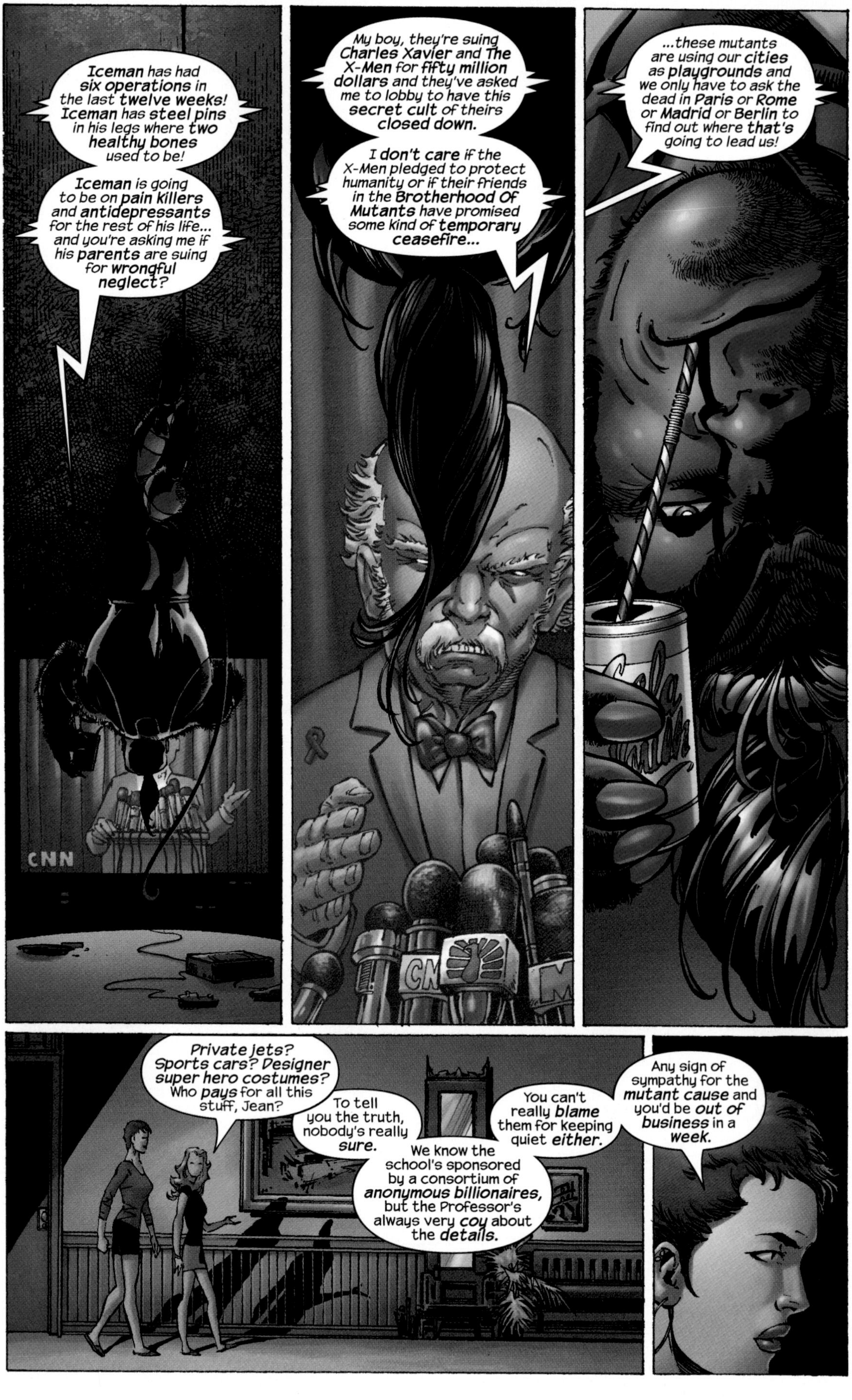
Iceman has had six operations in the last twelve weeks! Iceman has steel pins in his legs where two healthy bones used to be!
Iceman is going to be on pain killers and antidepressants for the rest of his life... and you're asking me if his parents are suing for wrongful neglect?
CNN
My boy, they're suing Charles Xavier and The X-Men for fifty million dollars and they've asked me to lobby to have this secret cult of theirs closed down.
I don't care if the X-Men pledged to protect humanity or if their friends in the Brotherhood Of Mutants have promised some kind of temporary ceasefire...
...these mutants are using our cities as playgrounds and we only have to ask the dead in Paris or Rome or Madrid or Berlin to find out where that's going to lead us!
Private jets? Sports cars? Designer super hero costumes? Who pays for all this stuff, Jean?
To tell you the truth, nobody's really sure.
We know the school's sponsored by a consortium of anonymous billionaires, but the Professor's always very coy about the details.
You can't really blame them for keeping quiet either.
Any sign of sympathy for the mutant cause and you'd be out of business in a week.

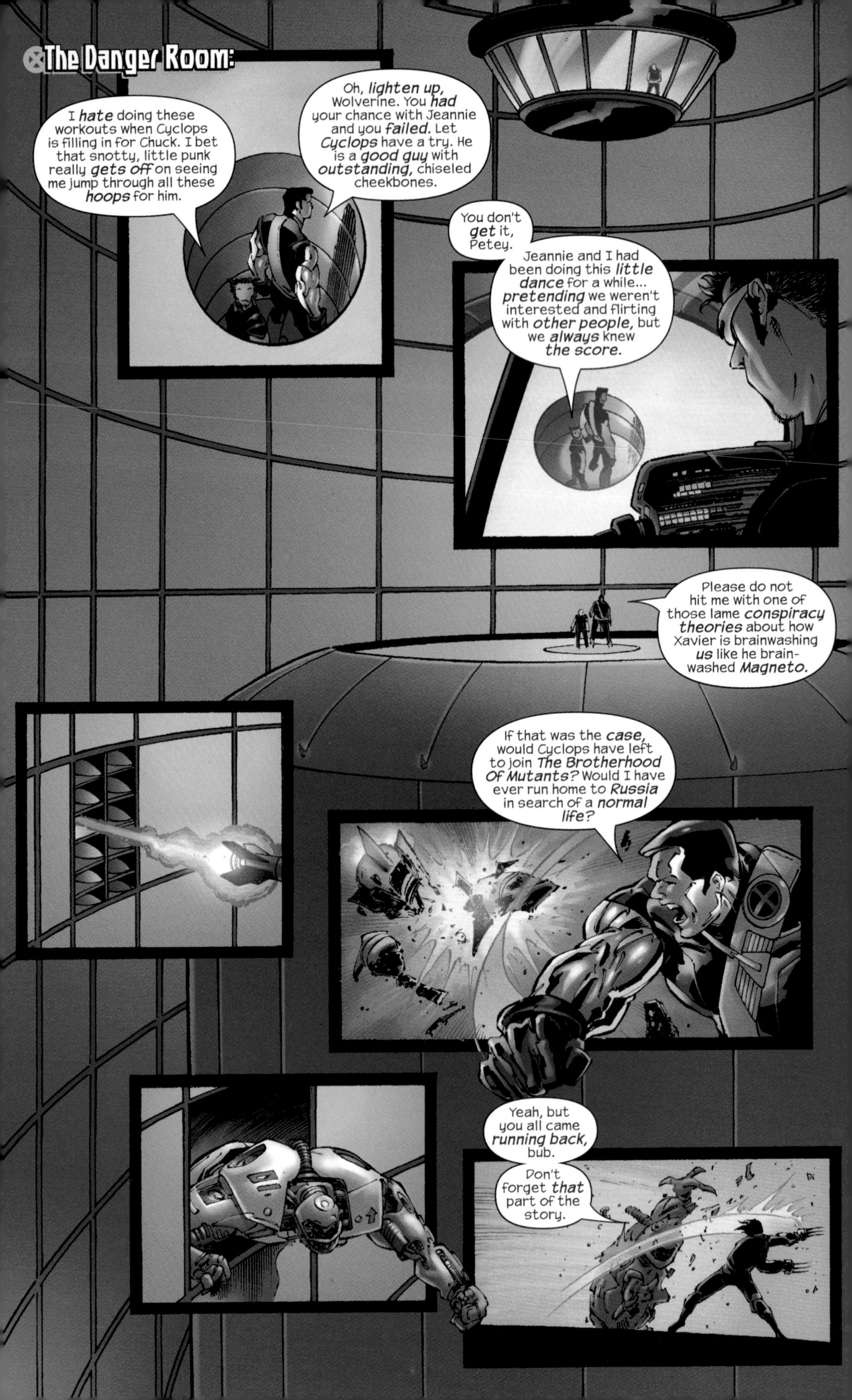
The Danger Room:
I hate doing these workouts when Cyclops is filling in for Chuck. I bet that snotty, little punk really gets off on seeing me jump through all these hoops for him.
Oh, lighten up, Wolverine. You had your chance with Jeannie and you failed. Let Cyclops have a try. He is a good guy with outstanding, chiseled cheekbones.
You don't get it, Petey.
Jeannie and I had been doing this little dance for a while... pretending we weren't interested and flirting with other people, but we always knew the score.
Please do not hit me with one of those lame conspiracy theories about how Xavier is brainwashing us like he brain-washed Magneto.
If that was the case, would Cyclops have left to join The Brotherhood Of Mutants? Would I have ever run home to Russia in search of a normal life?
Yeah, but you all came running back, bub.
Don't forget that part of the story.

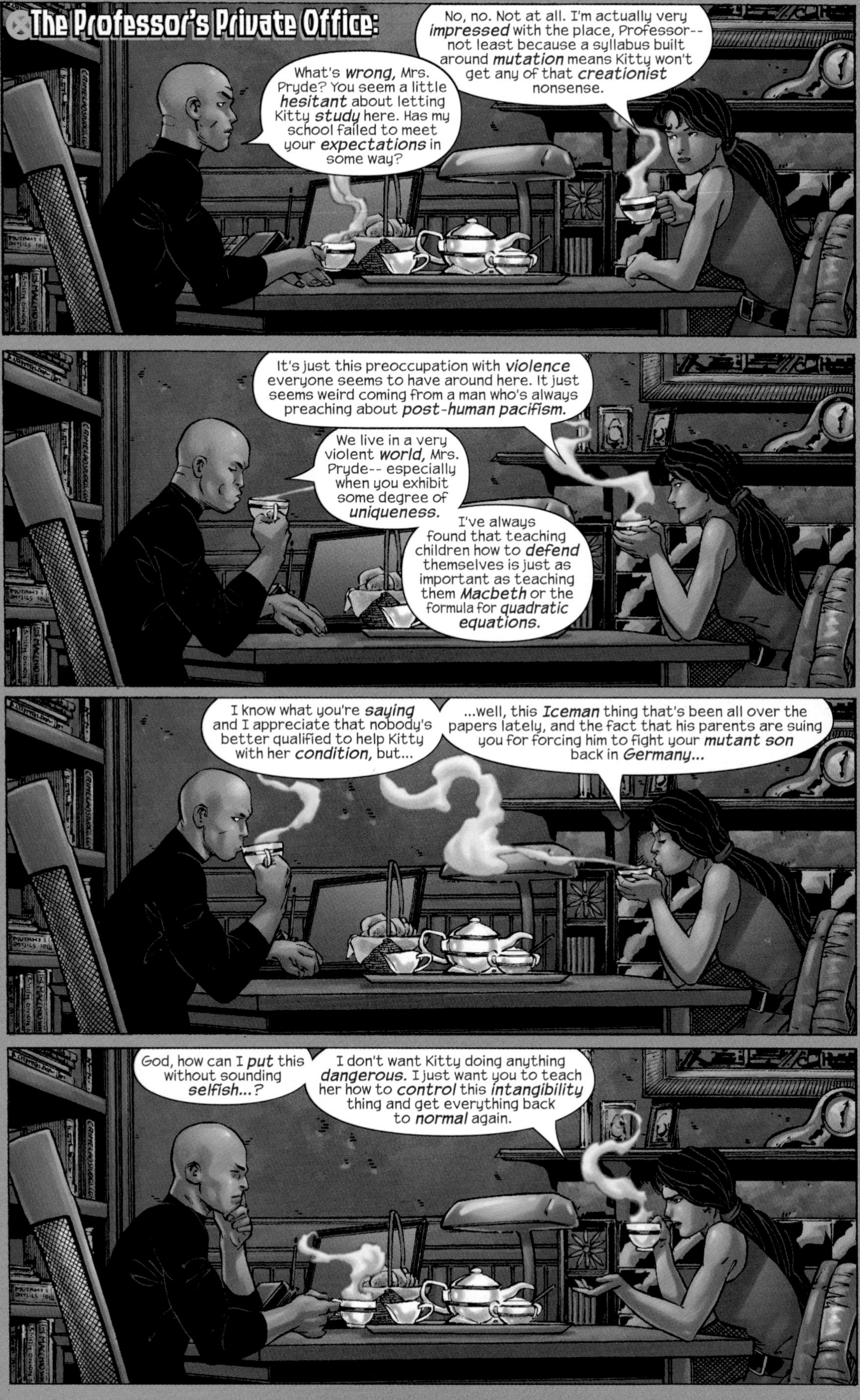
The Professor's Private Office:
What's wrong, Mrs. Pryde? You seem a little hesitant about letting Kitty study here. Has my school failed to meet your expectations in some way?
No, no. Not at all. I'm actually very impressed with the place, Professor-- not least because a syllabus built around mutation means Kitty won't get any of that creationist nonsense.
It's just this preoccupation with violence everyone seems to have around here. It just seems weird coming from a man who's always preaching about post-human pacifism.
We live in a very violent world, Mrs. Pryde-- especially when you exhibit some degree of uniqueness.
I've always found that teaching children how to defend themselves is just as important as teaching them Macbeth or the formula for quadratic equations.
I know what you're saying and I appreciate that nobody's better qualified to help Kitty with her condition, but...
...well, this Iceman thing that's been all over the papers lately, and the fact that his parents are suing you for forcing him to fight your mutant son back in Germany...
God, how can I put this without sounding selfish...?
I don't want Kitty doing anything dangerous. I just want you to teach her how to control this intangibility thing and get everything back to normal again.

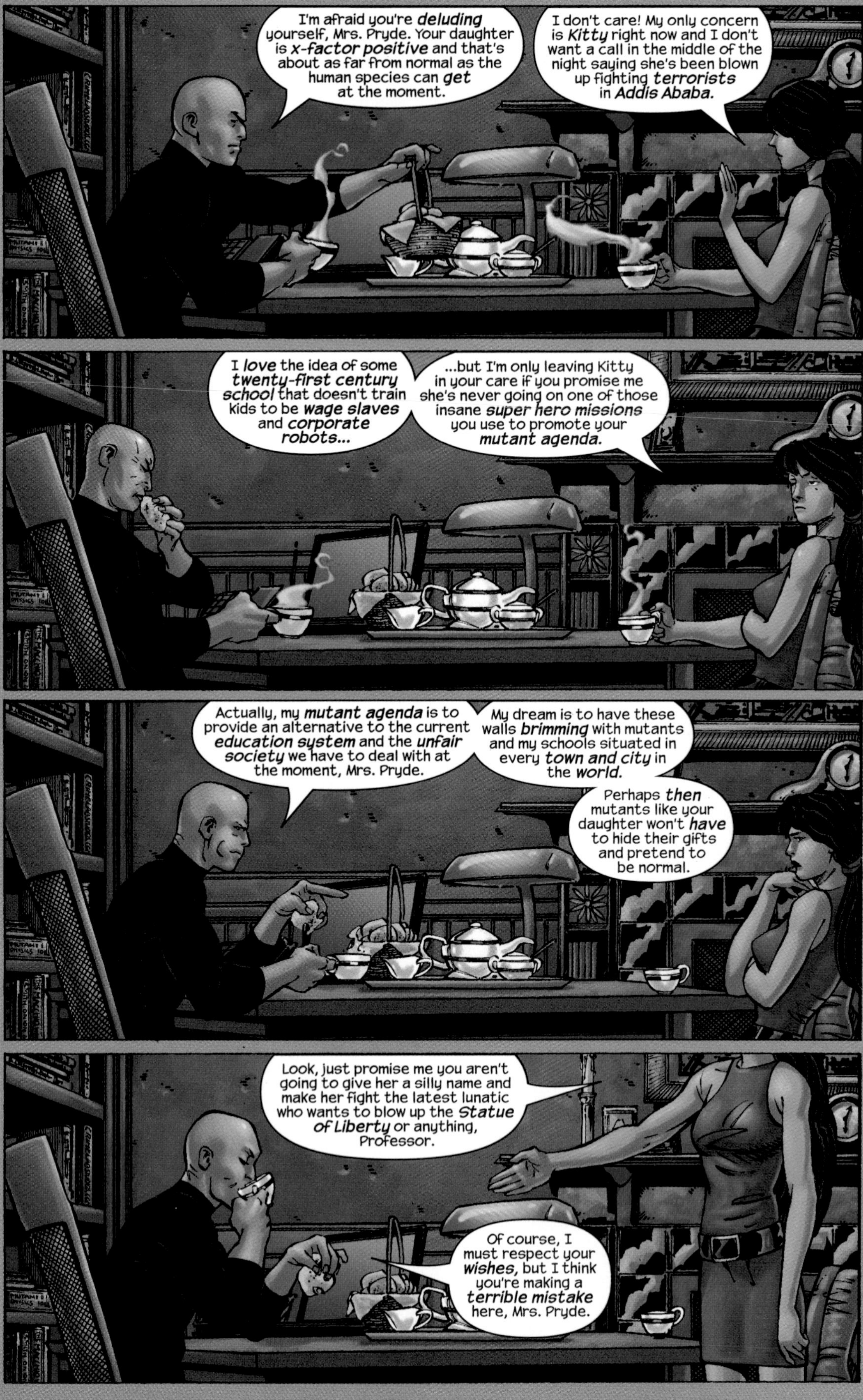

I'm afraid you're deluding yourself, Mrs. Pryde. Your daughter is x-factor positive and that's about as far from normal as the human species can get at the moment.
I don't care! My only concern is Kitty right now and I don't want a call in the middle of the night saying she's been blown up fighting terrorists in Addis Ababa.
I love the idea of some twenty-first century school that doesn't train kids to be wage slaves and corporate robots...
...but I'm only leaving Kitty in your care if you promise me she's never going on one of those insane super hero missions you use to promote your mutant agenda.
Actually, my mutant agenda is to provide an alternative to the current education system and the unfair society we have to deal with at the moment, Mrs. Pryde.
My dream is to have these walls brimming with mutants and my schools situated in every town and city in the world.
Perhaps then mutants like your daughter won't have to hide their gifts and pretend to be normal.
Look, just promise me you aren't going to give her a silly name and make her fight the latest lunatic who wants to blow up the Statue of Liberty or anything, Professor.
Of course, I must respect your wishes, but I think you're making a terrible mistake here, Mrs. Pryde.

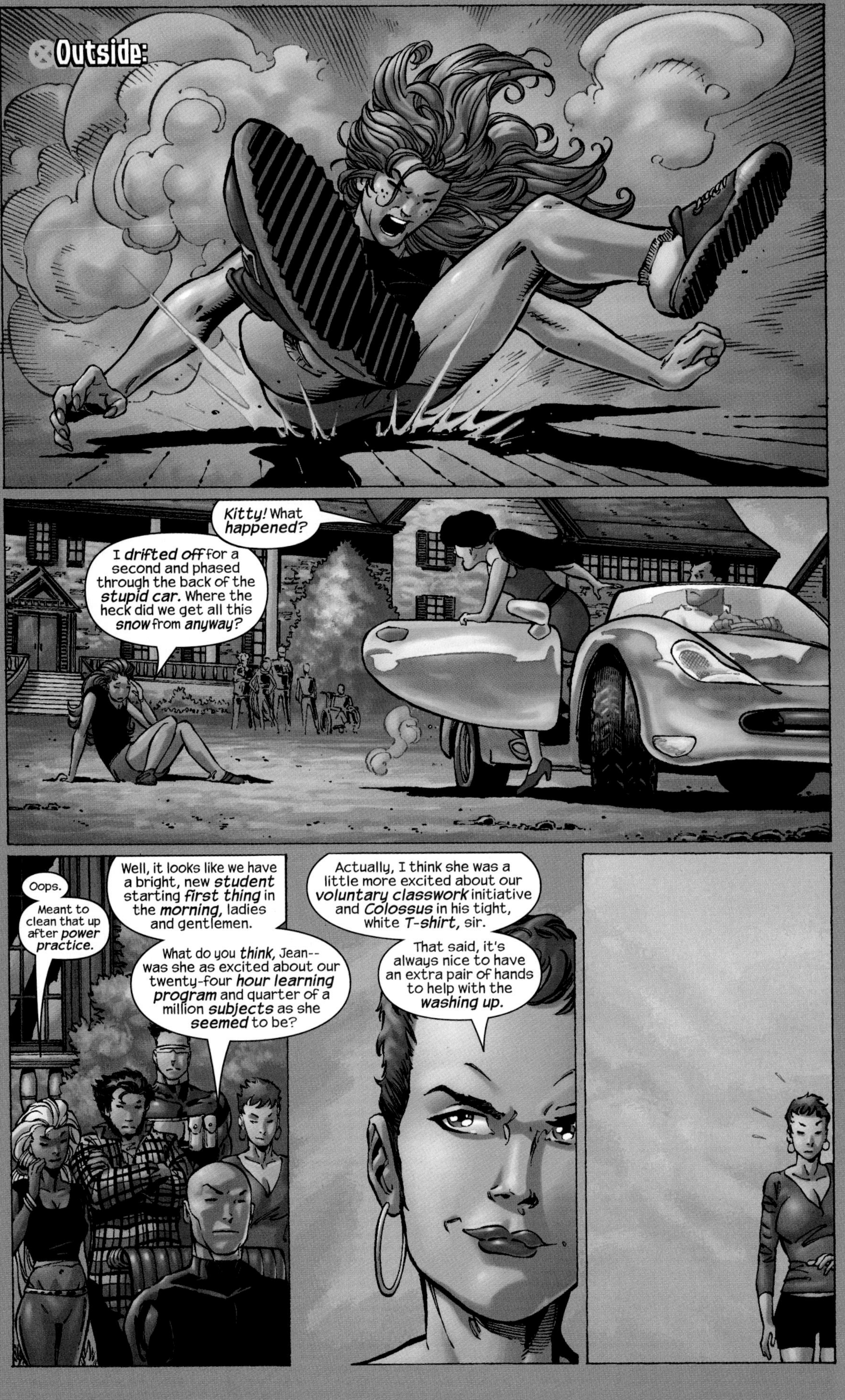
Outside:
Kitty! What happened?
I drifted off for a second and phased through the back of the stupid car. Where the heck did we get all this snow from anyway?
Oops.
Meant to clean that up after power practice.
Well, it looks like we have a bright, new student starting first thing in the morning, ladies and gentlemen.
What do you think, Jean-- was she as excited about our twenty-four hour learning program and quarter of a million subjects as she seemed to be?
Actually, I think she was a little more excited about our voluntary classwork initiative and Colossus in his tight, white T-shirt, sir.
That said, it's always nice to have an extra pair of hands to help with the washing up.

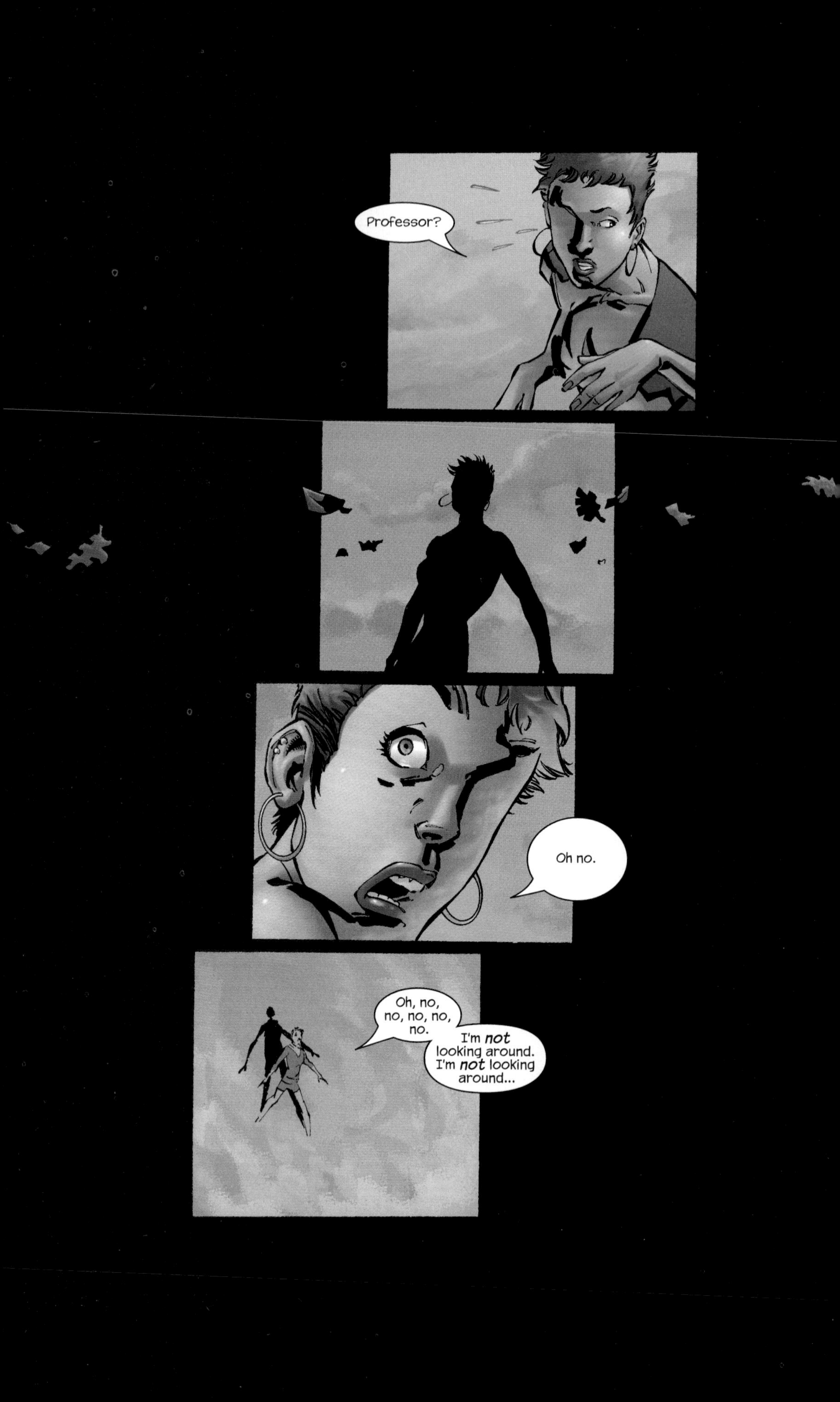
Professor?
Oh no.
Oh, no, no, no, no, no, no.
I'm *not* looking around. I'm *not* looking around...

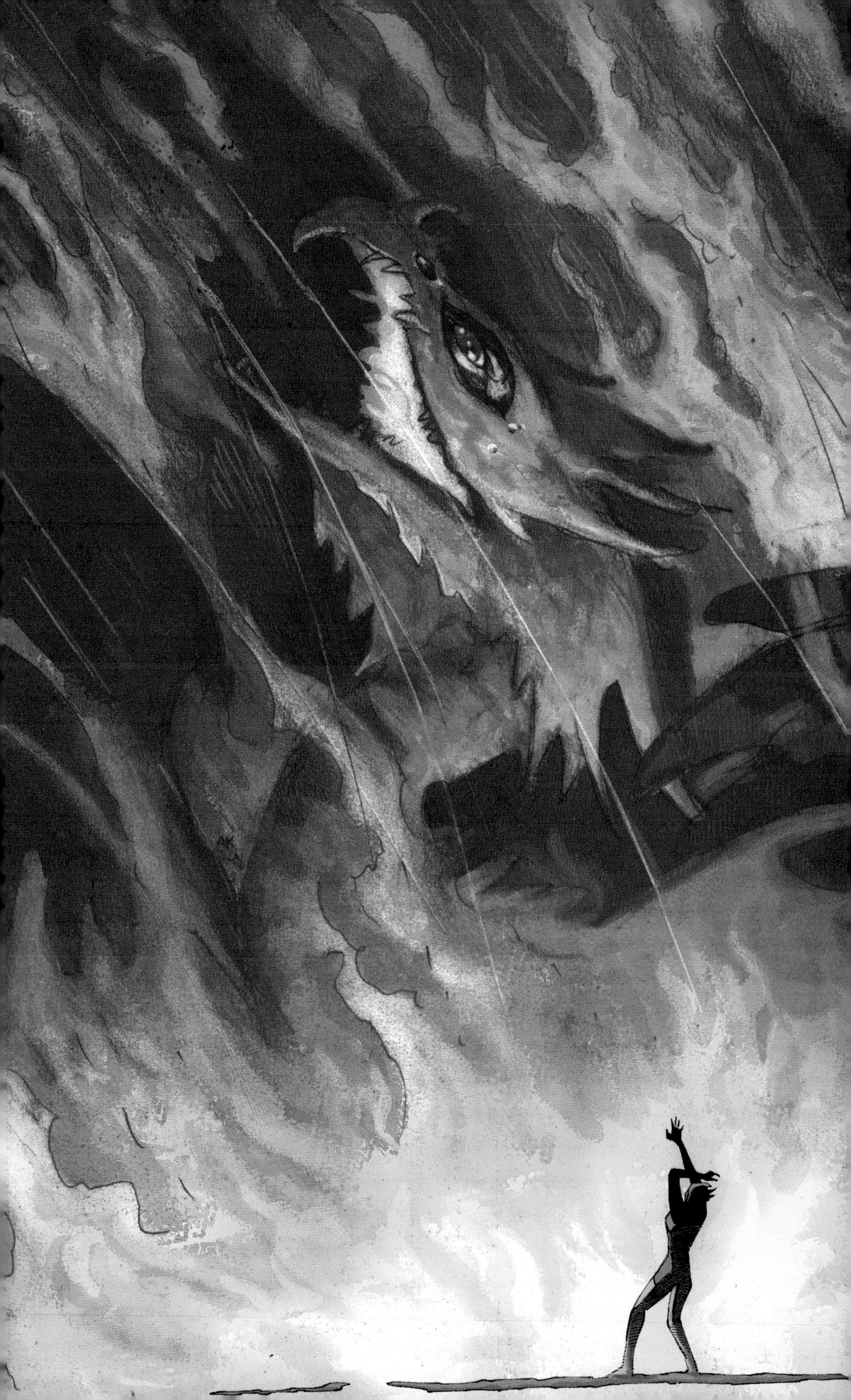

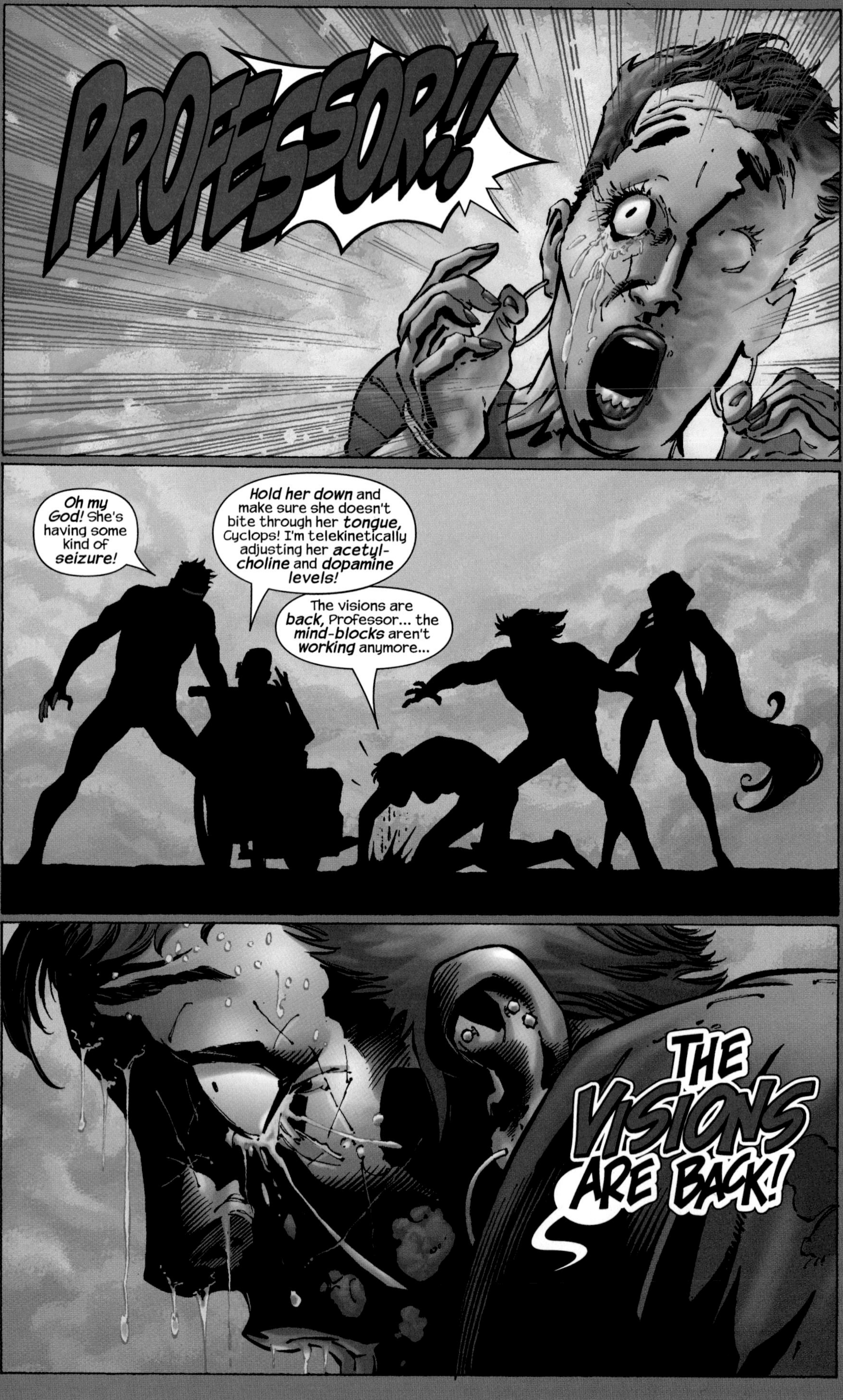
PROFESSOR!!
Oh my God! She's having some kind of seizure!
Hold her down and make sure she doesn't bite through her tongue, Cyclops! I'm telekinetically adjusting her acetyl-choline and dopamine levels!
The visions are back, Professor... the mind-blocks aren't working anymore...
THE VISIONS ARE BACK!

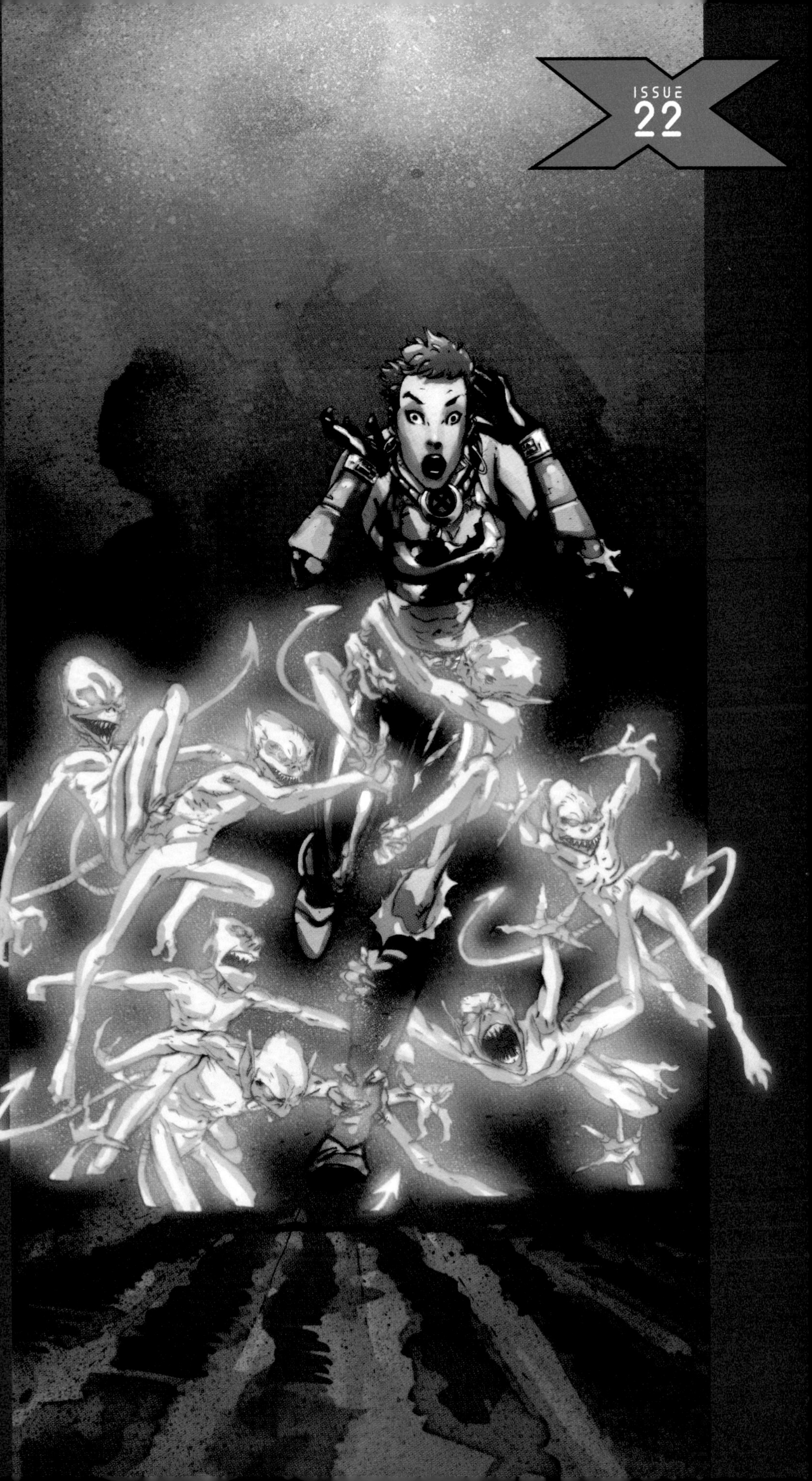
ISSUE
22

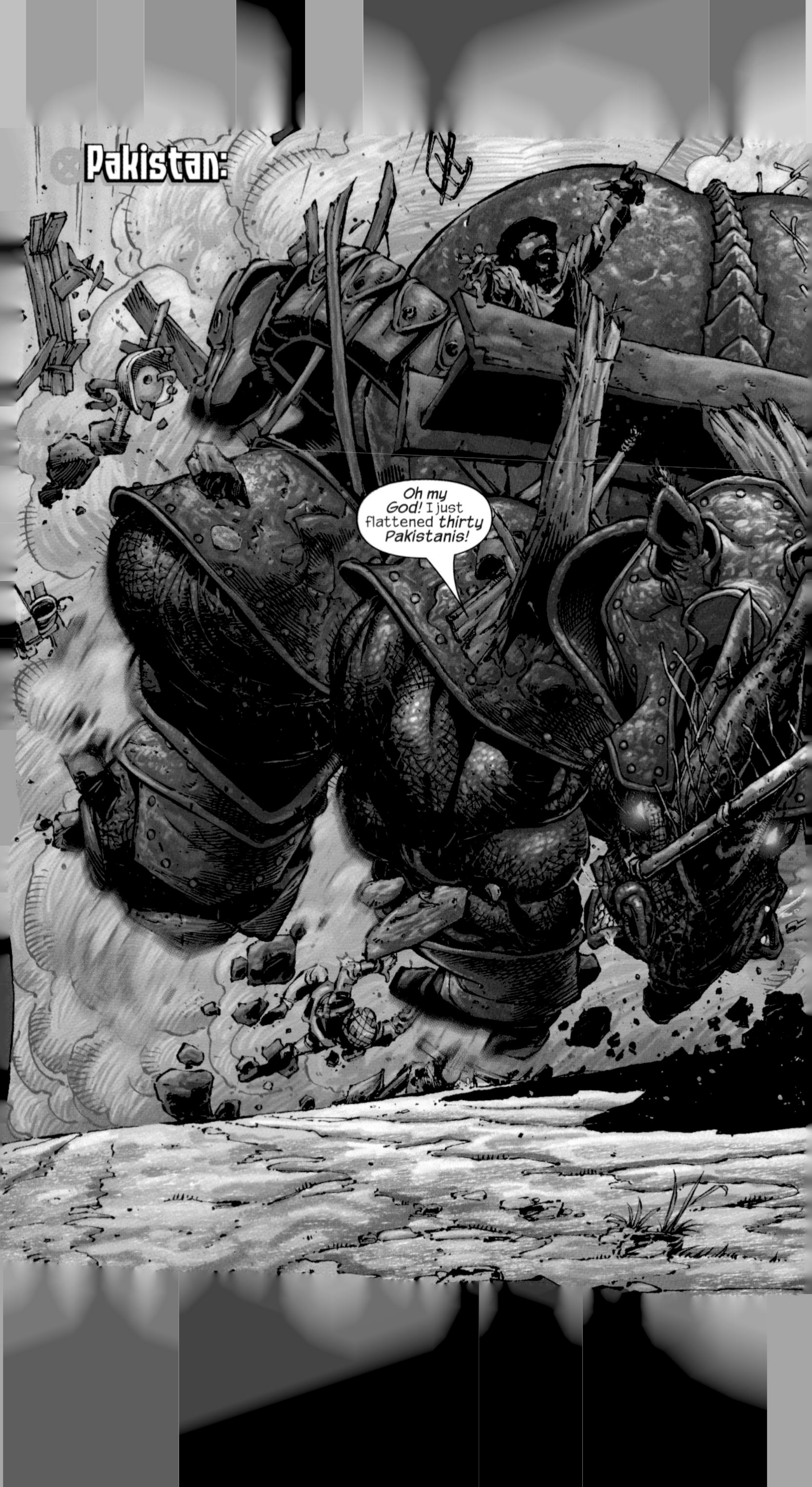
Pakistan:
Oh my God! I just flattened thirty Pakistanis!

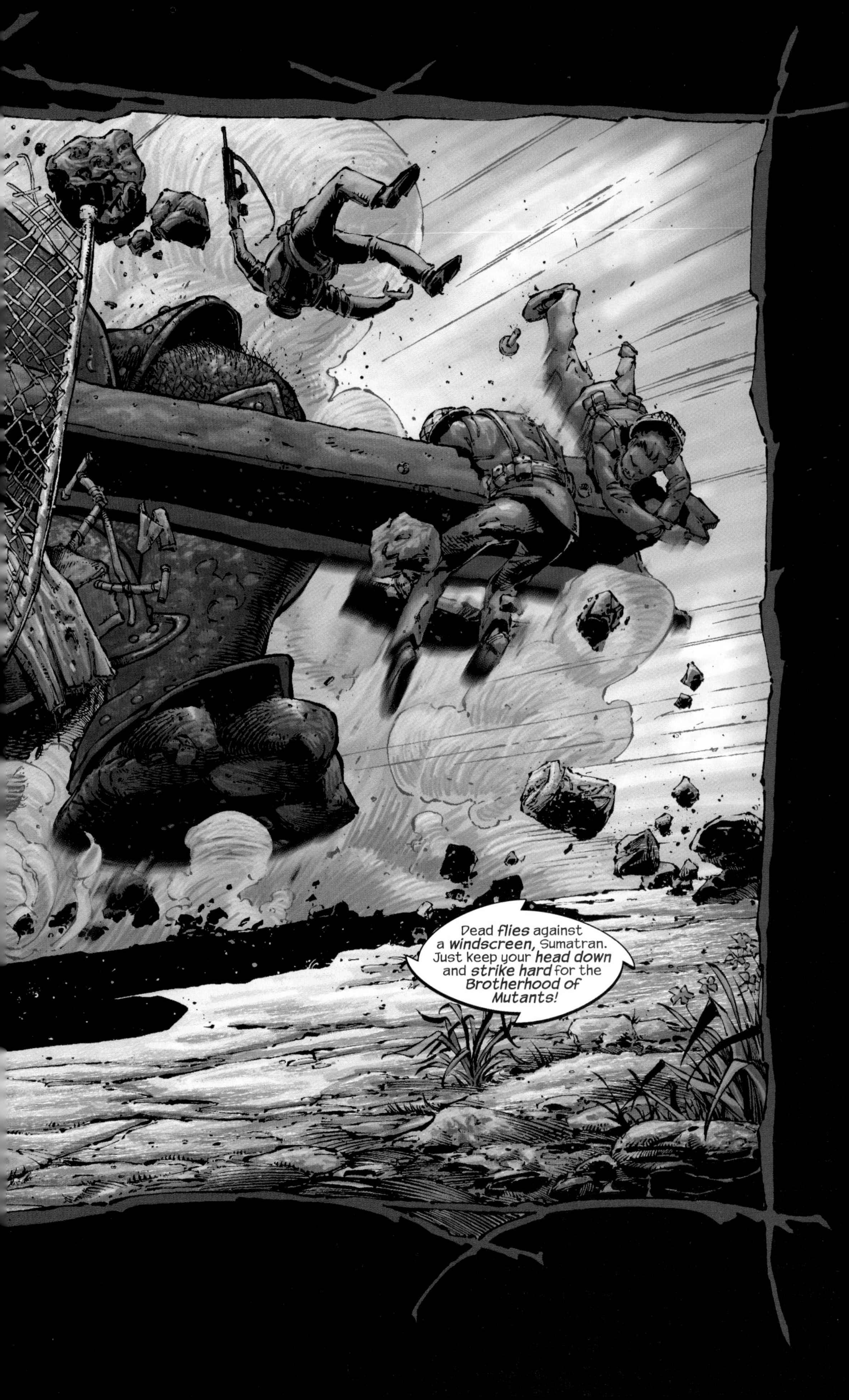
Dead *flies* against a ***windscreen,*** Sumatran. Just keep your ***head down*** and ***strike hard*** for the ***Brotherhood of Mutants!***

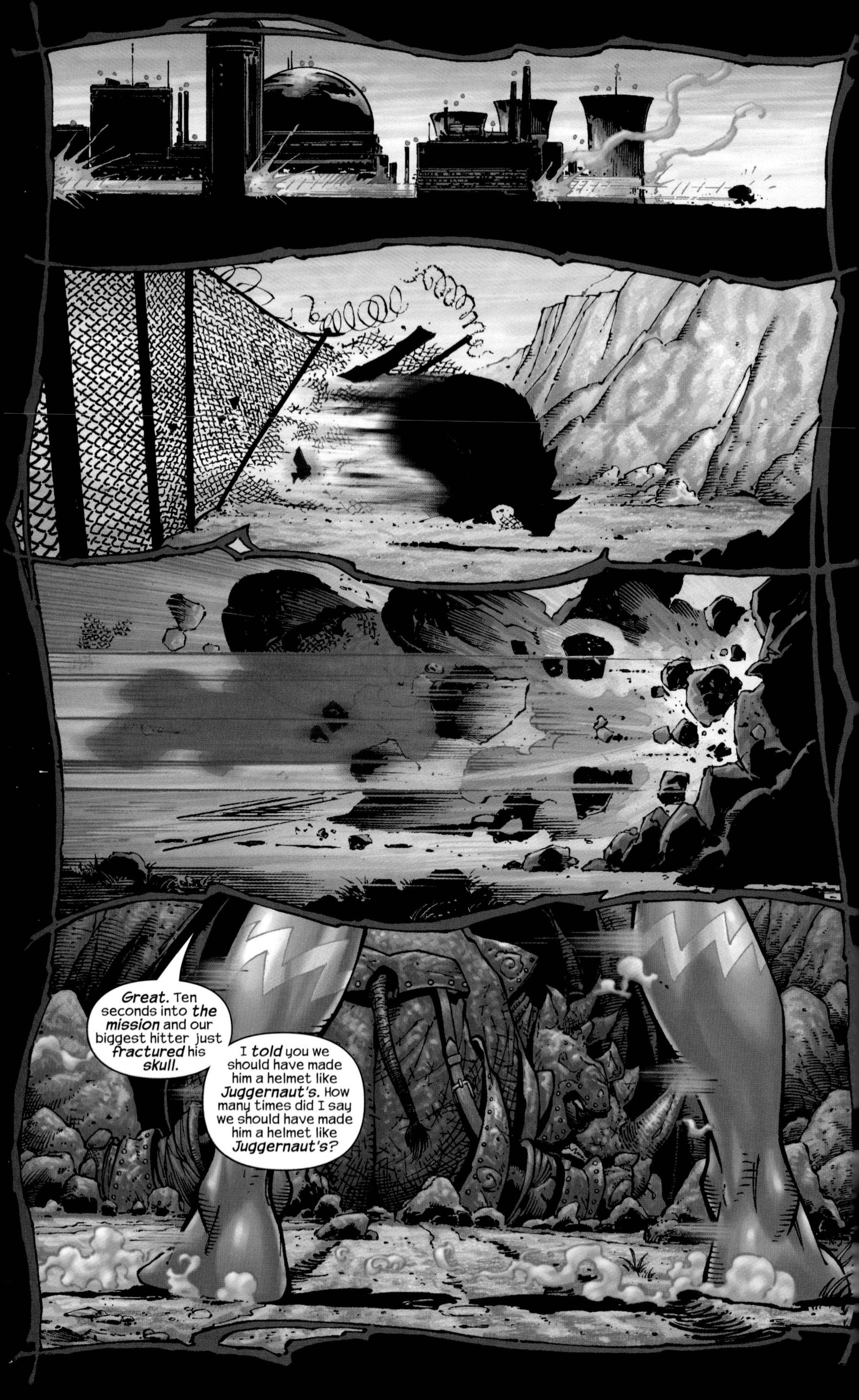
Great. Ten seconds into the mission and our biggest hitter just fractured his skull.
I told you we should have made him a helmet like Juggernaut's. How many times did I say we should have made him a helmet like Juggernaut's?

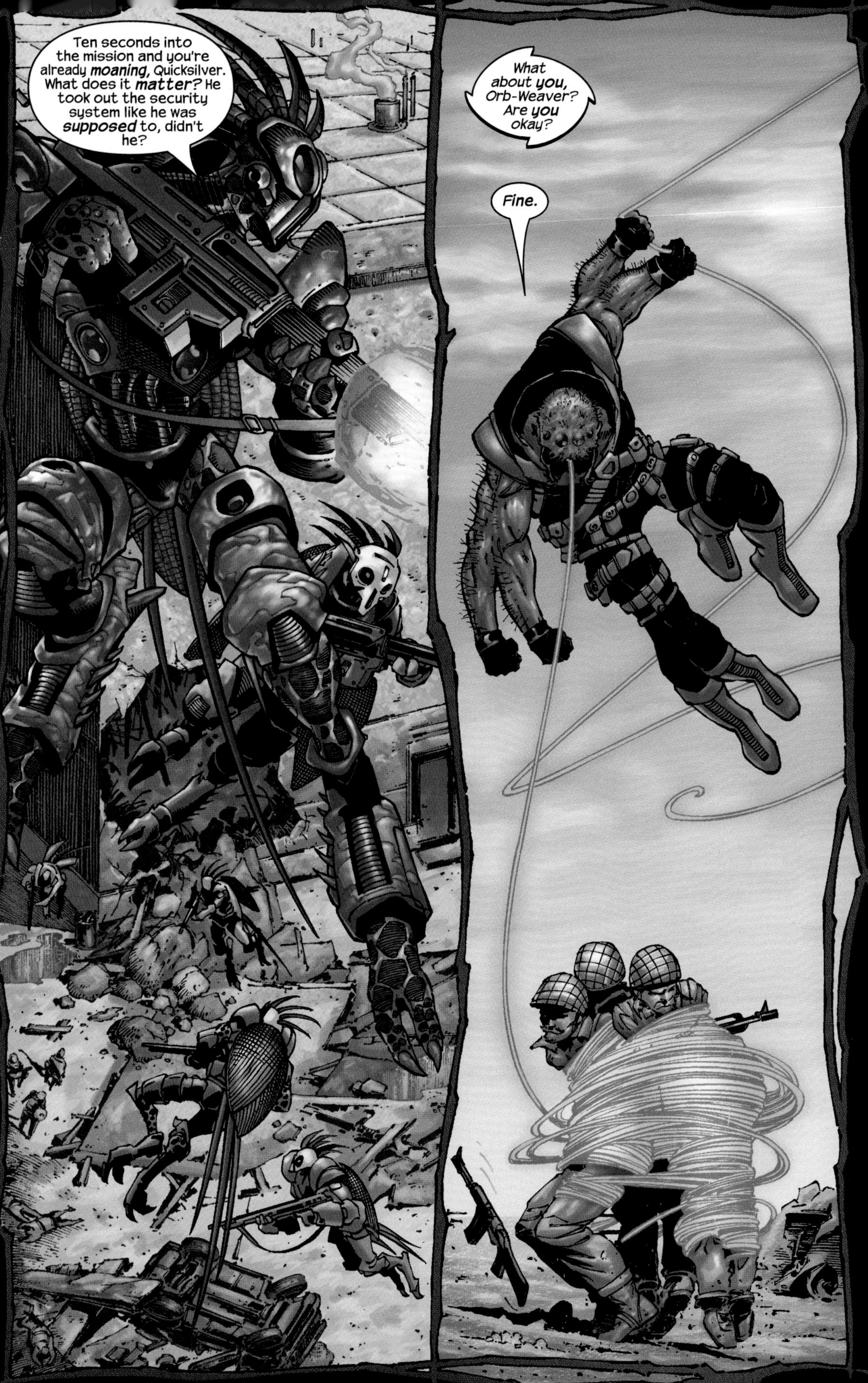
Ten seconds into the mission and you're already moaning, Quicksilver. What does it matter? He took out the security system like he was supposed to, didn't he?
What about you, Orb-Weaver? Are you okay?
Fine.

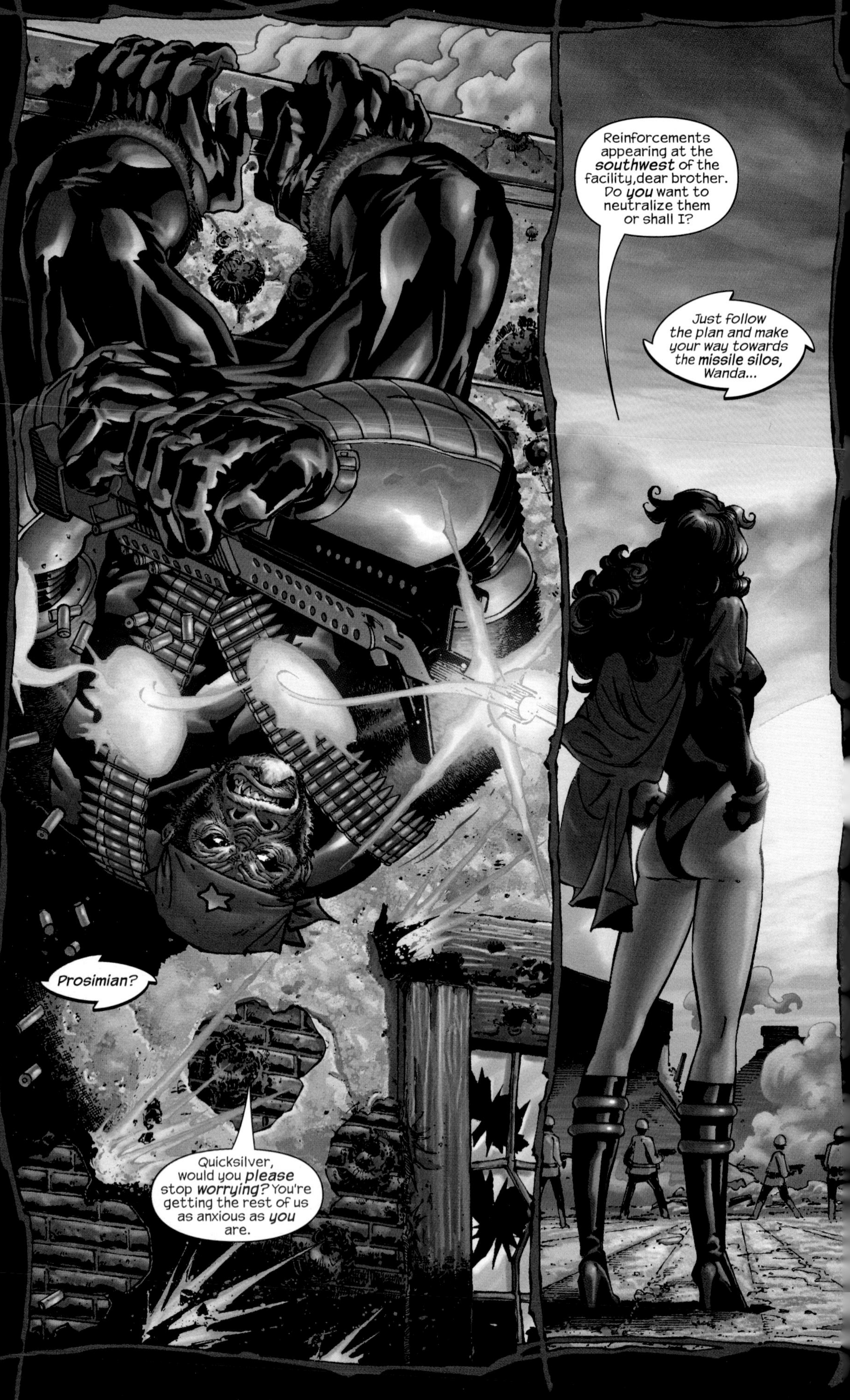
Reinforcements appearing at the southwest of the facility, dear brother. Do you want to neutralize them or shall I?
Just follow the plan and make your way towards the missile silos, Wanda...
Prosimian?
Quicksilver, would you please stop worrying? You're getting the rest of us as anxious as you are.

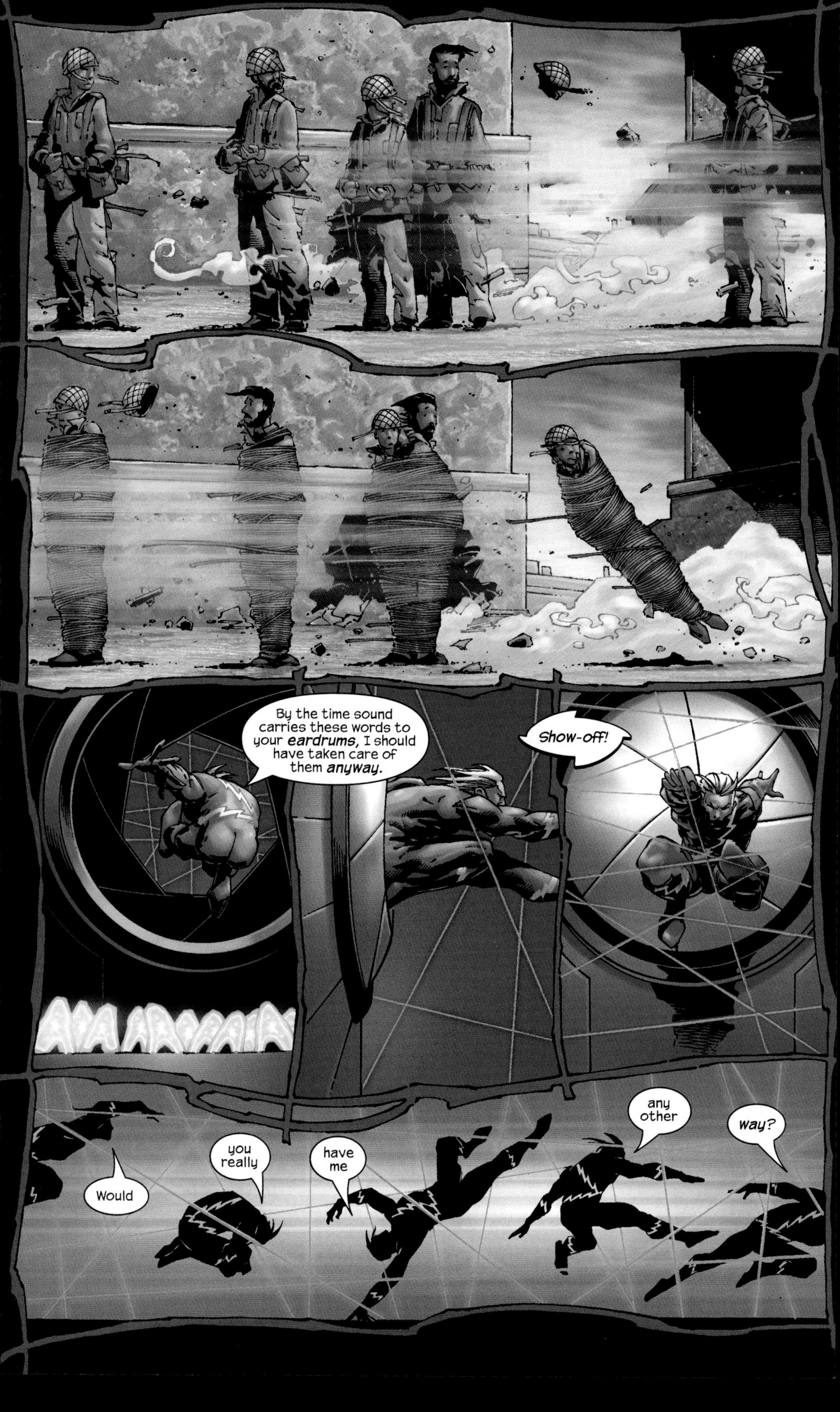

By the time sound carries these words to your *eardrums,* I should have taken care of them *anyway.*
*Show-off!*
Would
you really
have me
any other
*way?*

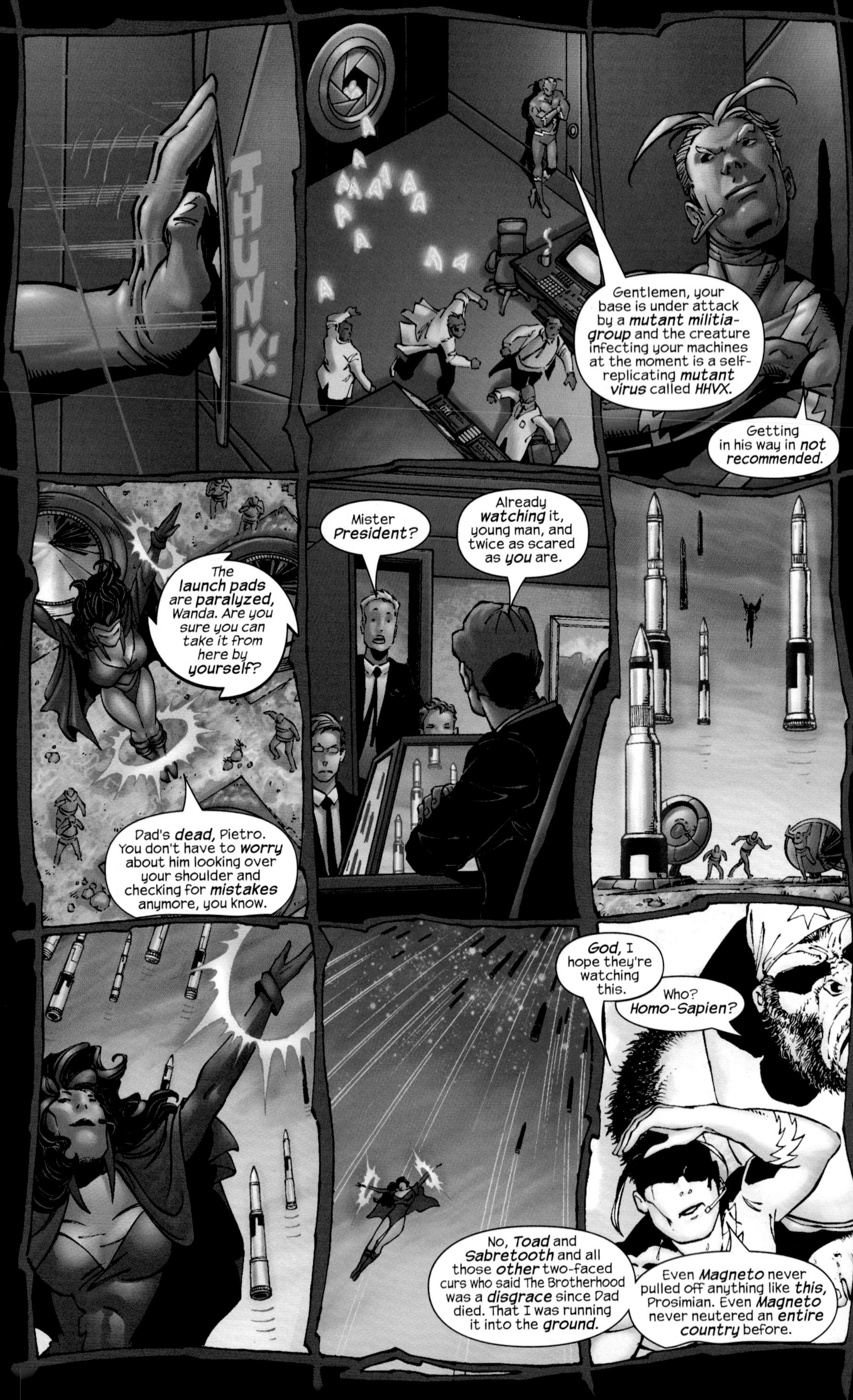
THUNK!
Gentlemen, your base is under attack by a mutant militia-group and the creature infecting your machines at the moment is a self-replicating mutant virus called HHVX.
Getting in his way in not recommended.
The launch pads are paralyzed, Wanda. Are you sure you can take it from here by yourself?
Dad's dead, Pietro. You don't have to worry about him looking over your shoulder and checking for mistakes anymore, you know.
Mister President?
Already watching it, young man, and twice as scared as you are.
God, I hope they're watching this.
Who? Homo-Sapien?
No, Toad and Sabretooth and all those other two-faced curs who said The Brotherhood was a disgrace since Dad died. That I was running it into the ground.
Even Magneto never pulled off anything like this, Prosimian. Even Magneto never neutered an entire country before.

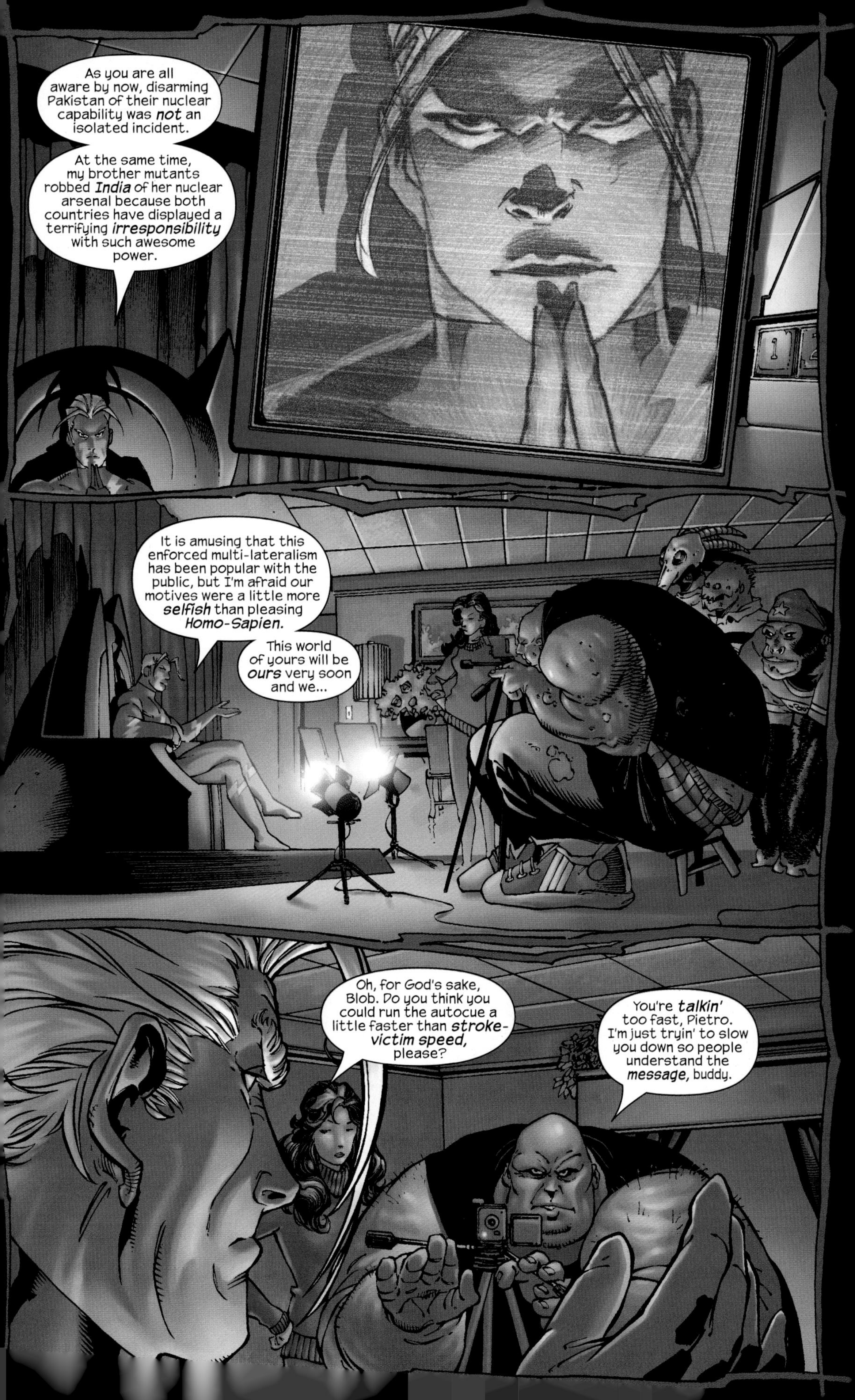

As you are all aware by now, disarming Pakistan of their nuclear capability was *not* an isolated incident.
At the same time, my brother mutants robbed *India* of her nuclear arsenal because both countries have displayed a terrifying *irresponsibility* with such awesome power.
It is amusing that this enforced multi-lateralism has been popular with the public, but I'm afraid our motives were a little more *selfish* than pleasing *Homo-Sapien.*
This world of yours will be *ours* very soon and we...
Oh, for God's sake, Blob. Do you think you could run the autocue a little faster than *stroke-victim speed,* please?
You're *talkin'* too fast, Pietro. I'm just tryin' to slow you down so people understand the *message,* buddy.

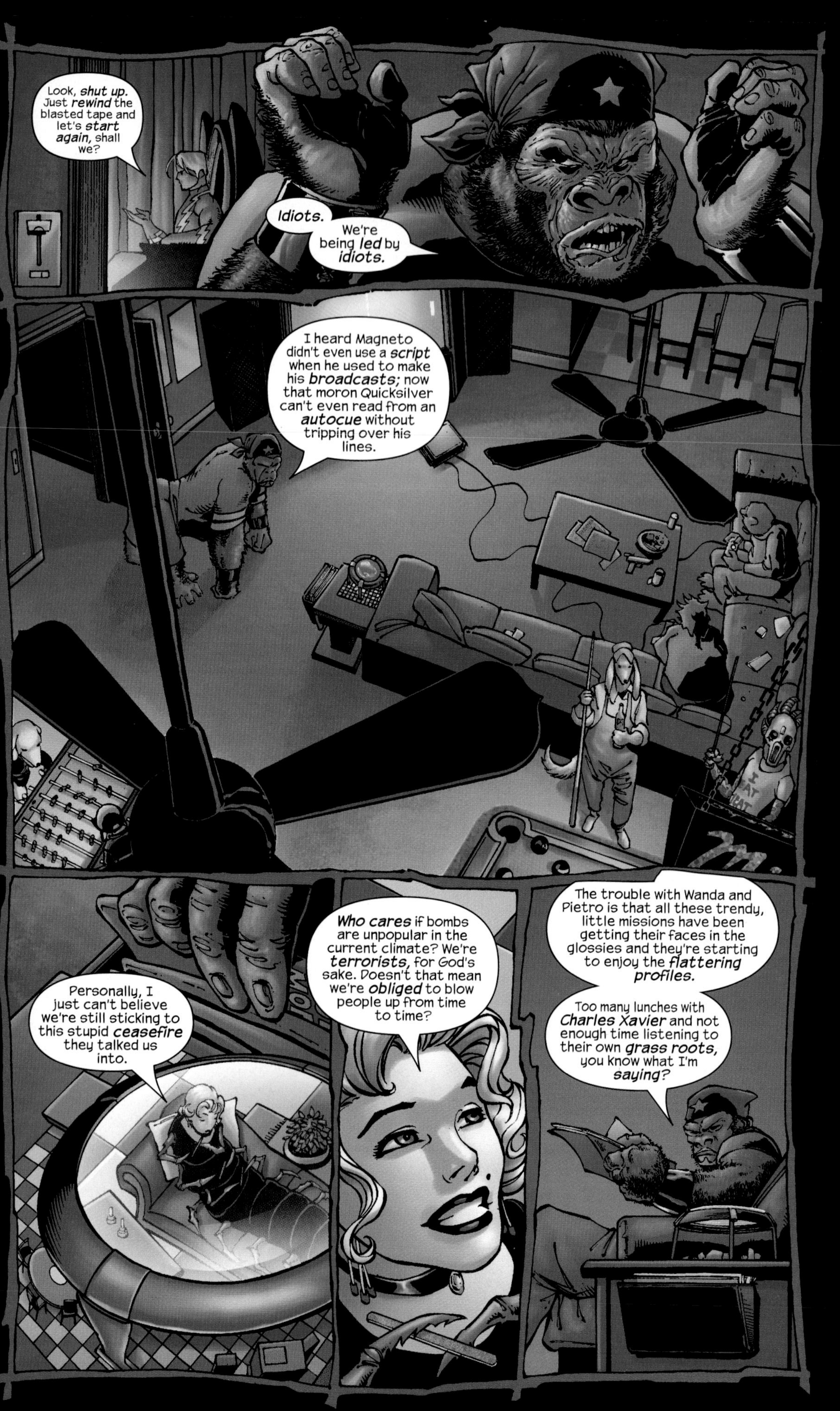
Look, shut up. Just rewind the blasted tape and let's start again, shall we?
Idiots.
We're being led by idiots.
I heard Magneto didn't even use a script when he used to make his broadcasts; now that moron Quicksilver can't even read from an autocue without tripping over his lines.
Personally, I just can't believe we're still sticking to this stupid ceasefire they talked us into.
Who cares if bombs are unpopular in the current climate? We're terrorists, for God's sake. Doesn't that mean we're obliged to blow people up from time to time?
The trouble with Wanda and Pietro is that all these trendy, little missions have been getting their faces in the glossies and they're starting to enjoy the flattering profiles.
Too many lunches with Charles Xavier and not enough time listening to their own grass roots, you know what I'm saying?

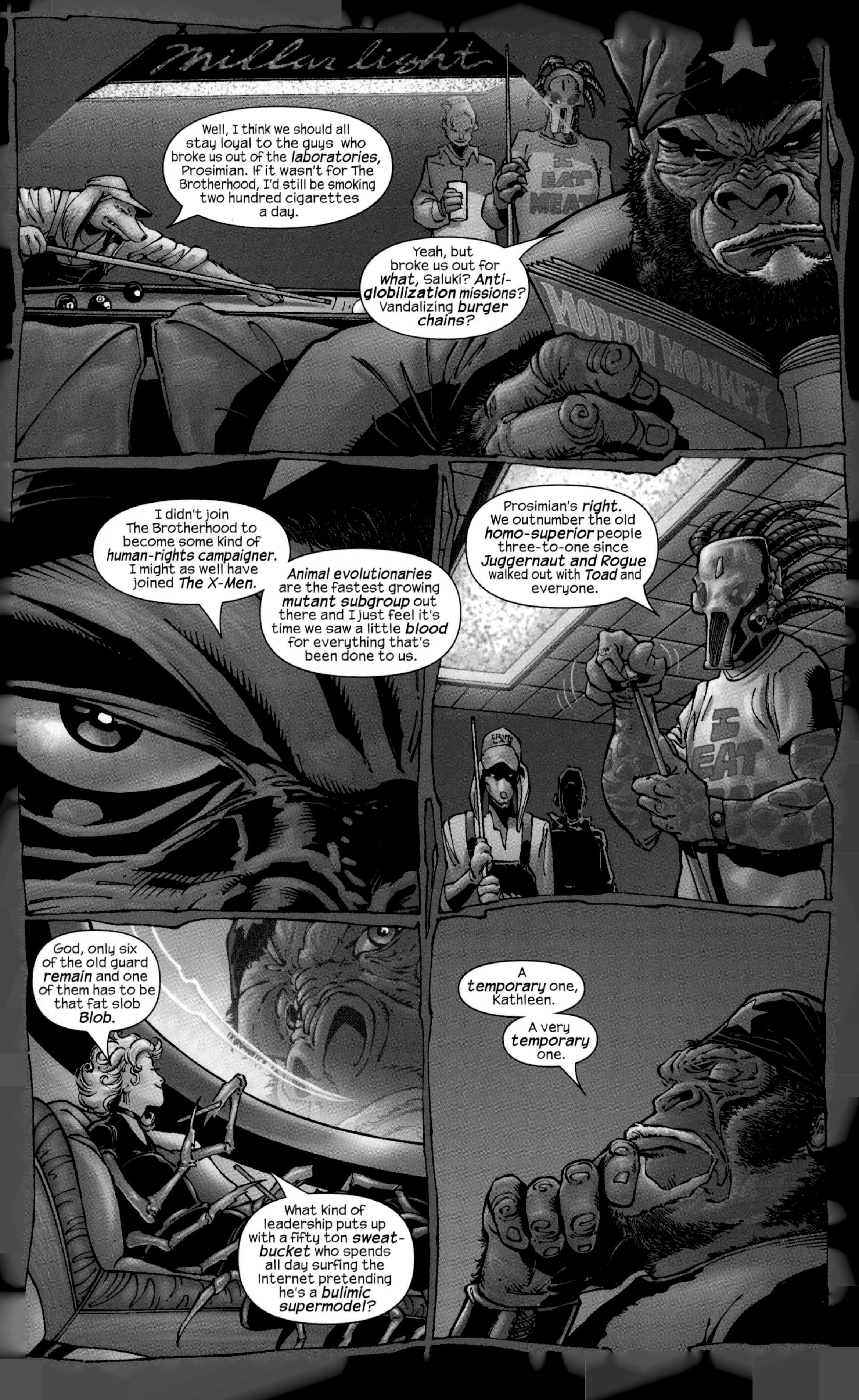
Millar light
Well, I think we should all stay loyal to the guys who broke us out of the *laboratories,* Prosimian. If it wasn't for The Brotherhood, I'd still be smoking two hundred cigarettes a day.
Yeah, but broke us out for *what,* Saluki? *Anti-globilization* missions? Vandalizing *burger chains?*
MODERN MONKEY
I didn't join The Brotherhood to become some kind of *human-rights campaigner.* I might as well have joined *The X-Men.*
*Animal evolutionaries* are the fastest growing *mutant subgroup* out there and I just feel it's time we saw a little *blood* for everything that's been done to us.
Prosimian's *right.* We outnumber the old *homo-superior* people three-to-one since *Juggernaut and Rogue* walked out with *Toad* and everyone.
God, only six of the old guard *remain* and one of them has to be that fat slob *Blob.*
What kind of leadership puts up with a fifty ton *sweat-bucket* who spends all day surfing the Internet pretending he's a *bulimic supermodel?*
A *temporary* one, Kathleen.
A very *temporary* one.

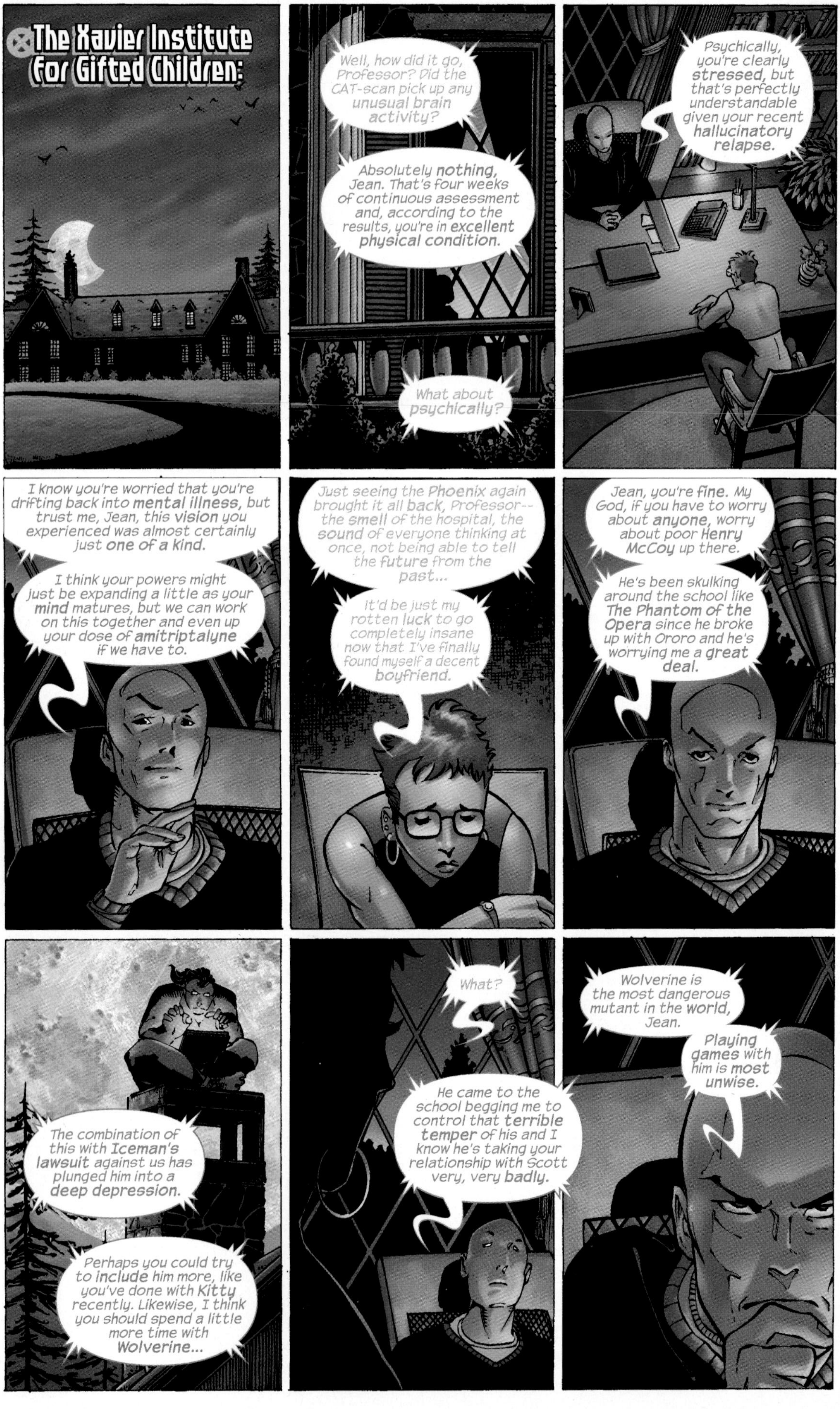

The Xavier Institute For Gifted Children:
Well, how did it go, Professor? Did the CAT-scan pick up any unusual brain activity?
Absolutely nothing, Jean. That's four weeks of continuous assessment and, according to the results, you're in excellent physical condition.
What about psychically?
Psychically, you're clearly stressed, but that's perfectly understandable given your recent hallucinatory relapse.
I know you're worried that you're drifting back into mental illness, but trust me, Jean, this vision you experienced was almost certainly just one of a kind.
I think your powers might just be expanding a little as your mind matures, but we can work on this together and even up your dose of amitriptalyne if we have to.
Just seeing the Phoenix again brought it all back, Professor-- the smell of the hospital, the sound of everyone thinking at once, not being able to tell the future from the past...
It'd be just my rotten luck to go completely insane now that I've finally found myself a decent boyfriend.
Jean, you're fine. My God, if you have to worry about anyone, worry about poor Henry McCoy up there.
He's been skulking around the school like The Phantom of the Opera since he broke up with Ororo and he's worrying me a great deal.
The combination of this with Iceman's lawsuit against us has plunged him into a deep depression.
Perhaps you could try to include him more, like you've done with Kitty recently. Likewise, I think you should spend a little more time with Wolverine...
What?
He came to the school begging me to control that terrible temper of his and I know he's taking your relationship with Scott very, very badly.
Wolverine is the most dangerous mutant in the world, Jean.
Playing games with him is most unwise.

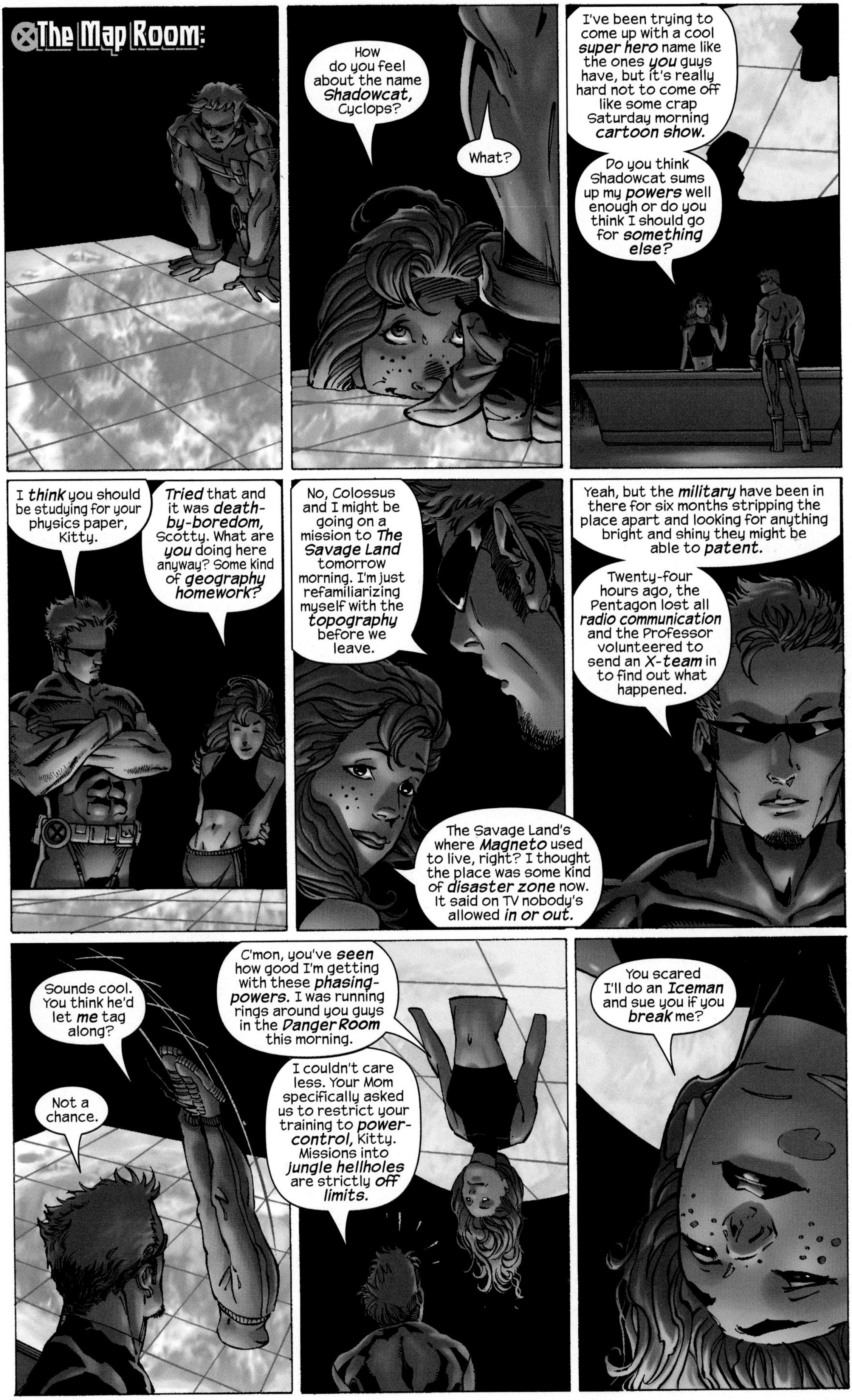
The Map Room:
How do you feel about the name Shadowcat, Cyclops?
What?
I've been trying to come up with a cool super hero name like the ones you guys have, but it's really hard not to come off like some crap Saturday morning cartoon show.
Do you think Shadowcat sums up my powers well enough or do you think I should go for something else?
I think you should be studying for your physics paper, Kitty.
Tried that and it was death-by-boredom, Scotty. What are you doing here anyway? Some kind of geography homework?
No, Colossus and I might be going on a mission to The Savage Land tomorrow morning. I'm just refamiliarizing myself with the topography before we leave.
The Savage Land's where Magneto used to live, right? I thought the place was some kind of disaster zone now. It said on TV nobody's allowed in or out.
Yeah, but the military have been in there for six months stripping the place apart and looking for anything bright and shiny they might be able to patent.
Twenty-four hours ago, the Pentagon lost all radio communication and the Professor volunteered to send an X-team in to find out what happened.
Sounds cool. You think he'd let me tag along?
Not a chance.
C'mon, you've seen how good I'm getting with these phasing-powers. I was running rings around you guys in the Danger Room this morning.
I couldn't care less. Your Mom specifically asked us to restrict your training to power-control, Kitty. Missions into jungle hellholes are strictly off limits.
You scared I'll do an Iceman and sue you if you break me?

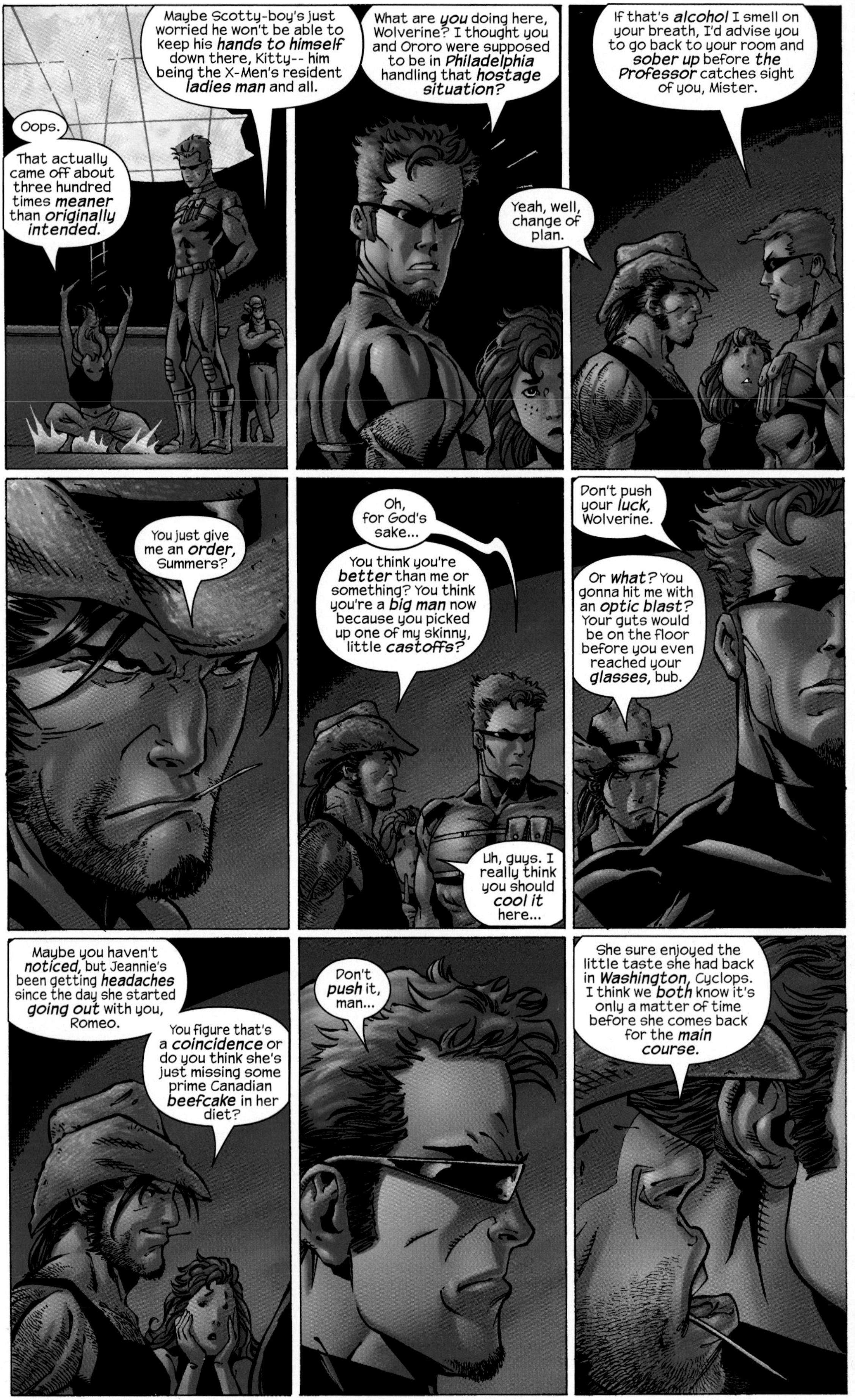
Maybe Scotty-boy's just worried he won't be able to keep his hands to himself down there, Kitty-- him being the X-Men's resident ladies man and all.
Oops.
That actually came off about three hundred times meaner than originally intended.
What are you doing here, Wolverine? I thought you and Ororo were supposed to be in Philadelphia handling that hostage situation?
Yeah, well, change of plan.
If that's alcohol I smell on your breath, I'd advise you to go back to your room and sober up before the Professor catches sight of you, Mister.
You just give me an order, Summers?
Oh, for God's sake...
You think you're better than me or something? You think you're a big man now because you picked up one of my skinny, little castoffs?
Uh, guys. I really think you should cool it here...
Don't push your luck, Wolverine.
Or what? You gonna hit me with an optic blast? Your guts would be on the floor before you even reached your glasses, bub.
Maybe you haven't noticed, but Jeannie's been getting headaches since the day she started going out with you, Romeo.
You figure that's a coincidence or do you think she's just missing some prime Canadian beefcake in her diet?
Don't push it, man...
She sure enjoyed the little taste she had back in Washington, Cyclops. I think we both know it's only a matter of time before she comes back for the main course.

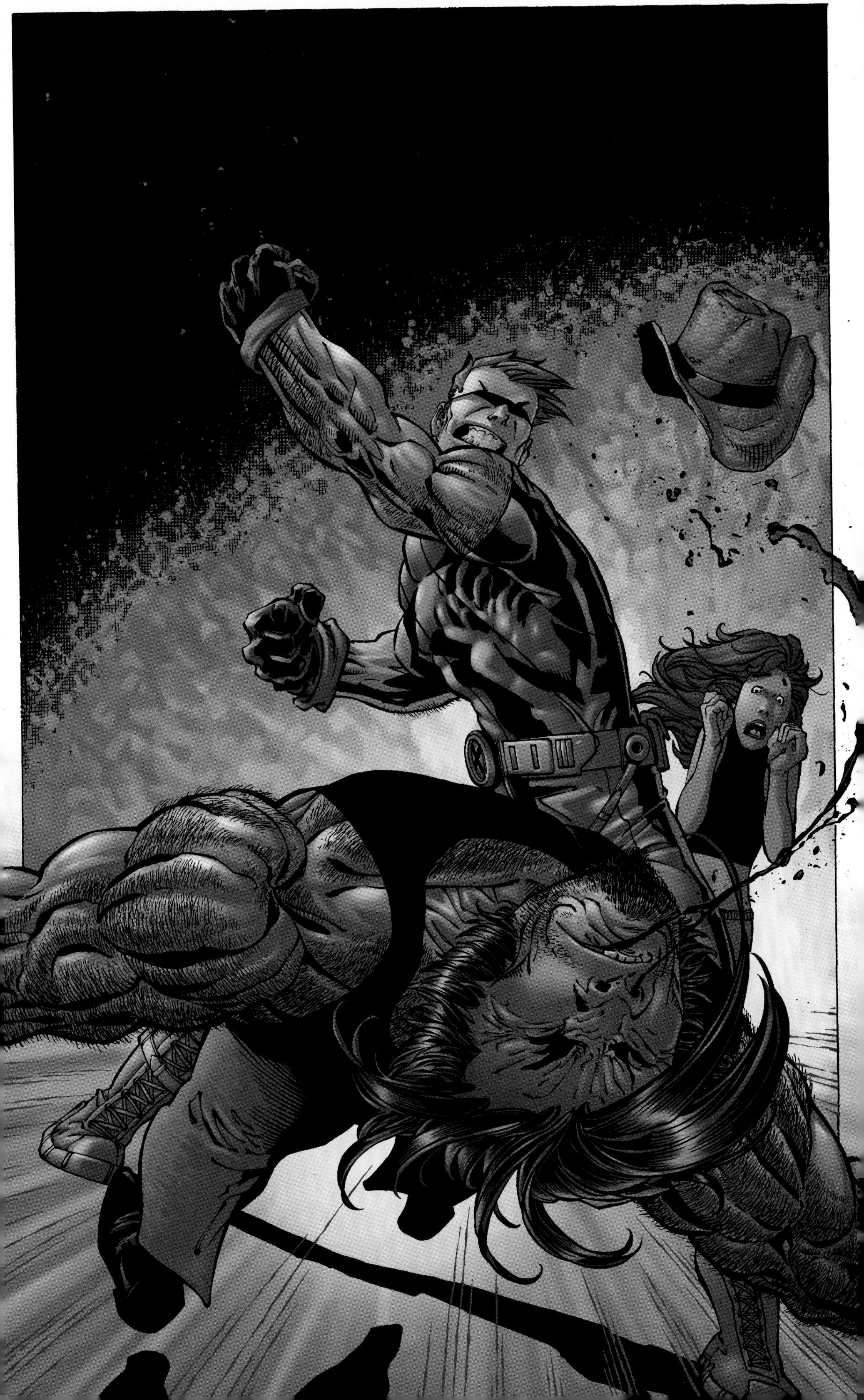

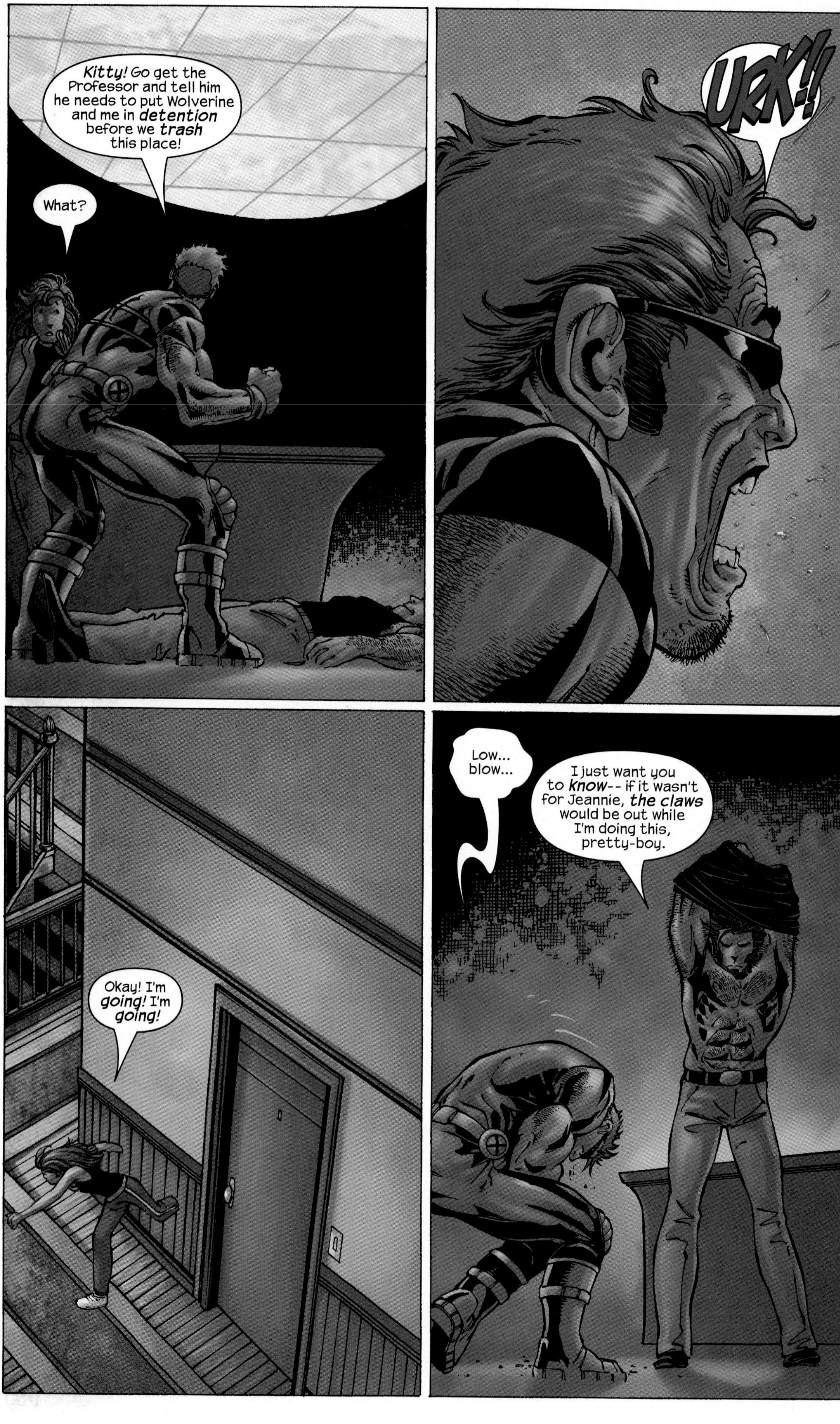
Kitty! Go get the Professor and tell him he needs to put Wolverine and me in detention before we trash this place!
What?
URK!!
Okay! I'm going! I'm going!
Low... blow...
I just want you to know-- if it wasn't for Jeannie, the claws would be out while I'm doing this, pretty-boy.

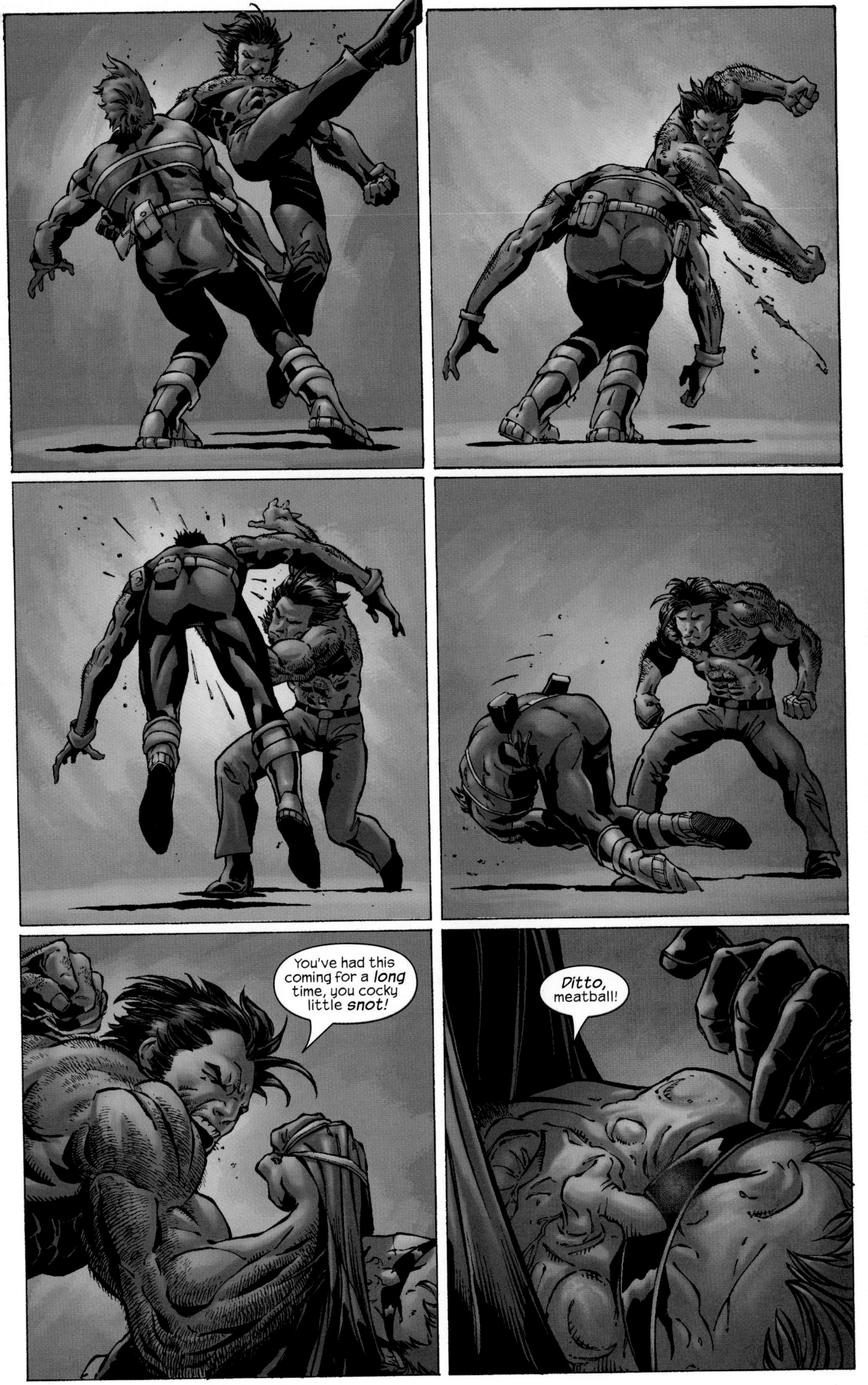
You've had this coming for a *long* time, you cocky little *snot!*
*Ditto,* meatball!

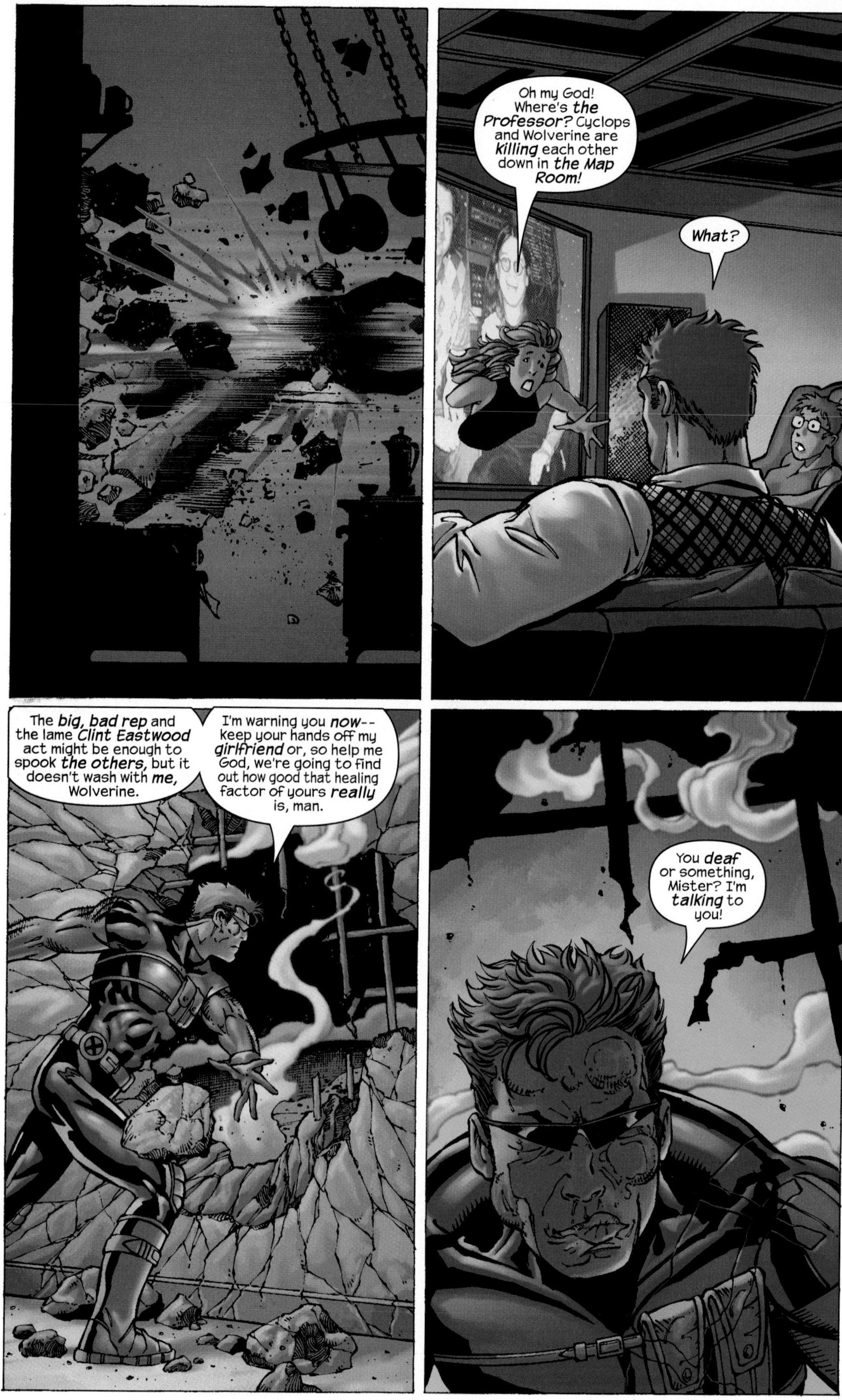

Oh my God! Where's the Professor? Cyclops and Wolverine are killing each other down in the Map Room!
What?
The big, bad rep and the lame Clint Eastwood act might be enough to spook the others, but it doesn't wash with me, Wolverine.
I'm warning you now-- keep your hands off my girlfriend or, so help me God, we're going to find out how good that healing factor of yours really is, man.
You deaf or something, Mister? I'm talking to you!

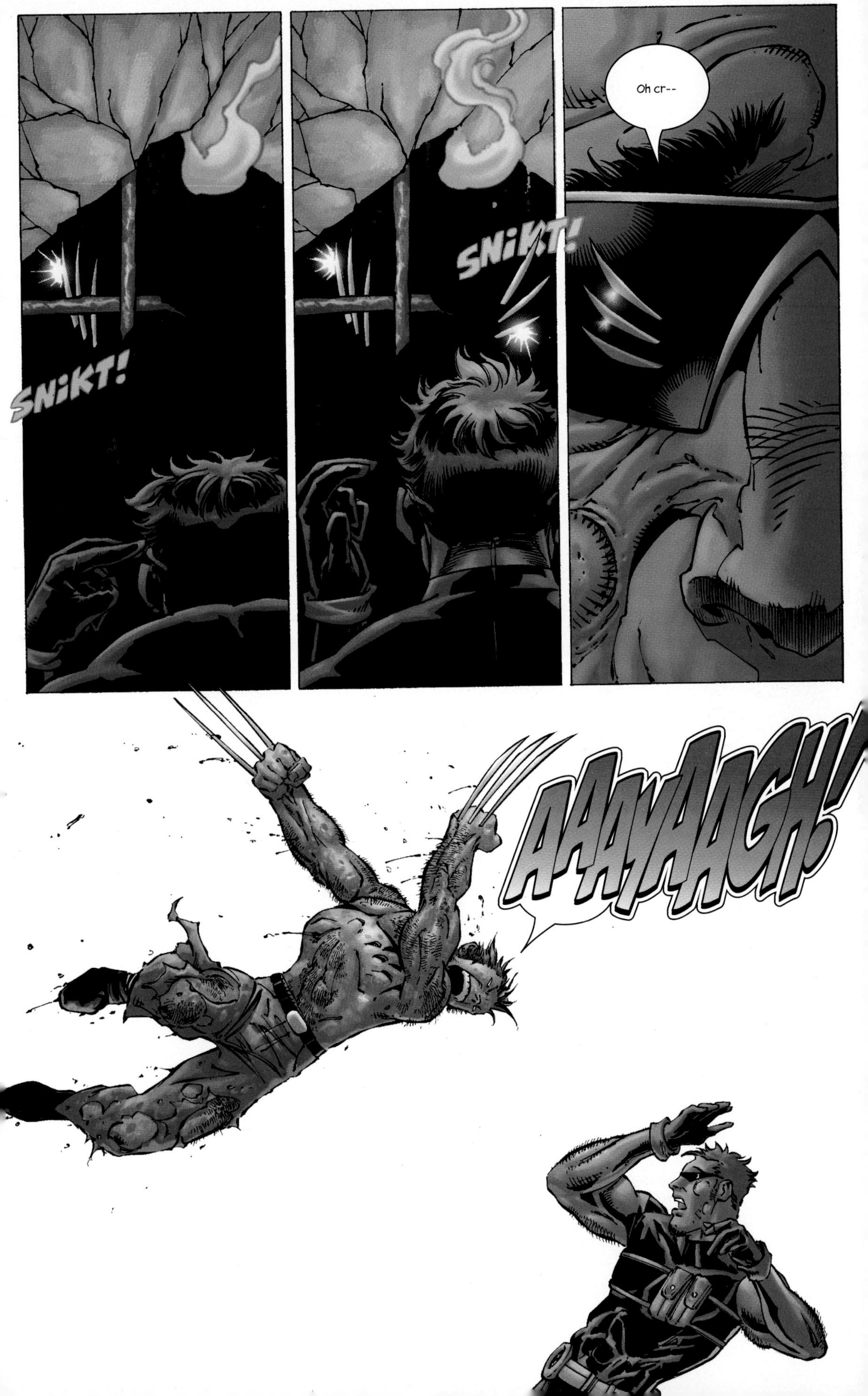
SNIKT!
SNIKT!
Oh cr--
AAAYAAGH!

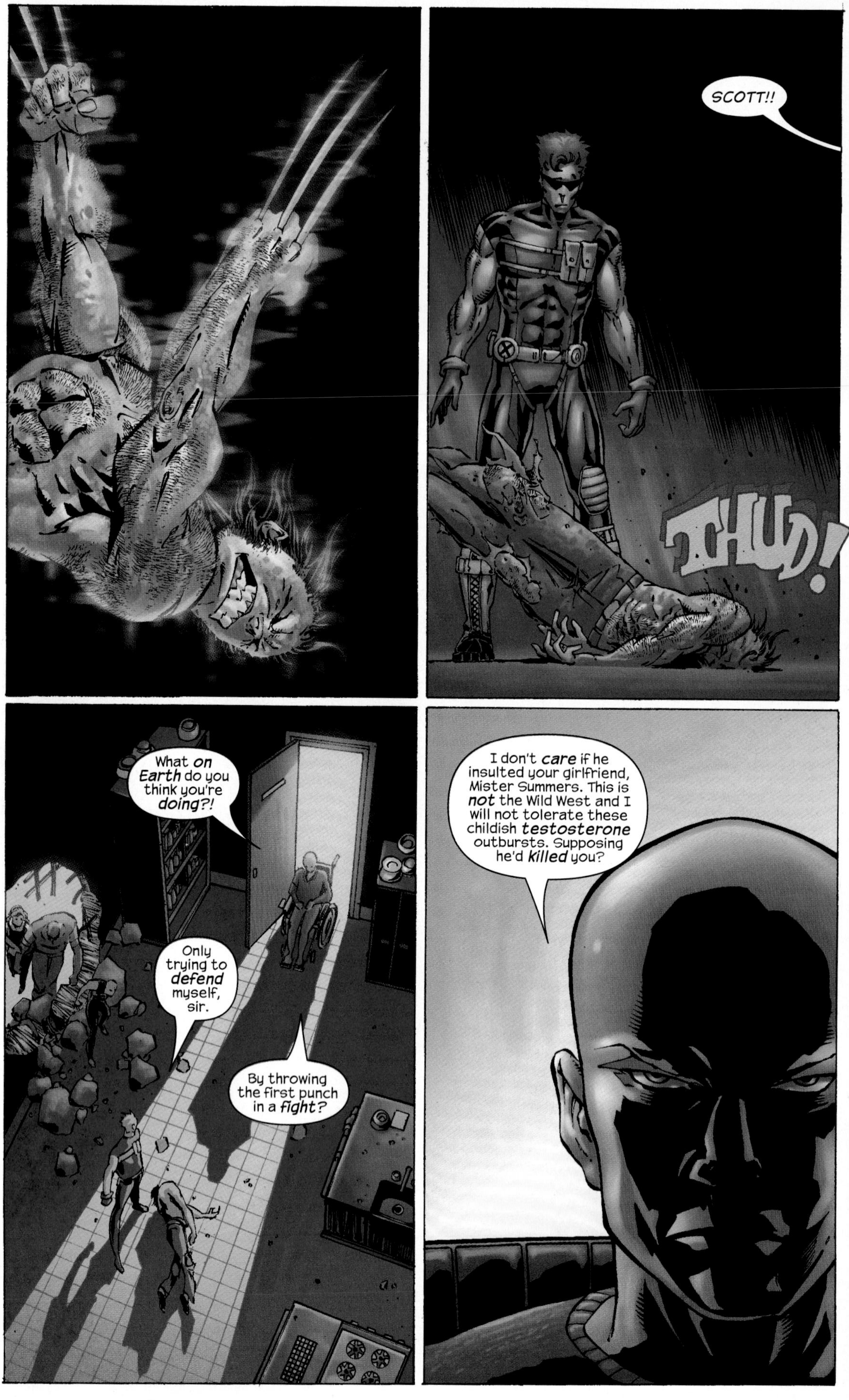
SCOTT!!
THUD!
What on Earth do you think you're doing?!
Only trying to defend myself, sir.
By throwing the first punch in a fight?
I don't care if he insulted your girlfriend, Mister Summers. This is not the Wild West and I will not tolerate these childish testosterone outbursts. Supposing he'd killed you?

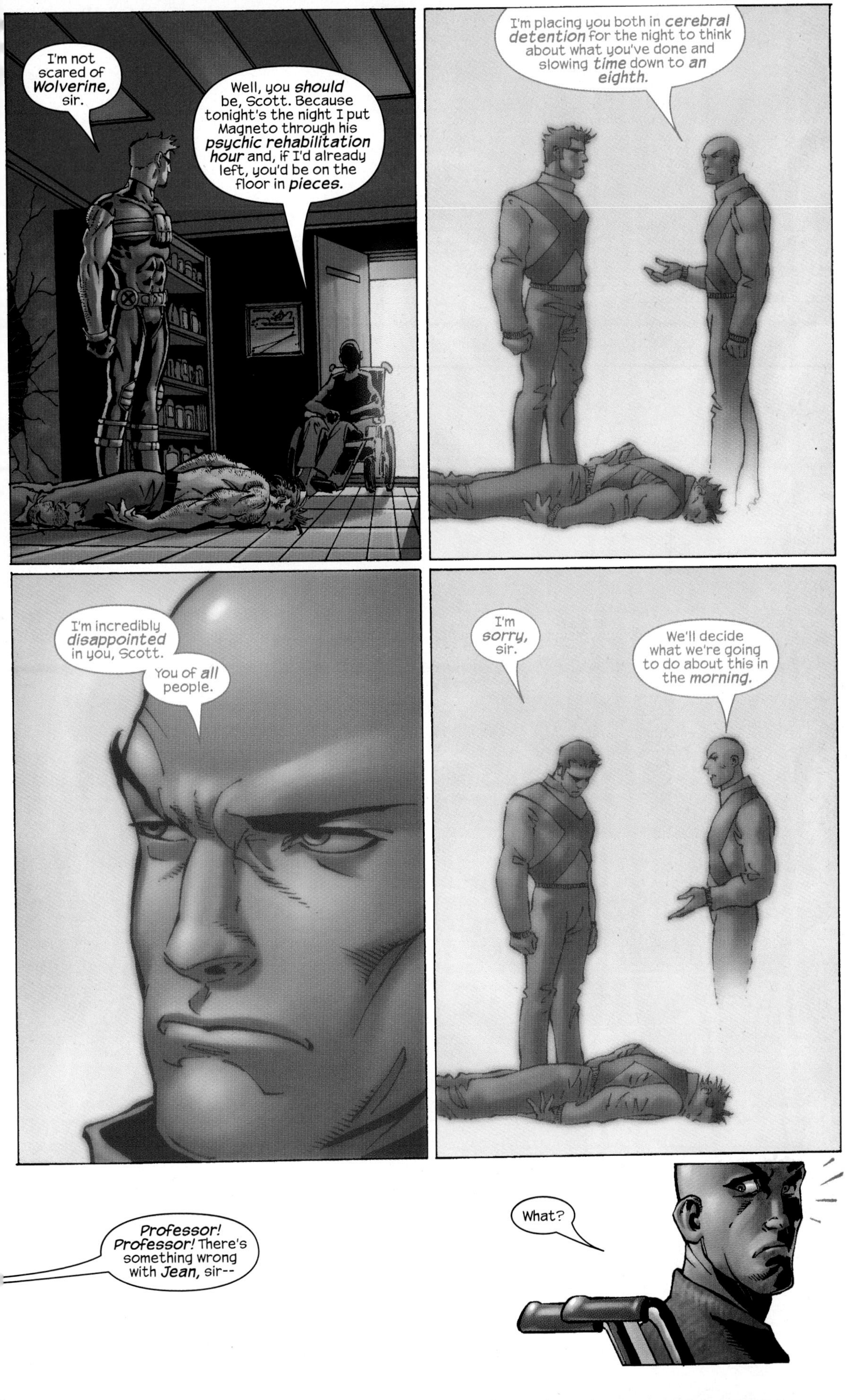
I'm not scared of Wolverine, sir.
Well, you should be, Scott. Because tonight's the night I put Magneto through his psychic rehabilitation hour and, if I'd already left, you'd be on the floor in pieces.
I'm placing you both in cerebral detention for the night to think about what you've done and slowing time down to an eighth.
I'm incredibly disappointed in you, Scott.
You of all people.
I'm sorry, sir.
We'll decide what we're going to do about this in the morning.
Professor! Professor! There's something wrong with Jean, sir--
What?

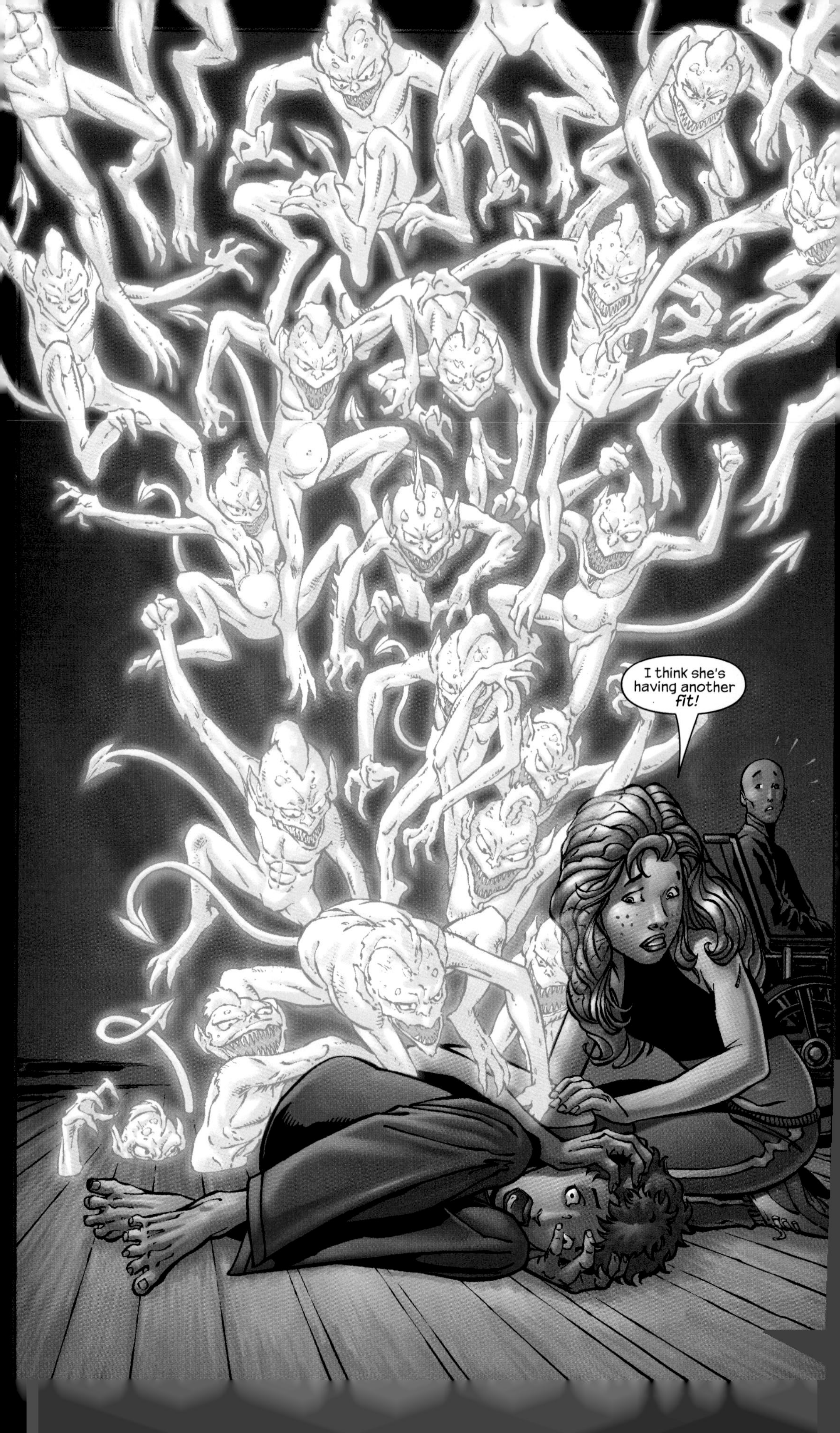
I think she's having another *fit!*

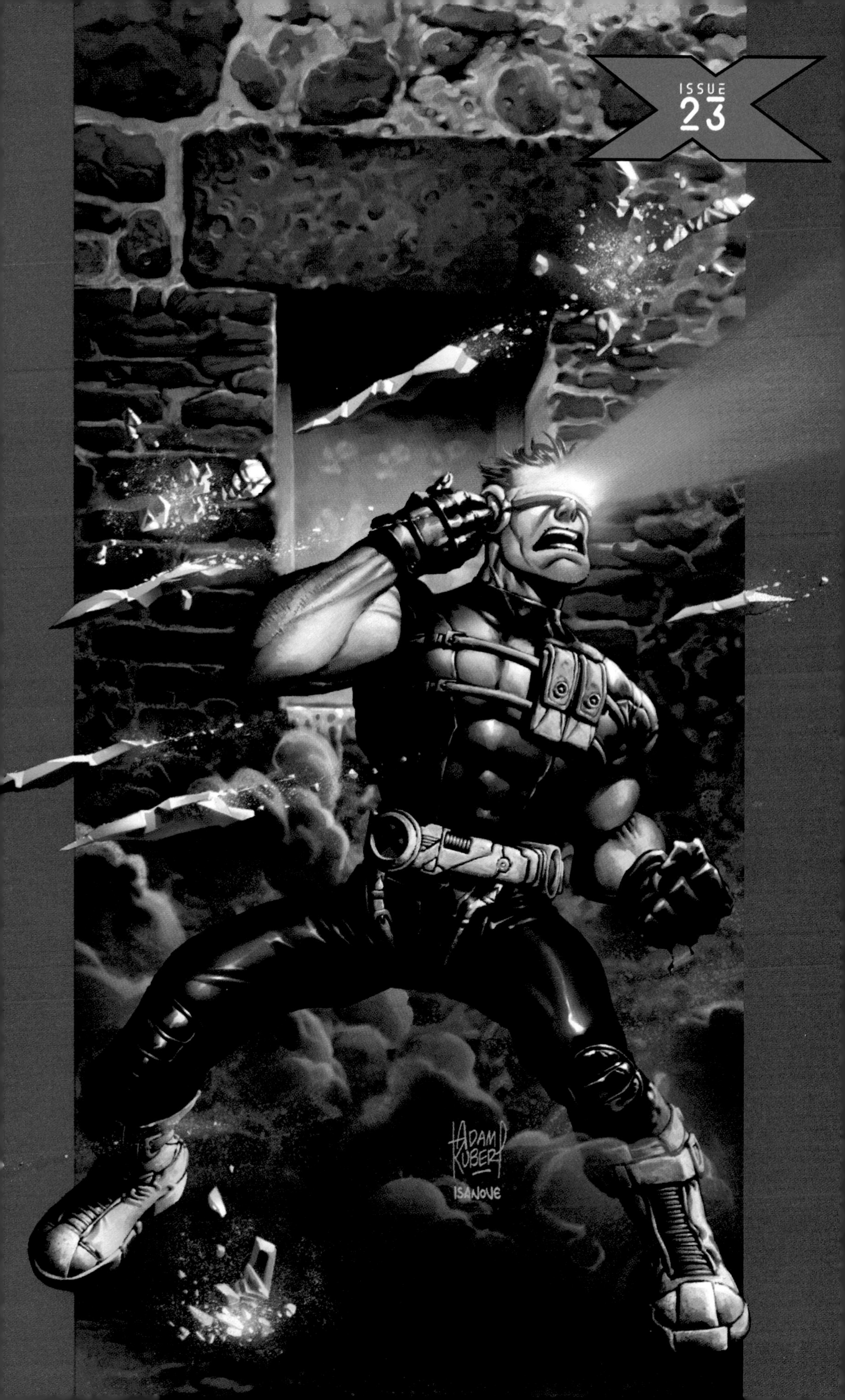
ISSUE
23
ADAM KUBERT
ISANOVE

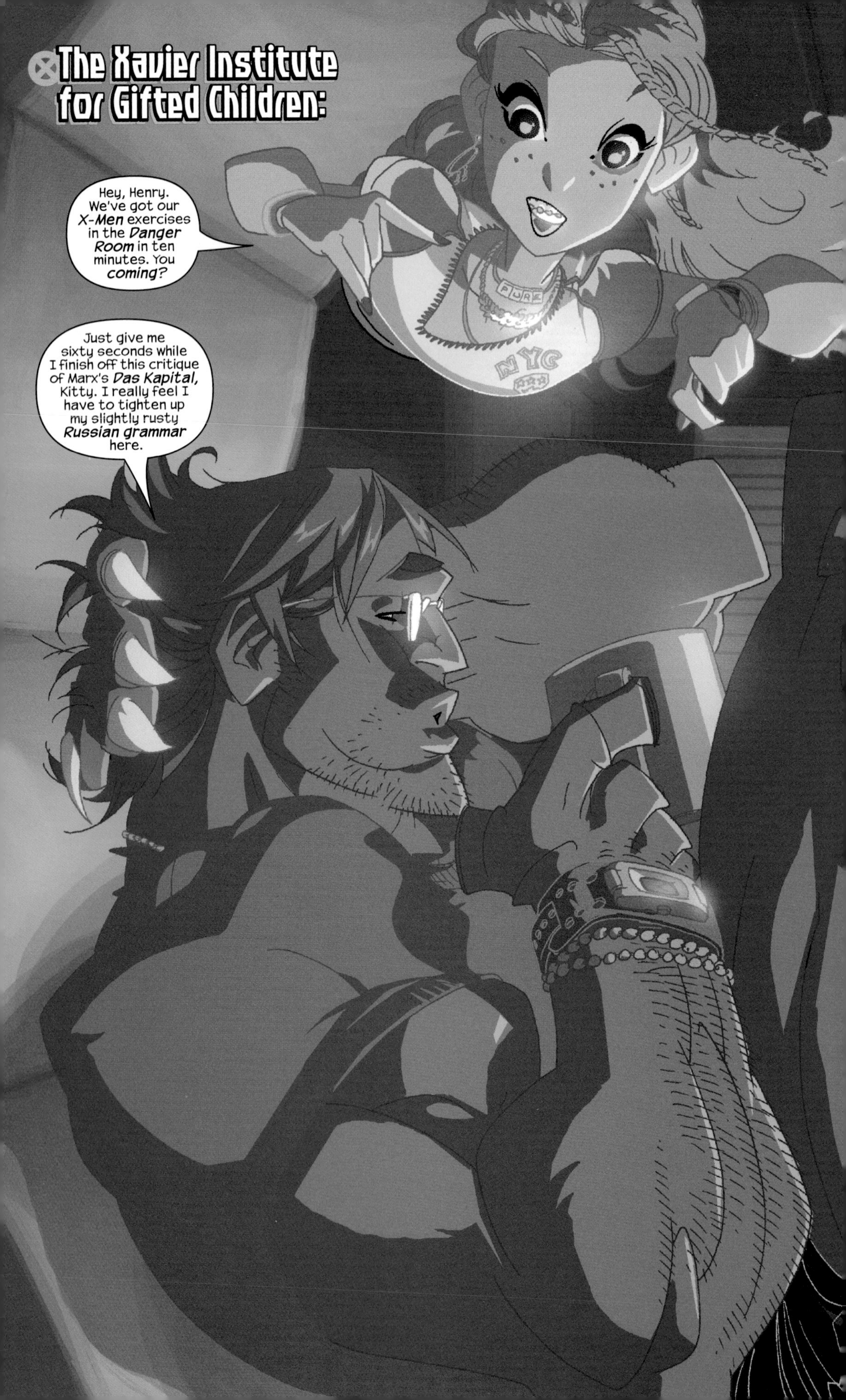
The Xavier Institute for Gifted Children:
Hey, Henry. We've got our X-Men exercises in the Danger Room in ten minutes. You coming?
Just give me sixty seconds while I finish off this critique of Marx's Das Kapital, Kitty. I really feel I have to tighten up my slightly rusty Russian grammar here.
PURE
NYC

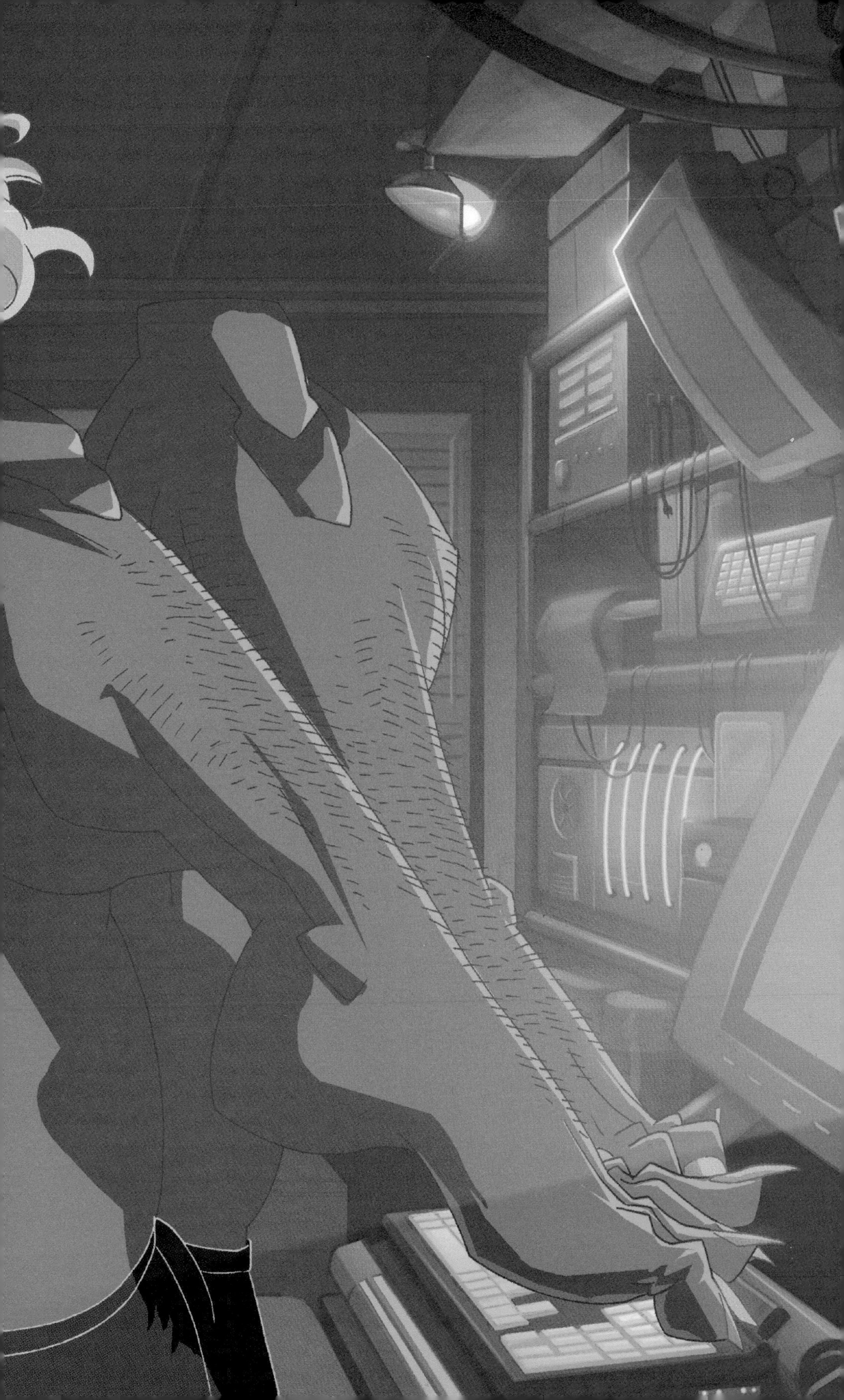

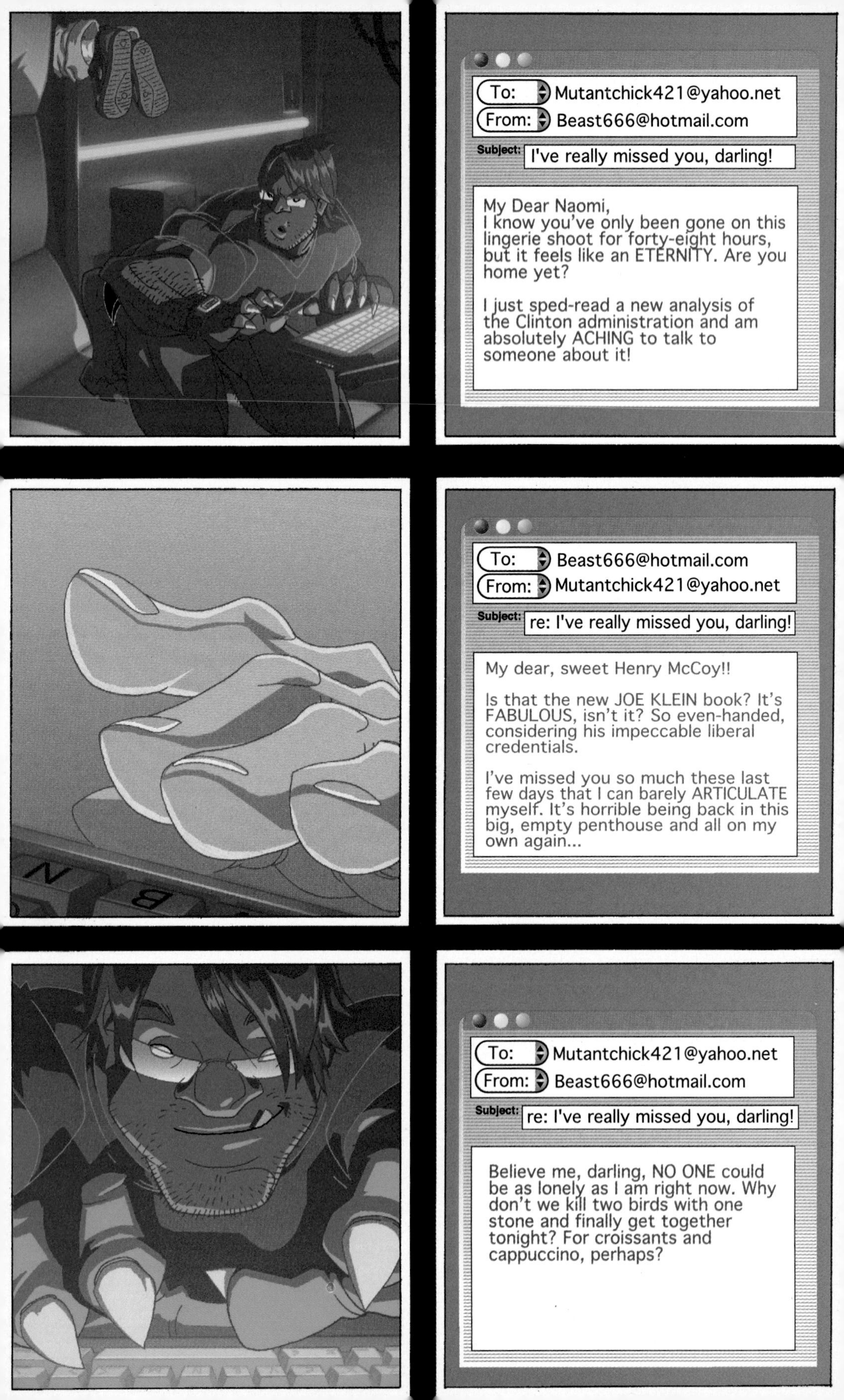
To: Mutantchick421@yahoo.net
From: Beast666@hotmail.com
Subject: I've really missed you, darling!
My Dear Naomi,
I know you've only been gone on this lingerie shoot for forty-eight hours, but it feels like an ETERNITY. Are you home yet?
I just sped-read a new analysis of the Clinton administration and am absolutely ACHING to talk to someone about it!
To: Beast666@hotmail.com
From: Mutantchick421@yahoo.net
Subject: re: I've really missed you, darling!
My dear, sweet Henry McCoy!!
Is that the new JOE KLEIN book? It's FABULOUS, isn't it? So even-handed, considering his impeccable liberal credentials.
I've missed you so much these last few days that I can barely ARTICULATE myself. It's horrible being back in this big, empty penthouse and all on my own again...
To: Mutantchick421@yahoo.net
From: Beast666@hotmail.com
Subject: re: I've really missed you, darling!
Believe me, darling, NO ONE could be as lonely as I am right now. Why don't we kill two birds with one stone and finally get together tonight? For croissants and cappuccino, perhaps?

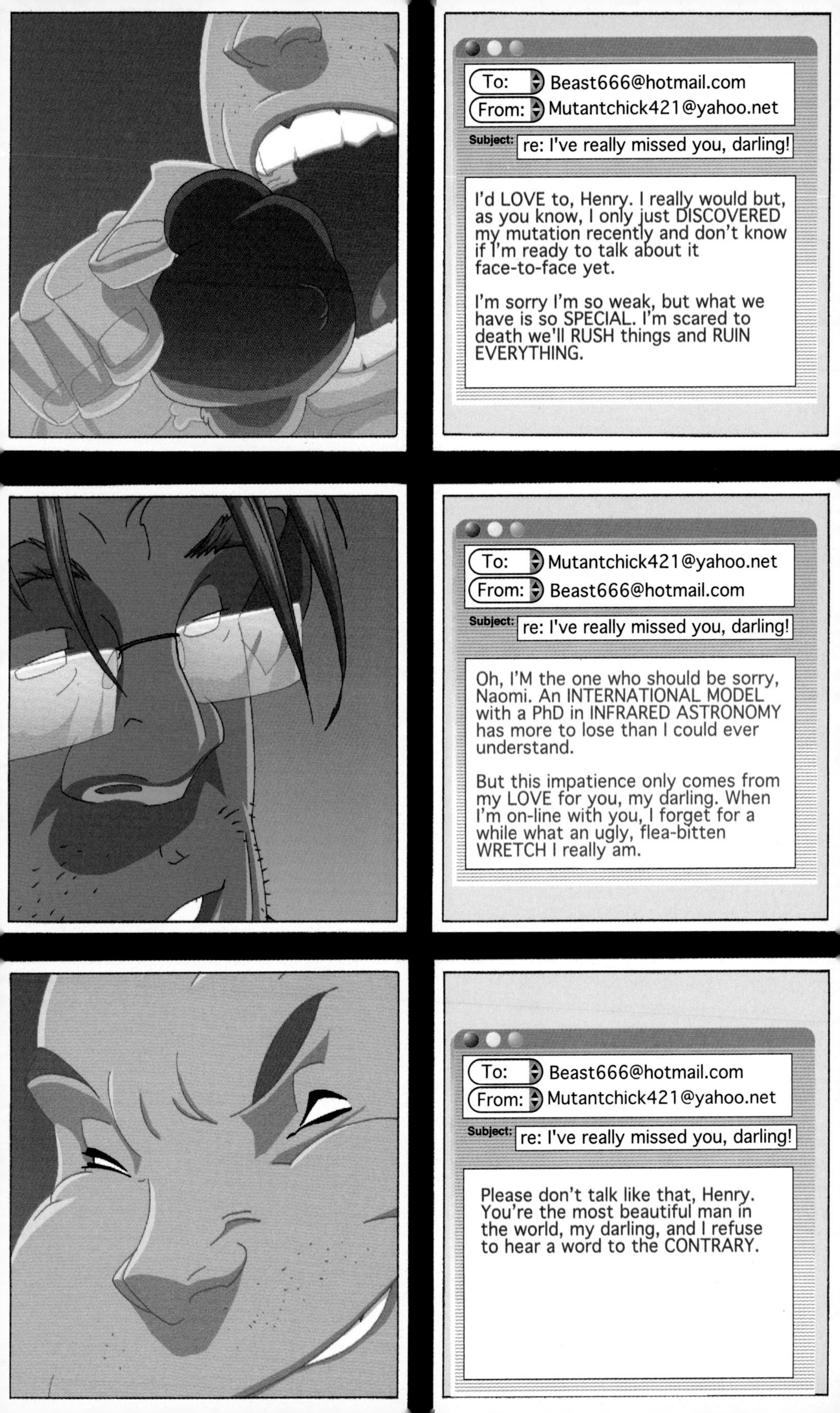
To: Beast666@hotmail.com
From: Mutantchick421@yahoo.net
Subject: re: I've really missed you, darling!
I'd LOVE to, Henry. I really would but, as you know, I only just DISCOVERED my mutation recently and don't know if I'm ready to talk about it face-to-face yet.
I'm sorry I'm so weak, but what we have is so SPECIAL. I'm scared to death we'll RUSH things and RUIN EVERYTHING.
To: Mutantchick421@yahoo.net
From: Beast666@hotmail.com
Subject: re: I've really missed you, darling!
Oh, I'M the one who should be sorry, Naomi. An INTERNATIONAL MODEL with a PhD in INFRARED ASTRONOMY has more to lose than I could ever understand.
But this impatience only comes from my LOVE for you, my darling. When I'm on-line with you, I forget for a while what an ugly, flea-bitten WRETCH I really am.
To: Beast666@hotmail.com
From: Mutantchick421@yahoo.net
Subject: re: I've really missed you, darling!
Please don't talk like that, Henry. You're the most beautiful man in the world, my darling, and I refuse to hear a word to the CONTRARY.

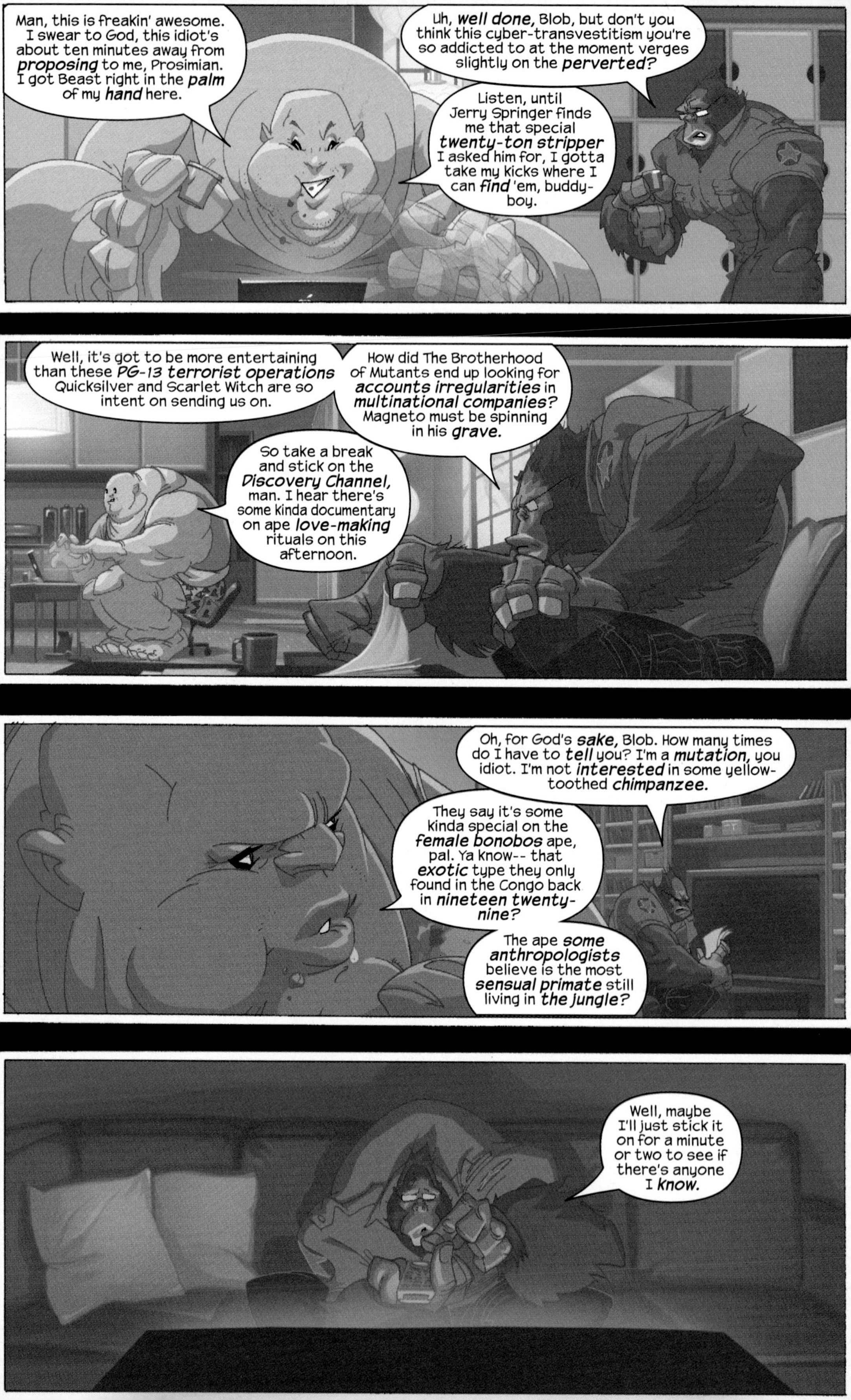

Man, this is freakin' awesome. I swear to God, this idiot's about ten minutes away from proposing to me, Prosimian. I got Beast right in the palm of my hand here.
Uh, well done, Blob, but don't you think this cyber-transvestitism you're so addicted to at the moment verges slightly on the perverted?
Listen, until Jerry Springer finds me that special twenty-ton stripper I asked him for, I gotta take my kicks where I can find 'em, buddy-boy.
Well, it's got to be more entertaining than these PG-13 terrorist operations Quicksilver and Scarlet Witch are so intent on sending us on.
How did The Brotherhood of Mutants end up looking for accounts irregularities in multinational companies? Magneto must be spinning in his grave.
So take a break and stick on the Discovery Channel, man. I hear there's some kinda documentary on ape love-making rituals on this afternoon.
Oh, for God's sake, Blob. How many times do I have to tell you? I'm a mutation, you idiot. I'm not interested in some yellow-toothed chimpanzee.
They say it's some kinda special on the female bonobos ape, pal. Ya know-- that exotic type they only found in the Congo back in nineteen twenty-nine?
The ape some anthropologists believe is the most sensual primate still living in the jungle?
Well, maybe I'll just stick it on for a minute or two to see if there's anyone I know.

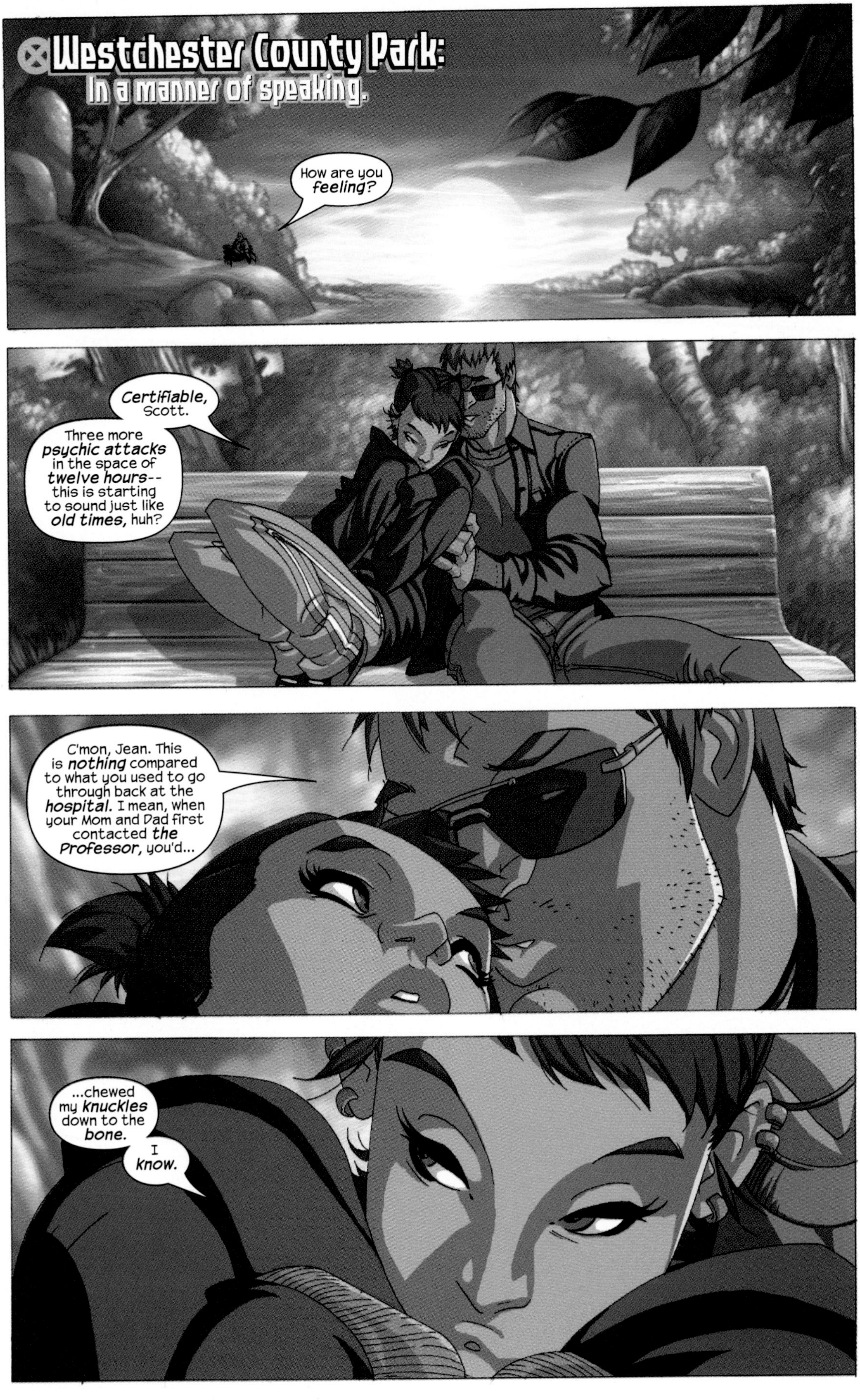
Westchester County Park:
In a manner of speaking.
How are you feeling?
Certifiable, Scott.
Three more psychic attacks in the space of twelve hours-- this is starting to sound just like old times, huh?
C'mon, Jean. This is nothing compared to what you used to go through back at the hospital. I mean, when your Mom and Dad first contacted the Professor, you'd...
...chewed my knuckles down to the bone.
I know.

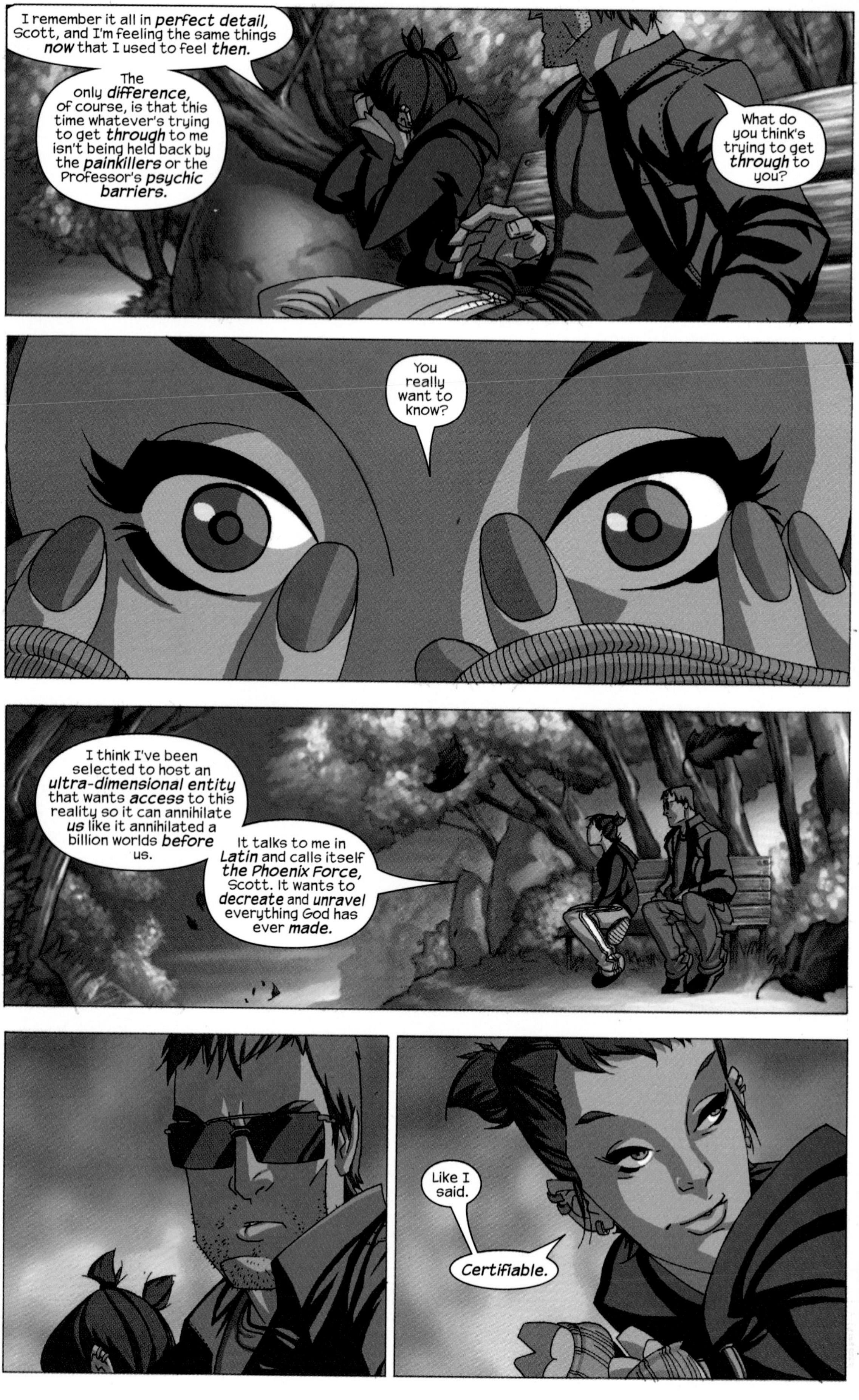
I remember it all in perfect detail, Scott, and I'm feeling the same things now that I used to feel then.
The only difference, of course, is that this time whatever's trying to get through to me isn't being held back by the painkillers or the Professor's psychic barriers.
What do you think's trying to get through to you?
You really want to know?
I think I've been selected to host an ultra-dimensional entity that wants access to this reality so it can annihilate us like it annihilated a billion worlds before us.
It talks to me in Latin and calls itself the Phoenix Force, Scott. It wants to decreate and unravel everything God has ever made.
Like I said.
Certifiable.

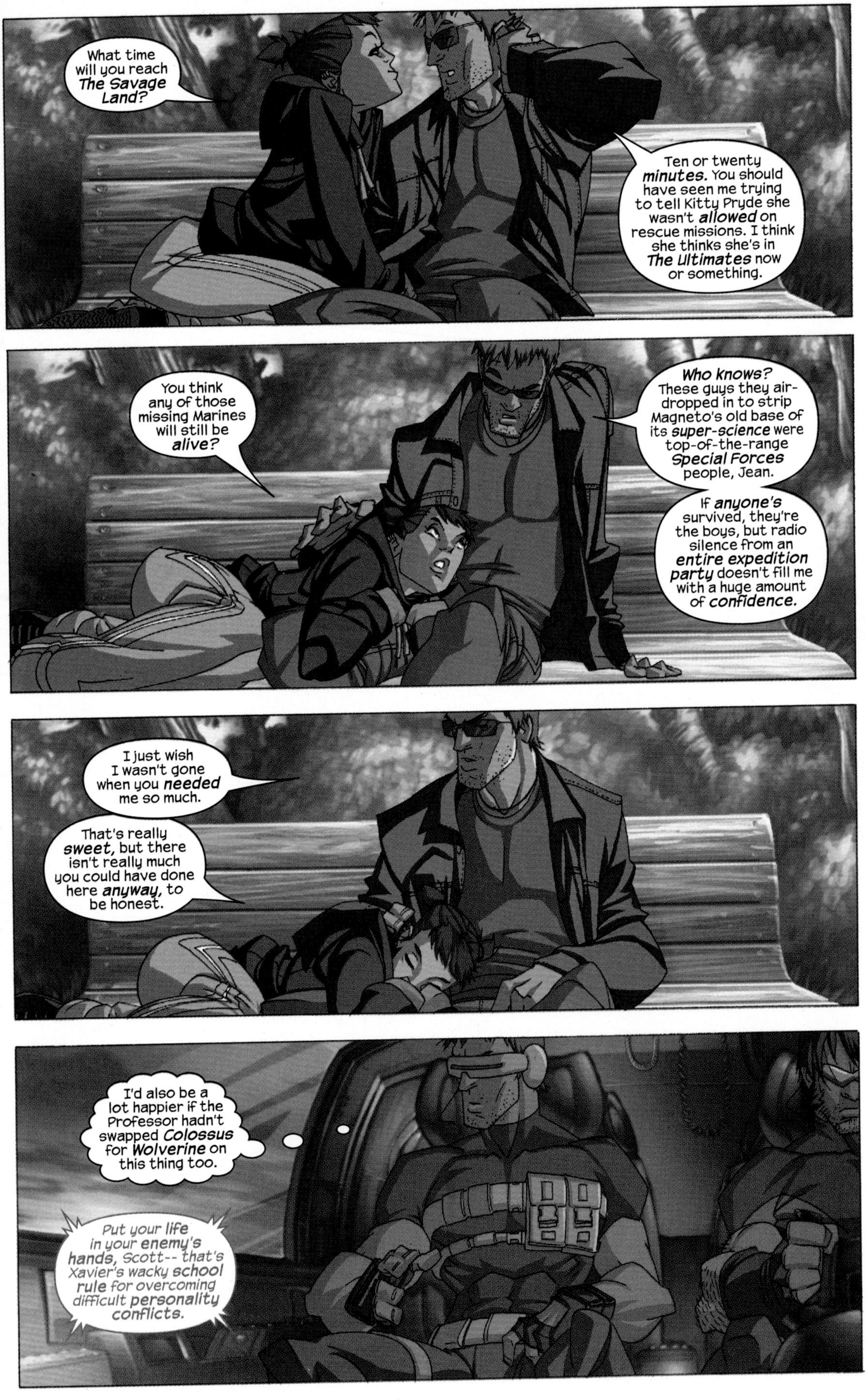
What time will you reach The Savage Land?
Ten or twenty minutes. You should have seen me trying to tell Kitty Pryde she wasn't allowed on rescue missions. I think she thinks she's in The Ultimates now or something.
You think any of those missing Marines will still be alive?
Who knows? These guys they air-dropped in to strip Magneto's old base of its super-science were top-of-the-range Special Forces people, Jean.
If anyone's survived, they're the boys, but radio silence from an entire expedition party doesn't fill me with a huge amount of confidence.
I just wish I wasn't gone when you needed me so much.
That's really sweet, but there isn't really much you could have done here anyway, to be honest.
I'd also be a lot happier if the Professor hadn't swapped Colossus for Wolverine on this thing too.
Put your life in your enemy's hands, Scott-- that's Xavier's wacky school rule for overcoming difficult personality conflicts.

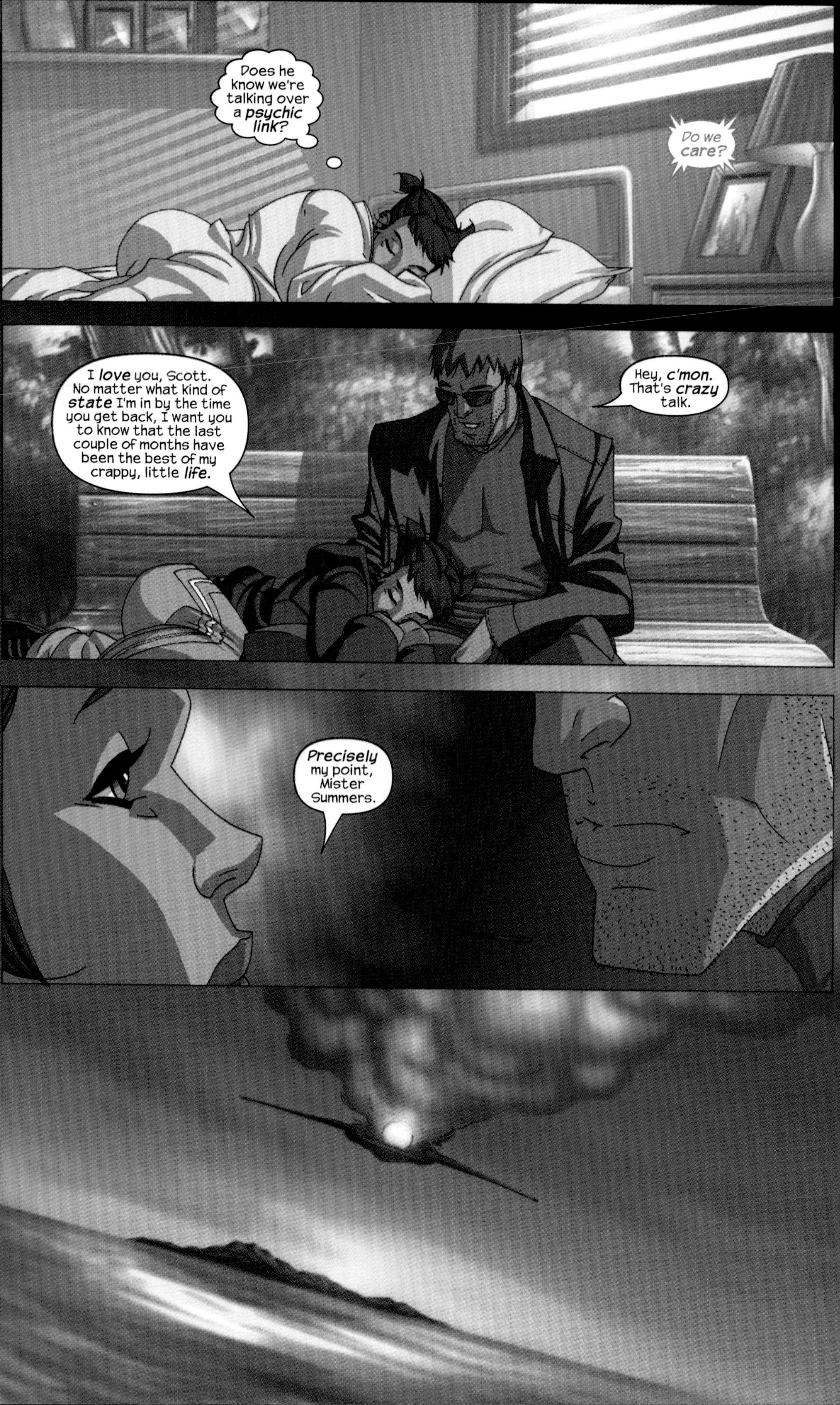
Does he know we're talking over a *psychic* link?
Do we care?
I *love* you, Scott. No matter what kind of *state* I'm in by the time you get back, I want you to know that the last couple of months have been the best of my crappy, little *life.*
Hey, *c'mon.* That's *crazy* talk.
*Precisely* my point, Mister Summers.

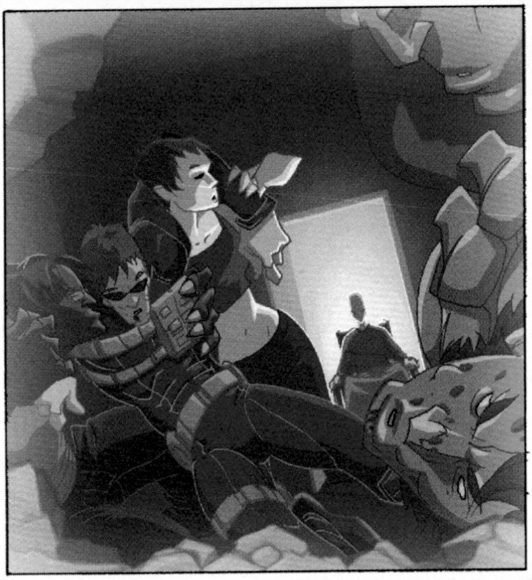

I still can't BELIEVE what happened here last night, Naomi! Cyclops and Wolverine almost KILLED each other over Wolverine's little crush on MARVEL GIRL.

The Professor put them both in a psychic detention room for an hour to settle their differences and now he's sent them off to find some missing U.S. Marines in The Savage Land together!

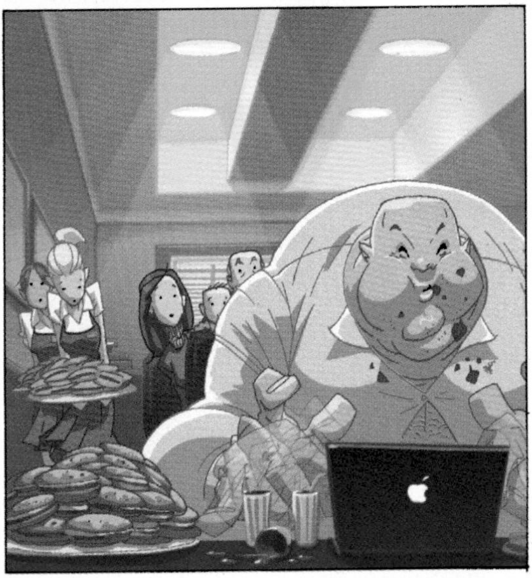

God, why does Xavier keep sucking up to the establishment like this, Henry? The U.S. Army were only STATIONED in The Savage Land to steal advanced MUTANT TECHNOLOGY.

I realize Cyclops and Wolverine know the area better than anyone, but why risk mutant lives for a species who are openly conspiring AGAINST us?

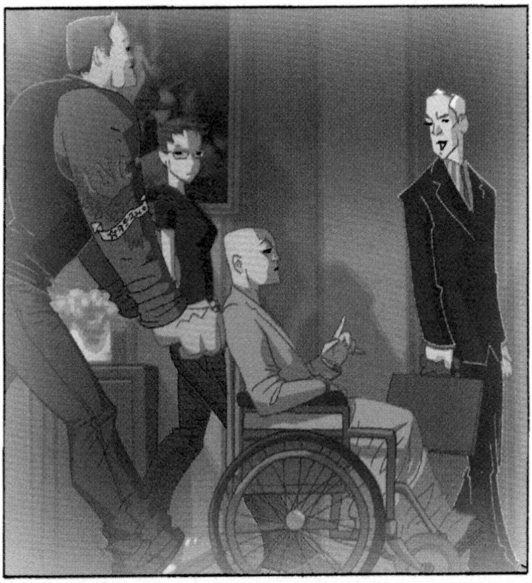

They aren't ALL against us, Naomi. In fact, our secret sponsors sent a representative this afternoon to see how much money we wanted for this legal battle against Iceman's parents.

I'm really MISSING Bobby right now, you know. I spent all afternoon just sitting in his room listening to that awful CD collection of his.

Poor baby. I wish I'd been there to hold your hand. :(

But what makes you think the X-Men's FINANCIERS are acting out of ALTRUISM, Henry? Isn't their anonymity a sign that Xavier could be controlling their MINDS?

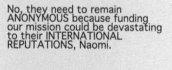

No, they need to remain ANONYMOUS because funding our mission could be devastating to their INTERNATIONAL REPUTATIONS, Naomi.

Ororo and Kitty raised a similar point at a recent TUTORIAL, but I sincerely believe this is one instance where the Professor isn't meddling with ANYONE'S neurons.

Meaning WHAT? That this HELLFIRE CLUB you told me about buys you JUMP-JETS and STATE-OF-THE-ART SECURITY SYSTEMS out of the goodness of their HEARTS? LOL!!!

That's what I LOVE about you, Henry McCoy; your almost child-like belief that human beings AREN'T the most stupid, self-centered species that ever walked the Earth. :)

It's so SWEET!

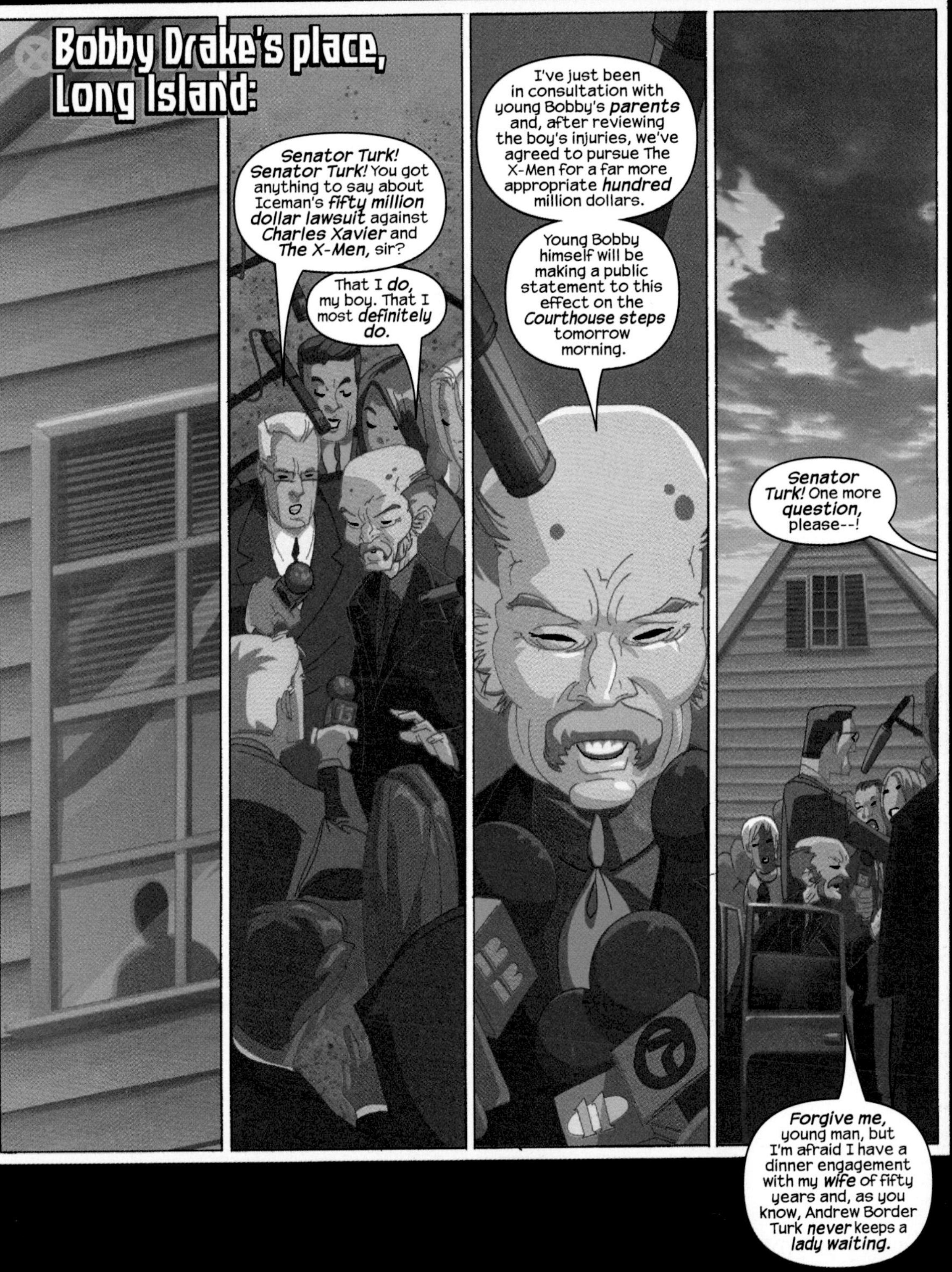

Bobby Drake's place, Long Island:
Senator Turk! Senator Turk! You got anything to say about Iceman's fifty million dollar lawsuit against Charles Xavier and The X-Men, sir?
That I do, my boy. That I most definitely do.
I've just been in consultation with young Bobby's parents and, after reviewing the boy's injuries, we've agreed to pursue The X-Men for a far more appropriate hundred million dollars.
Young Bobby himself will be making a public statement to this effect on the Courthouse steps tomorrow morning.
Senator Turk! One more question, please--!
Forgive me, young man, but I'm afraid I have a dinner engagement with my wife of fifty years and, as you know, Andrew Border Turk never keeps a lady waiting.

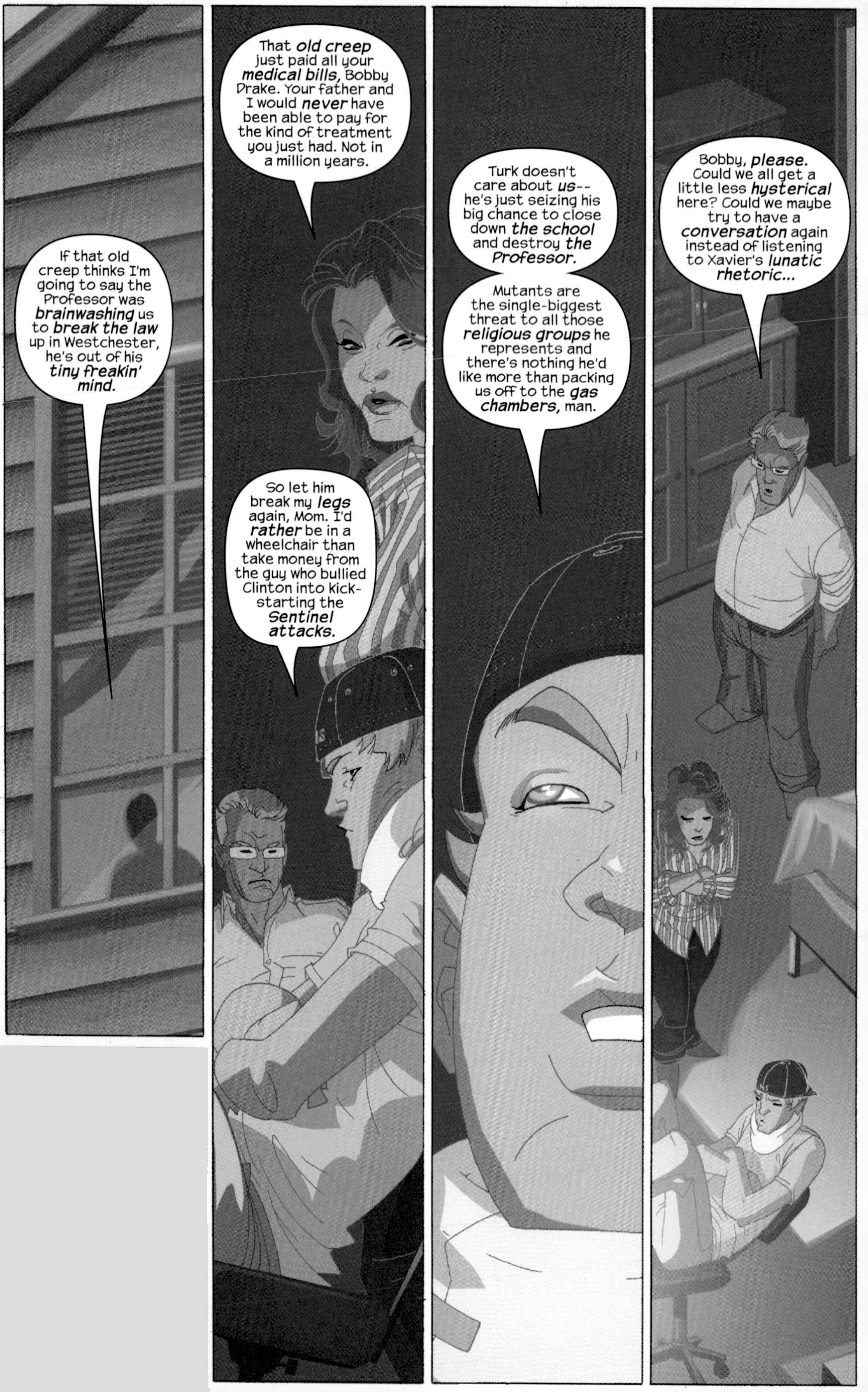

If that old creep thinks I'm going to say the Professor was brainwashing us to break the law up in Westchester, he's out of his tiny freakin' mind.
That old creep just paid all your medical bills, Bobby Drake. Your father and I would never have been able to pay for the kind of treatment you just had. Not in a million years.
So let him break my legs again, Mom. I'd rather be in a wheelchair than take money from the guy who bullied Clinton into kick-starting the Sentinel attacks.
Turk doesn't care about us-- he's just seizing his big chance to close down the school and destroy the Professor.
Mutants are the single-biggest threat to all those religious groups he represents and there's nothing he'd like more than packing us off to the gas chambers, man.
Bobby, please. Could we all get a little less hysterical here? Could we maybe try to have a conversation again instead of listening to Xavier's lunatic rhetoric...

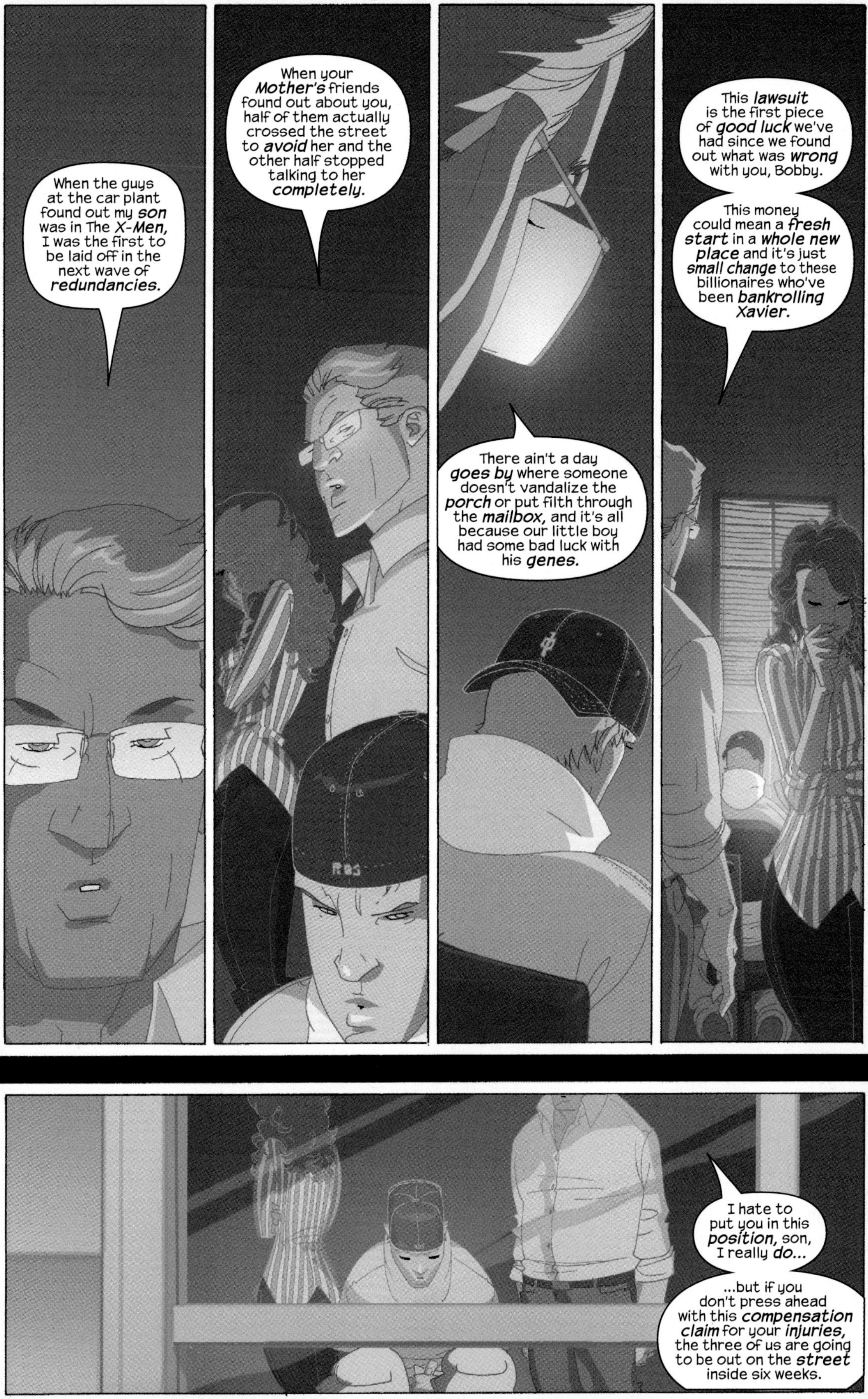
When the guys at the car plant found out my son was in The X-Men, I was the first to be laid off in the next wave of redundancies.
When your Mother's friends found out about you, half of them actually crossed the street to avoid her and the other half stopped talking to her completely.
There ain't a day goes by where someone doesn't vandalize the porch or put filth through the mailbox, and it's all because our little boy had some bad luck with his genes.
This lawsuit is the first piece of good luck we've had since we found out what was wrong with you, Bobby.
This money could mean a fresh start in a whole new place and it's just small change to these billionaires who've been bankrolling Xavier.
I hate to put you in this position, son, I really do...
...but if you don't press ahead with this compensation claim for your injuries, the three of us are going to be out on the street inside six weeks.

Hi Naomi :)

Storm and I were on DISHWASHING DUTY tonight and it all felt very STRANGE. She was telling me about a HOSTAGE CRISIS in LOUISIANA, but I wasn't even LISTENING.

I still can't believe we DATED all that time. What did we have in COMMON? Why do I feel so disconnected from anyone who isn't YOU at the moment?

Have you ever wondered if you've maybe joined the WRONG SIDE, Henry? Do you ever think you might be happier ATTACKING mankind instead of HELPING them?

After all, Homo Sapien has hardly been kind to YOU over the years :(

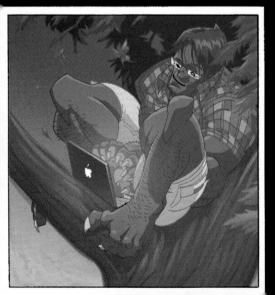

Nevertheless, I LIKE the Professor and appreciate that his ideas are the best chance of survival for EITHER species, Naomi.

Whether it's balancing chemical equations or building a car from scratch, kids can learn more here in a single day than you learn in a LIFETIME of regular schooling.

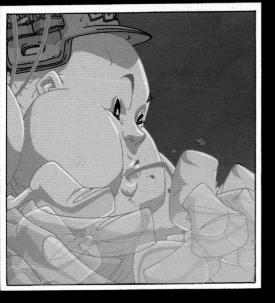

Personally, I just can't understand how an intelligent guy like you can follow the DOCTRINE of that hypocrite.

Where does he get the nerve to write these papers on non-violent solutions to post-human problems when he MURDERED MAGNETO in front of FIVE THOUSAND WITNESSES?

Well, between you and me, that's not exactly how things TRANSPIRED back in Washington, darling.

I'm telling you this in the STRICTEST CONFIDENCE and only because I know I can TRUST you with all my HEART...

...but MAGNETO isn't really DEAD, you know. The whole thing was an ELABORATE RUSE.

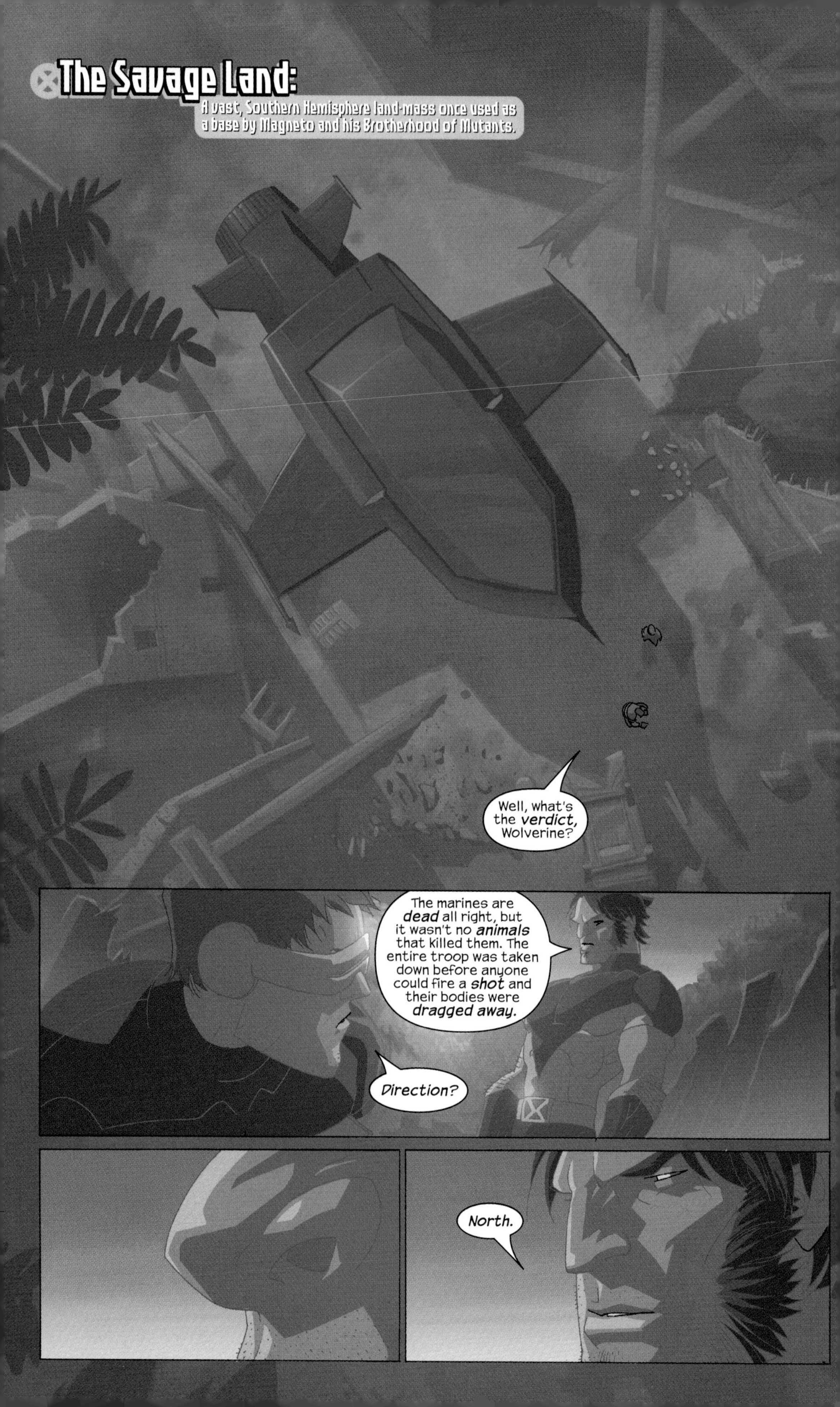

The Savage Land:
A vast, Southern Hemisphere land-mass once used as a base by Magneto and his Brotherhood of Mutants.
Well, what's the verdict, Wolverine?
The marines are dead all right, but it wasn't no animals that killed them. The entire troop was taken down before anyone could fire a shot and their bodies were dragged away.
Direction?
North.

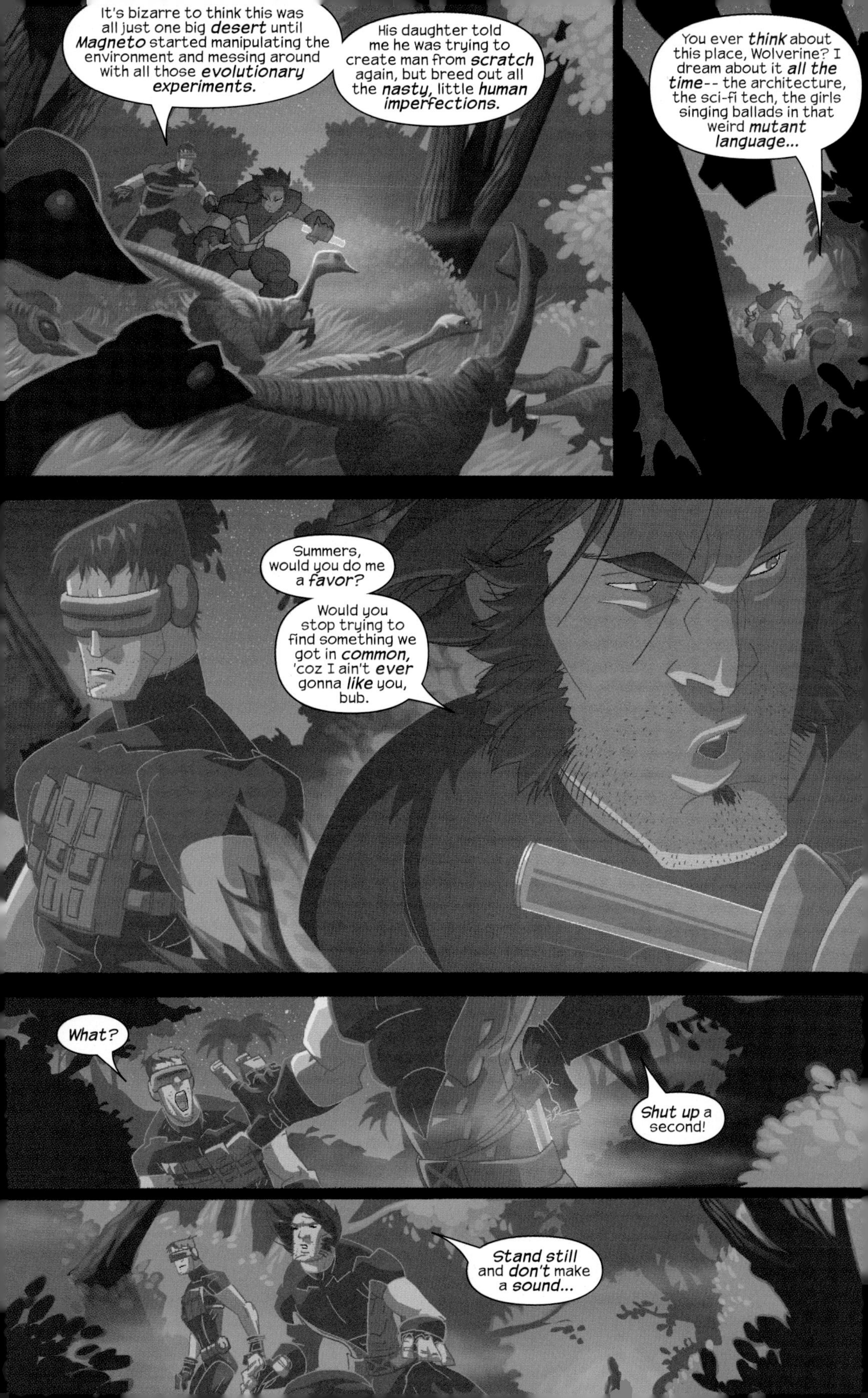
It's bizarre to think this was all just one big *desert* until *Magneto* started manipulating the environment and messing around with all those *evolutionary experiments.*
His daughter told me he was trying to create man from *scratch* again, but breed out all the *nasty,* little *human imperfections.*
You ever *think* about this place, Wolverine? I dream about it *all the time*-- the architecture, the sci-fi tech, the girls singing ballads in that weird *mutant language...*
Summers, would you do me a *favor?*
Would you stop trying to find something we got in *common,* 'coz I ain't *ever* gonna *like* you, bub.
*What?*
*Shut up* a second!
*Stand still* and *don't* make a *sound...*

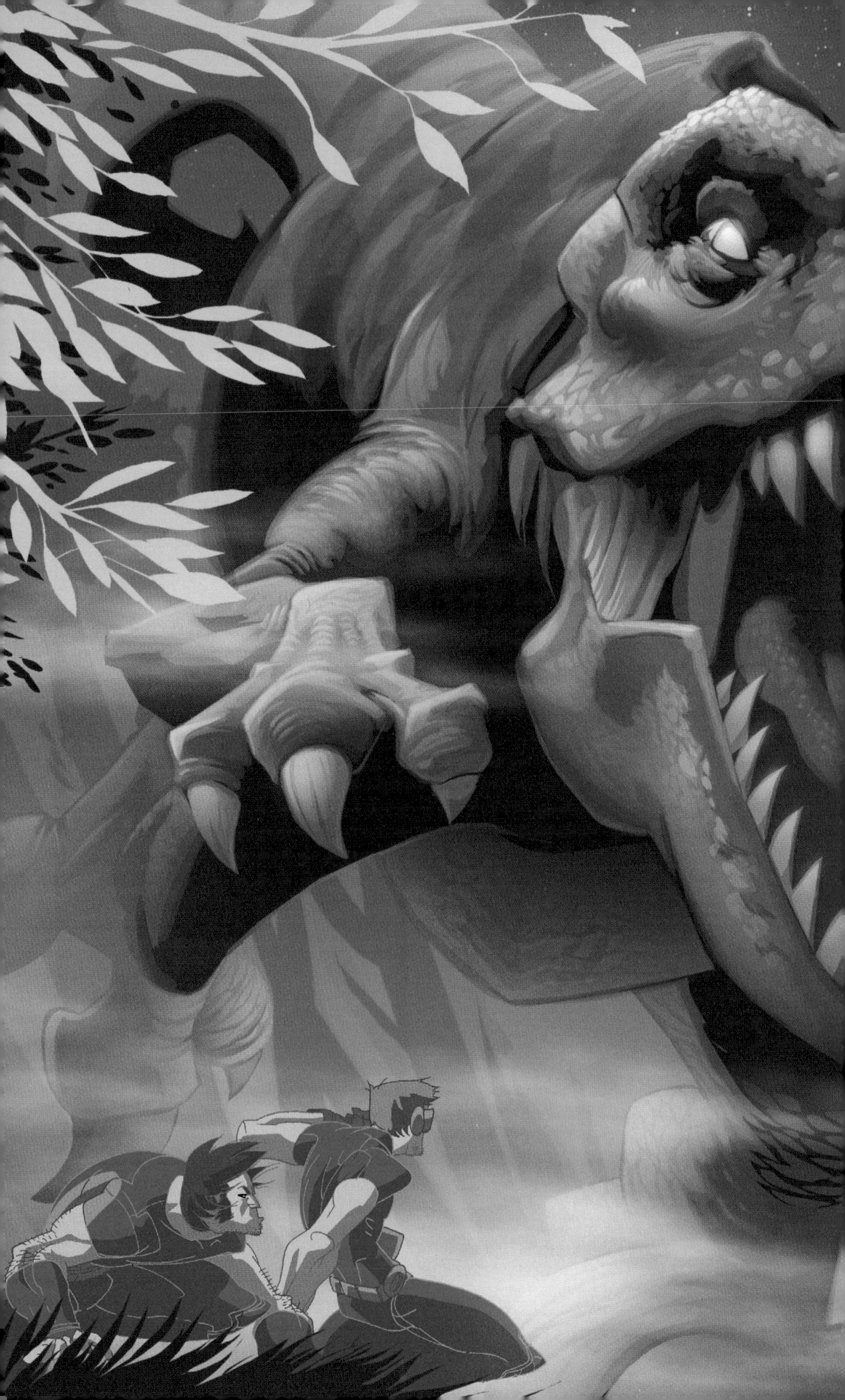

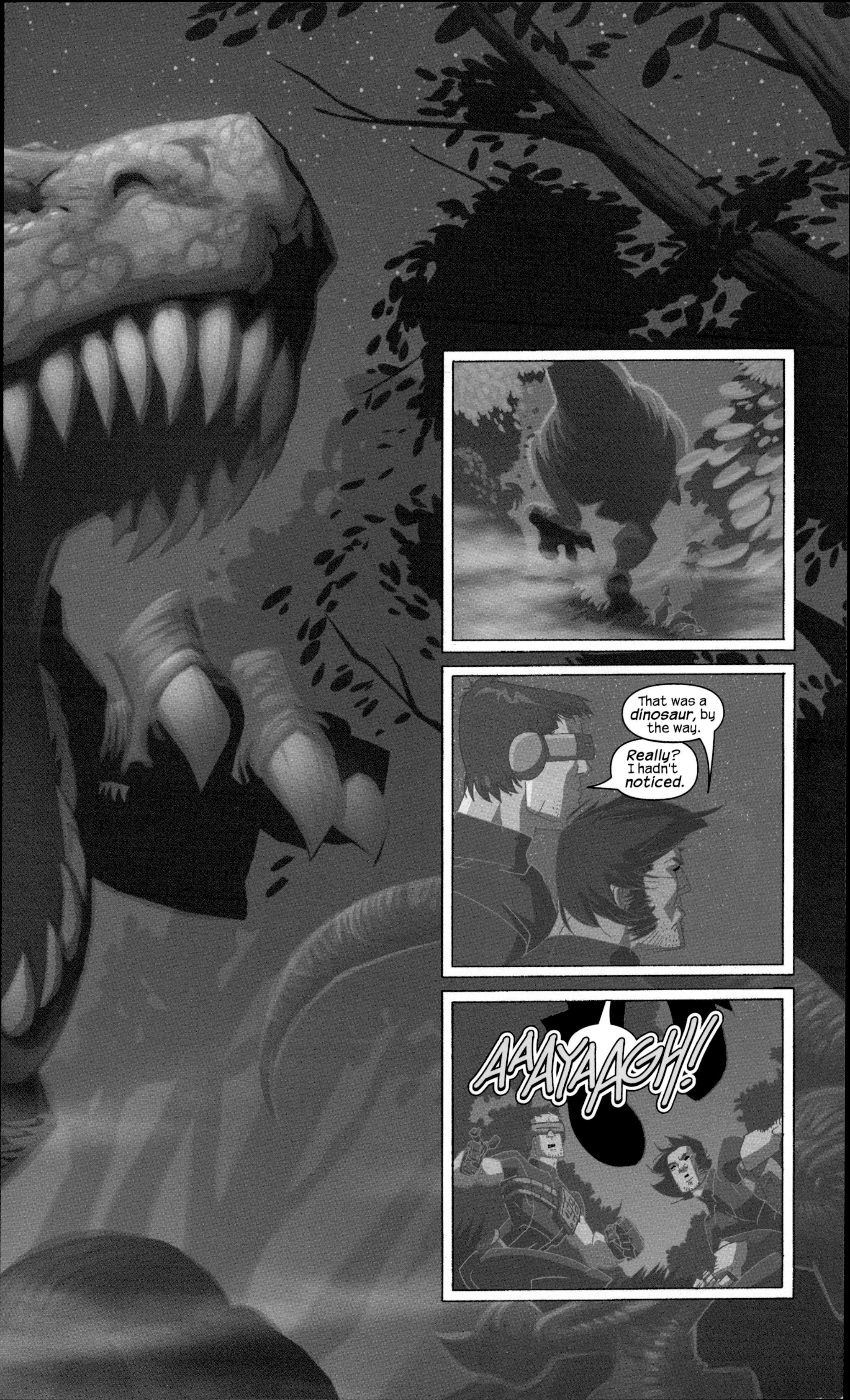
That was a dinosaur, by the way.
Really? I hadn't noticed.
AAAYAAGH!

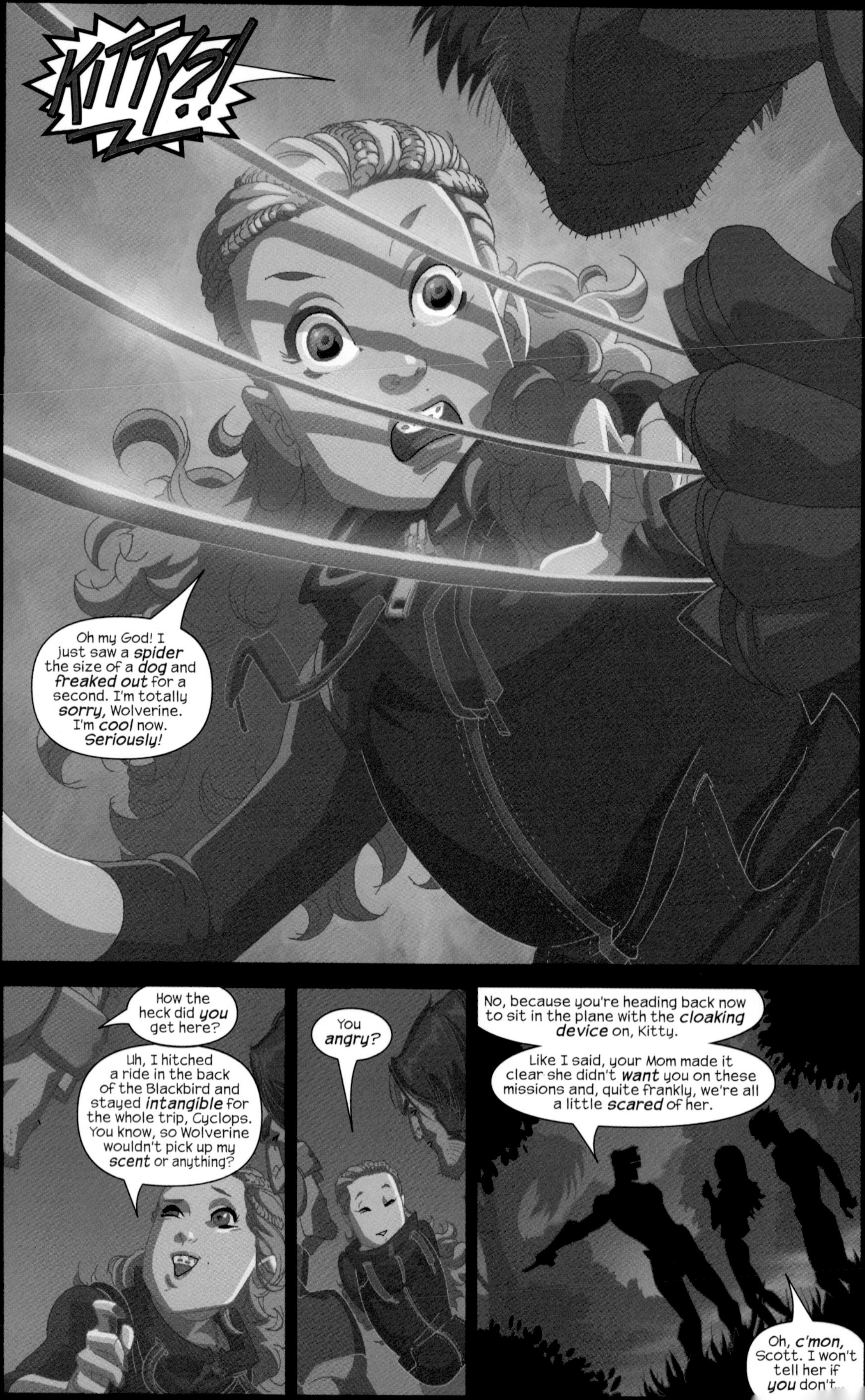
KITTY?!
Oh my God! I just saw a spider the size of a dog and freaked out for a second. I'm totally sorry, Wolverine. I'm cool now. Seriously!
How the heck did you get here?
Uh, I hitched a ride in the back of the Blackbird and stayed intangible for the whole trip, Cyclops. You know, so Wolverine wouldn't pick up my scent or anything?
You angry?
No, because you're heading back now to sit in the plane with the cloaking device on, Kitty.
Like I said, your Mom made it clear she didn't want you on these missions and, quite frankly, we're all a little scared of her.
Oh, c'mon, Scott. I won't tell her if you don't...

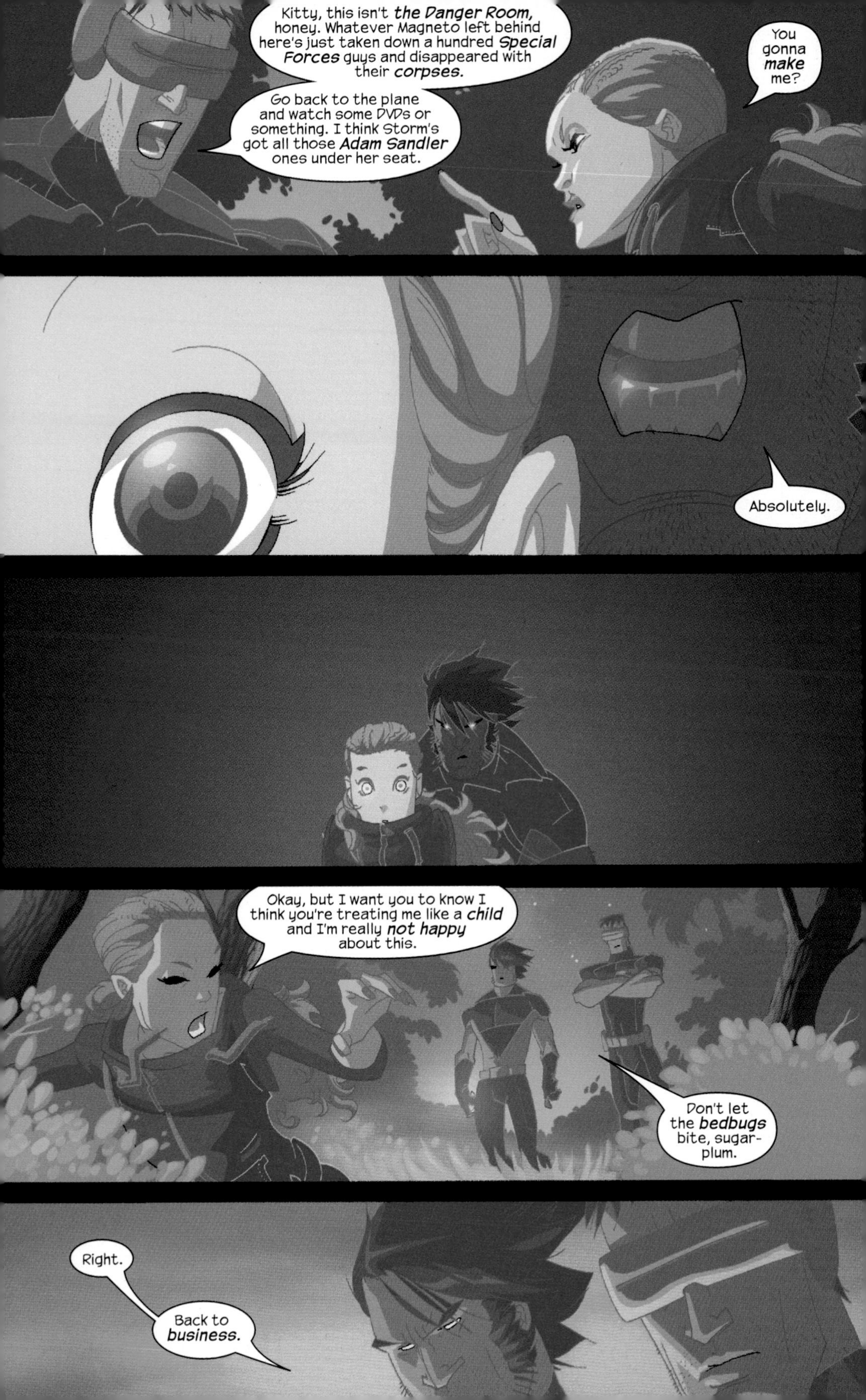
Kitty, this isn't the Danger Room, honey. Whatever Magneto left behind here's just taken down a hundred Special Forces guys and disappeared with their corpses.
Go back to the plane and watch some DVDs or something. I think Storm's got all those Adam Sandler ones under her seat.
You gonna make me?
Absolutely.
Okay, but I want you to know I think you're treating me like a child and I'm really not happy about this.
Don't let the bedbugs bite, sugar-plum.
Right.
Back to business.

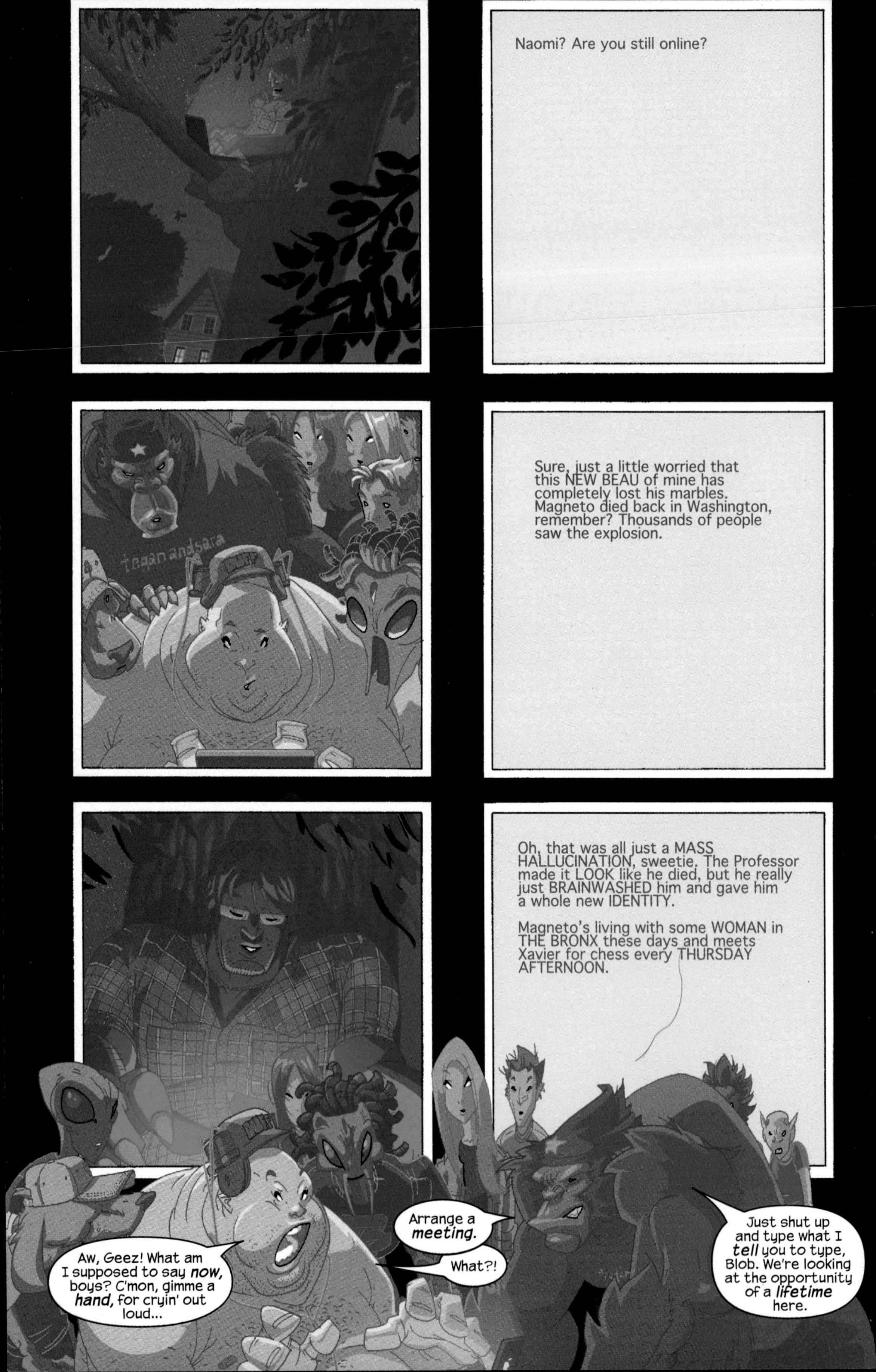
Naomi? Are you still online?
Sure, just a little worried that this NEW BEAU of mine has completely lost his marbles. Magneto died back in Washington, remember? Thousands of people saw the explosion.
tegan and sara
Oh, that was all just a MASS HALLUCINATION, sweetie. The Professor made it LOOK like he died, but he really just BRAINWASHED him and gave him a whole new IDENTITY.
Magneto's living with some WOMAN in THE BRONX these days and meets Xavier for chess every THURSDAY AFTERNOON.
Aw, Geez! What am I supposed to say *now,* boys? C'mon, gimme a *hand,* for cryin' out loud...
Arrange a *meeting.*
What?!
Just shut up and type what I *tell* you to type, Blob. We're looking at the opportunity of a *lifetime* here.

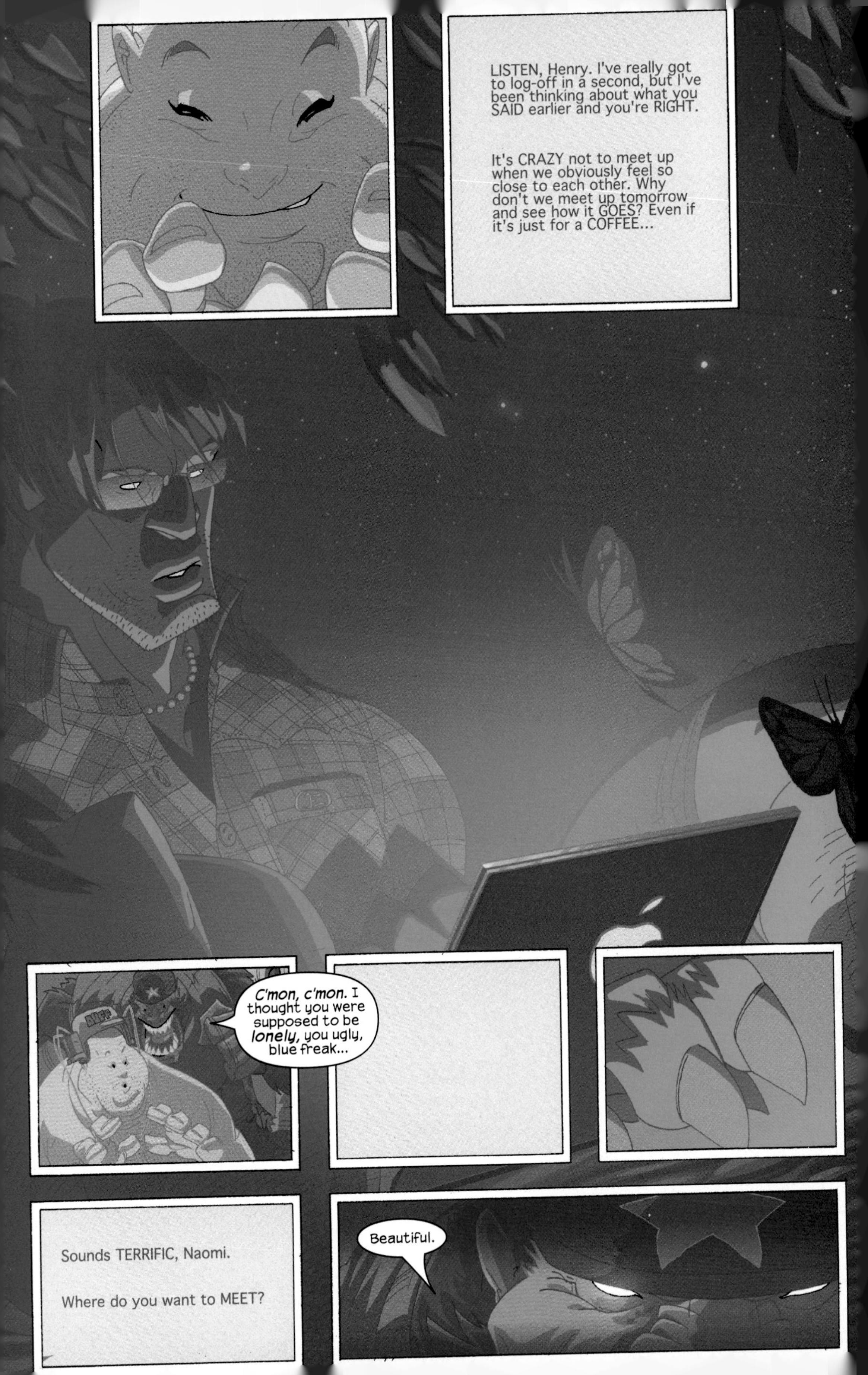

LISTEN, Henry. I've really got to log-off in a second, but I've been thinking about what you SAID earlier and you're RIGHT.
It's CRAZY not to meet up when we obviously feel so close to each other. Why don't we meet up tomorrow and see how it GOES? Even if it's just for a COFFEE...
C'mon, c'mon. I thought you were supposed to be lonely, you ugly, blue freak...
Sounds TERRIFIC, Naomi.
Where do you want to MEET?
Beautiful.

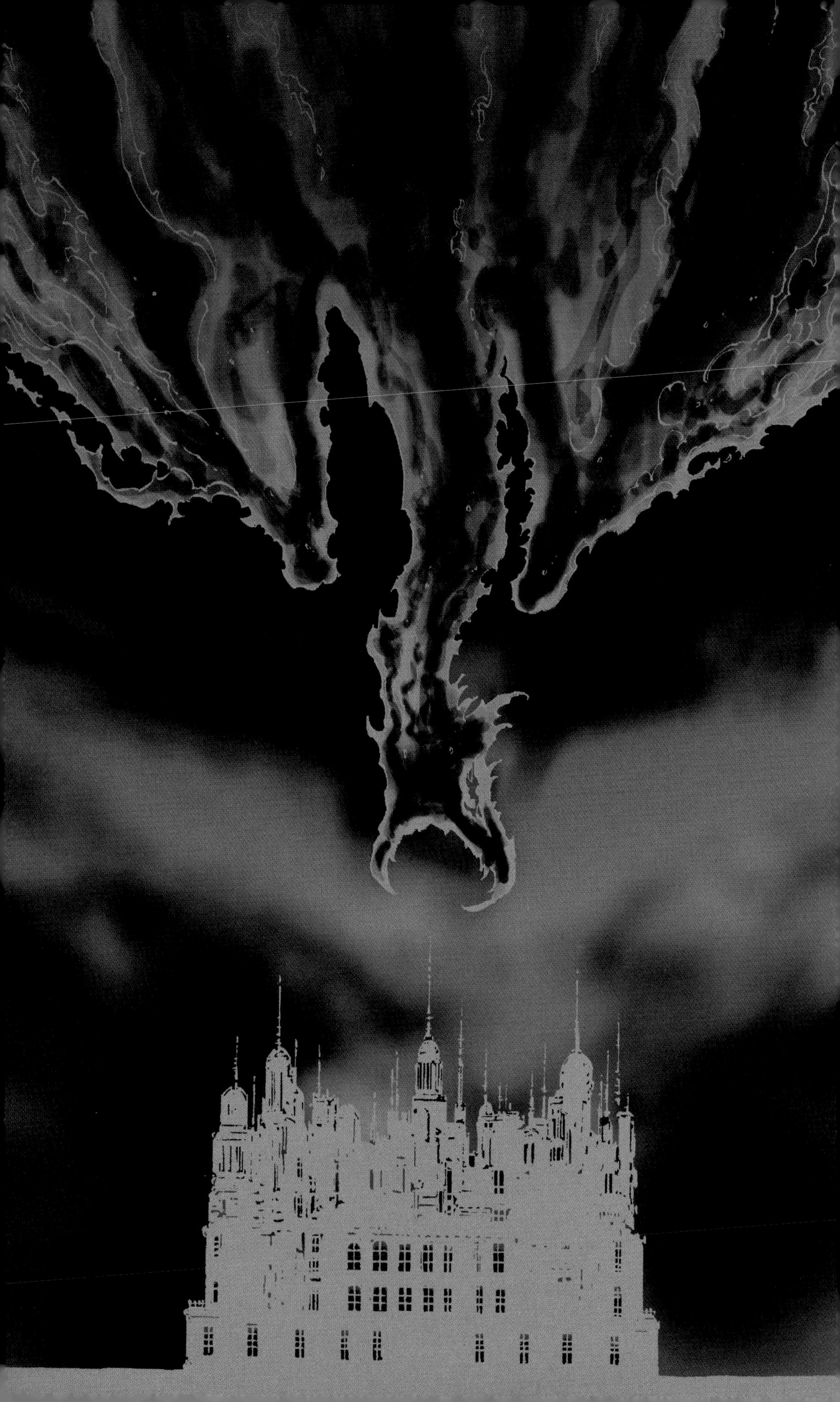

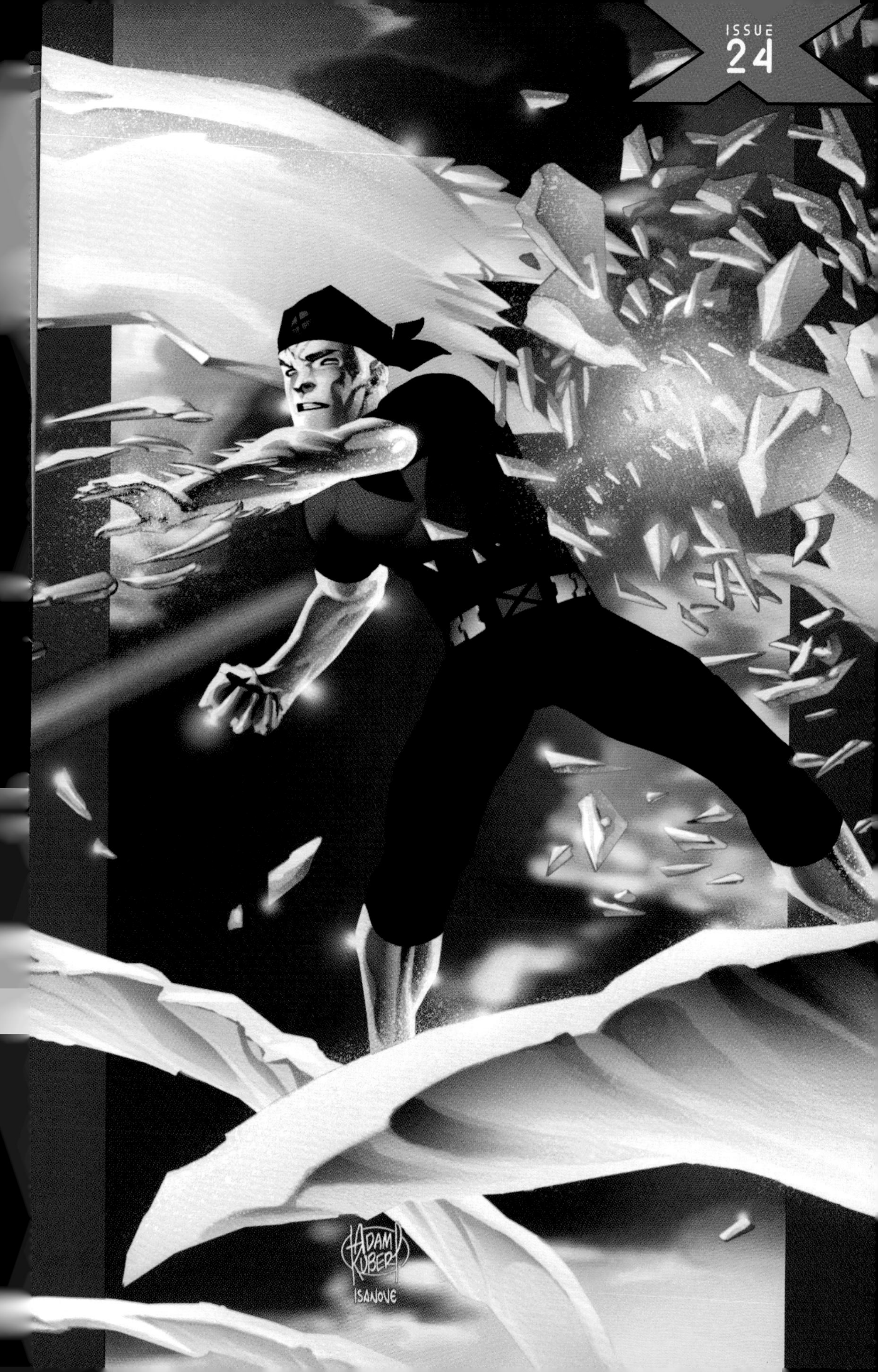
ISSUE
24
ADAM KUBERT
ISANOVE

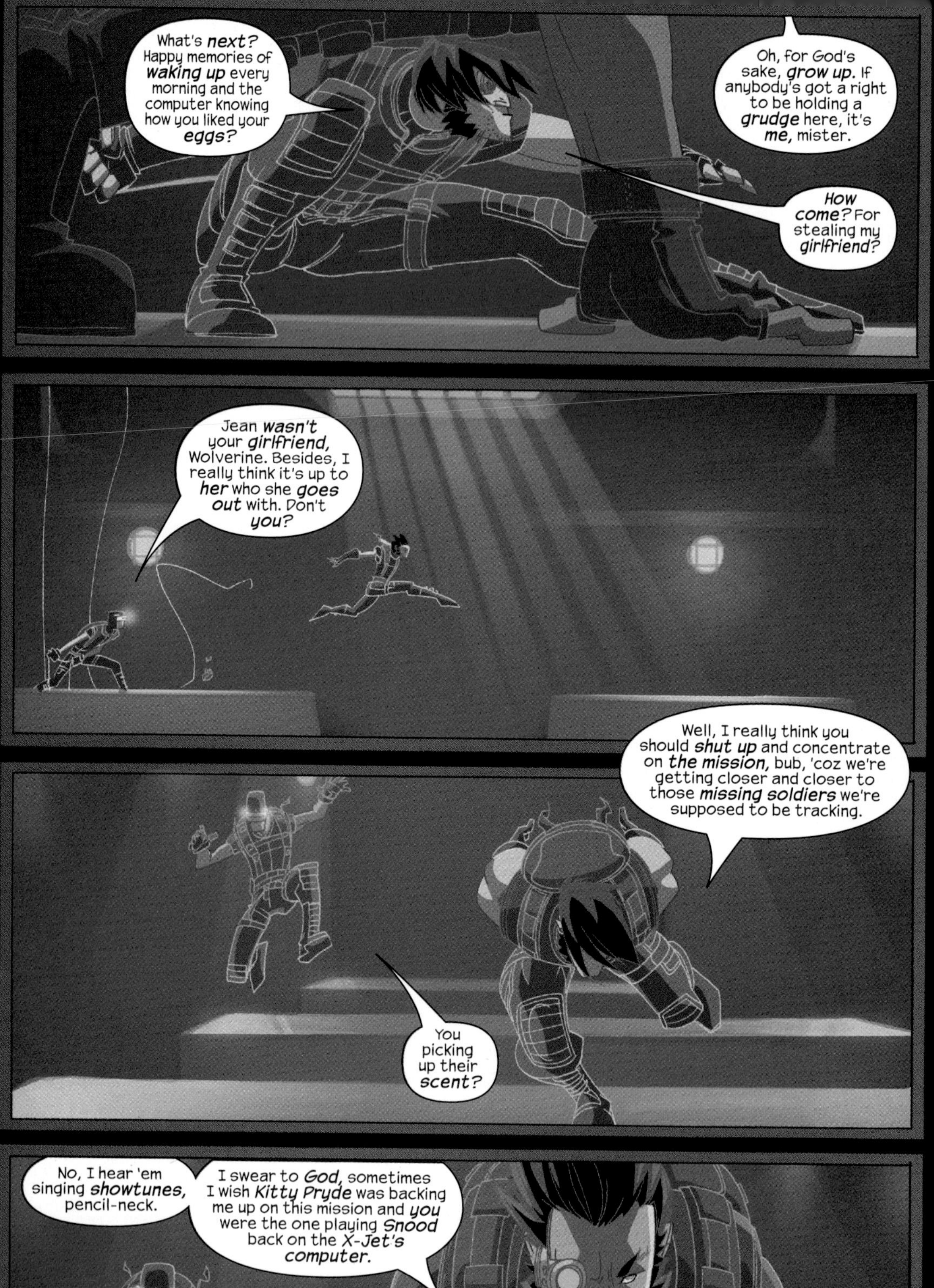
What's next? Happy memories of waking up every morning and the computer knowing how you liked your eggs?
Oh, for God's sake, grow up. If anybody's got a right to be holding a grudge here, it's me, mister.
How come? For stealing my girlfriend?
Jean wasn't your girlfriend, Wolverine. Besides, I really think it's up to her who she goes out with. Don't you?
Well, I really think you should shut up and concentrate on the mission, bub, 'coz we're getting closer and closer to those missing soldiers we're supposed to be tracking.
You picking up their scent?
No, I hear 'em singing showtunes, pencil-neck.
I swear to God, sometimes I wish Kitty Pryde was backing me up on this mission and you were the one playing Snood back on the X-Jet's computer.

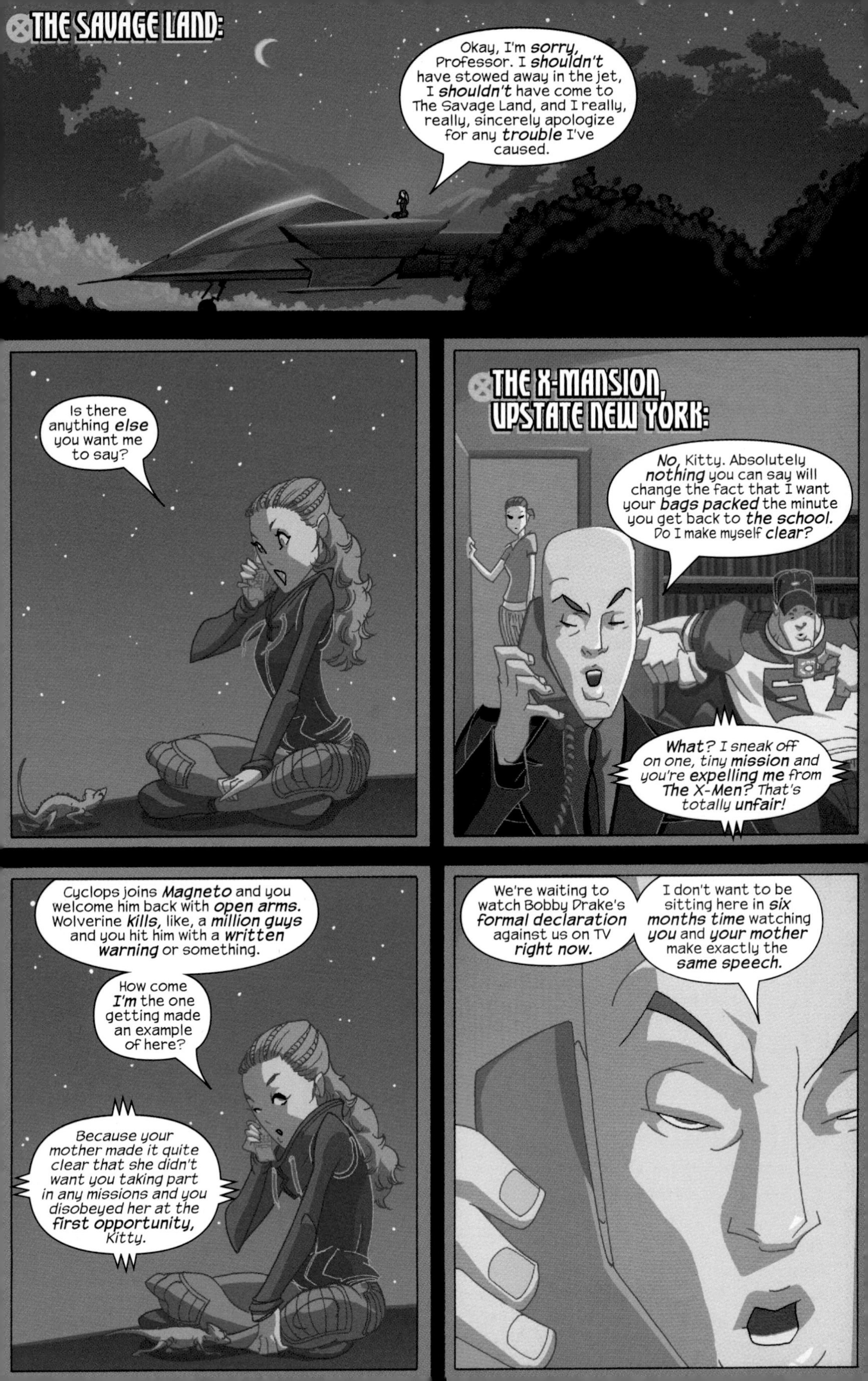
THE SAVAGE LAND:
Okay, I'm *sorry*, Professor. I *shouldn't* have stowed away in the jet, I *shouldn't* have come to The Savage Land, and I really, really, sincerely apologize for any *trouble* I've caused.
Is there anything *else* you want me to say?
THE X-MANSION, UPSTATE NEW YORK:
*No*, Kitty. Absolutely *nothing* you can say will change the fact that I want your *bags packed* the minute you get back to *the school*. Do I make myself *clear*?
*What*? I sneak off on one, tiny *mission* and you're *expelling me* from *The X-Men*? That's totally *unfair*!
Cyclops joins *Magneto* and you welcome him back with *open arms*. Wolverine *kills*, like, a *million guys* and you hit him with a *written warning* or something.
How come *I'm* the one getting made an example of here?
Because your mother made it quite clear that she didn't want you taking part in any missions and you disobeyed her at the *first opportunity*, Kitty.
We're waiting to watch Bobby Drake's *formal declaration* against us on TV *right now*.
I don't want to be sitting here in *six months time* watching *you* and *your mother* make exactly the *same speech*.

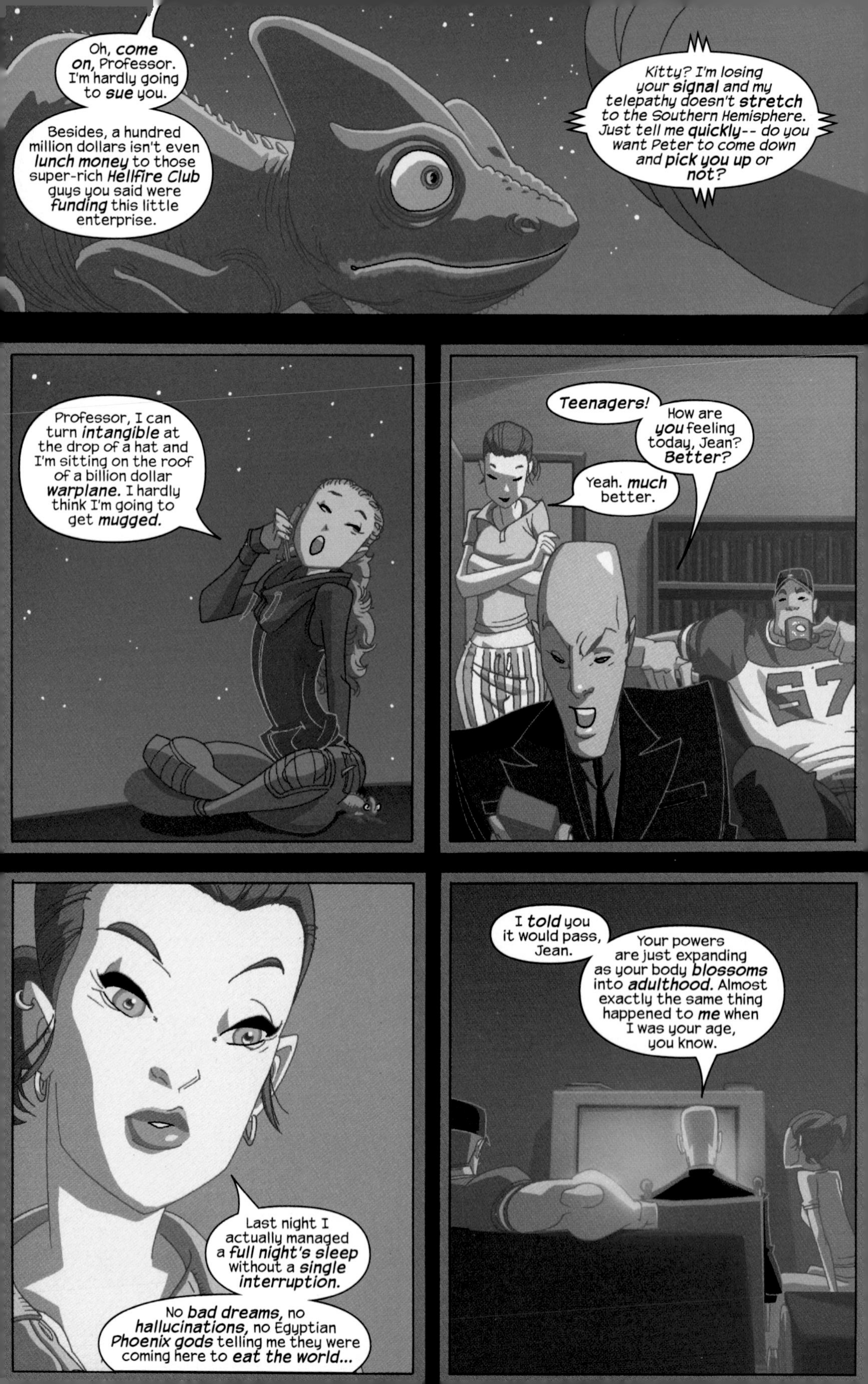

Oh, come on, Professor. I'm hardly going to sue you.
Besides, a hundred million dollars isn't even lunch money to those super-rich Hellfire Club guys you said were funding this little enterprise.
Kitty? I'm losing your signal and my telepathy doesn't stretch to the Southern Hemisphere. Just tell me quickly-- do you want Peter to come down and pick you up or not?
Professor, I can turn intangible at the drop of a hat and I'm sitting on the roof of a billion dollar warplane. I hardly think I'm going to get mugged.
Teenagers!
How are you feeling today, Jean? Better?
Yeah. much better.
Last night I actually managed a full night's sleep without a single interruption.
No bad dreams, no hallucinations, no Egyptian Phoenix gods telling me they were coming here to eat the world...
I told you it would pass, Jean.
Your powers are just expanding as your body blossoms into adulthood. Almost exactly the same thing happened to me when I was your age, you know.

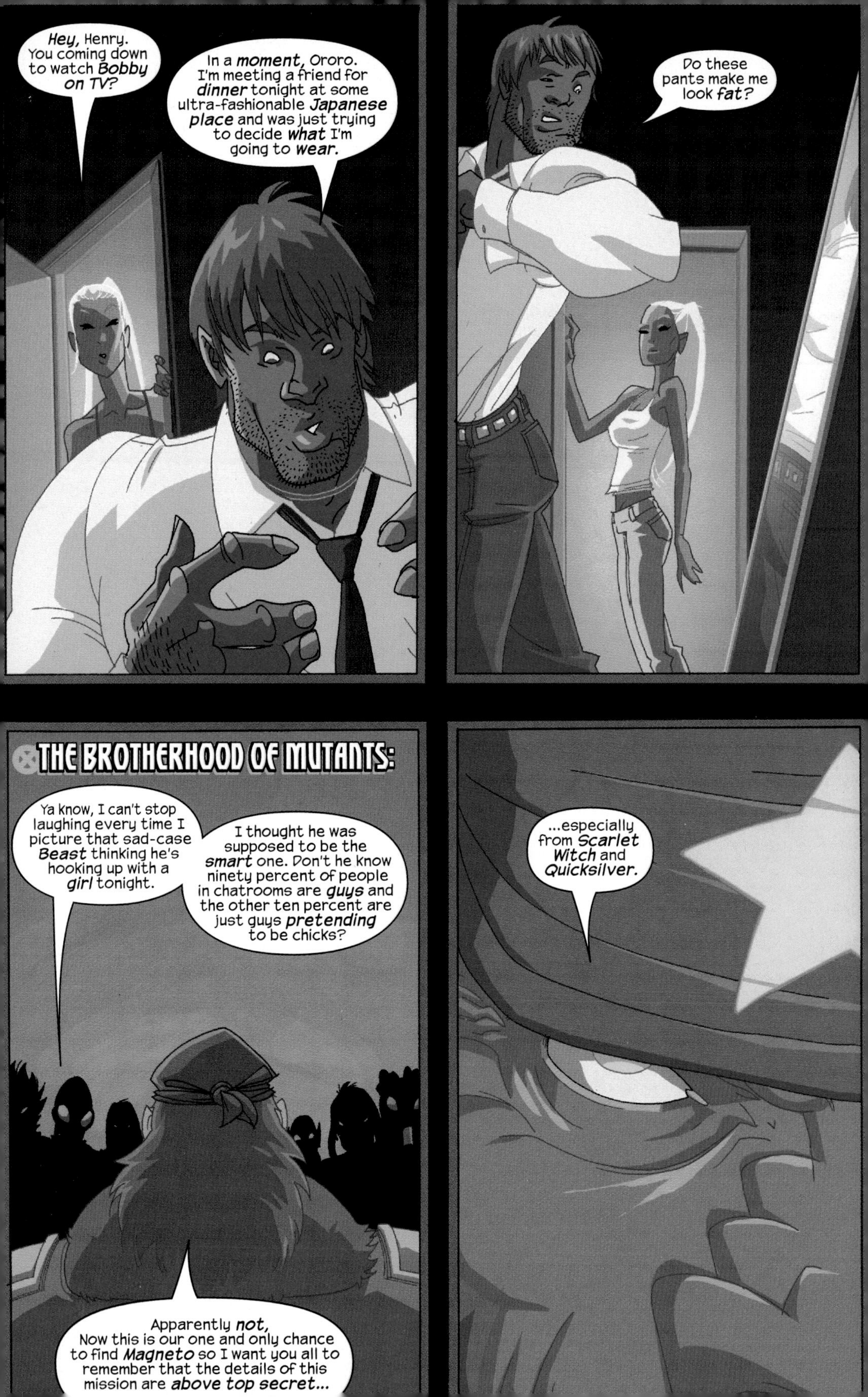
Hey, Henry. You coming down to watch Bobby on TV?
In a moment, Ororo. I'm meeting a friend for dinner tonight at some ultra-fashionable Japanese place and was just trying to decide what I'm going to wear.
Do these pants make me look fat?
THE BROTHERHOOD OF MUTANTS:
Ya know, I can't stop laughing every time I picture that sad-case Beast thinking he's hooking up with a girl tonight.
I thought he was supposed to be the smart one. Don't he know ninety percent of people in chatrooms are guys and the other ten percent are just guys pretending to be chicks?
Apparently not, Now this is our one and only chance to find Magneto so I want you all to remember that the details of this mission are above top secret...
...especially from Scarlet Witch and Quicksilver.

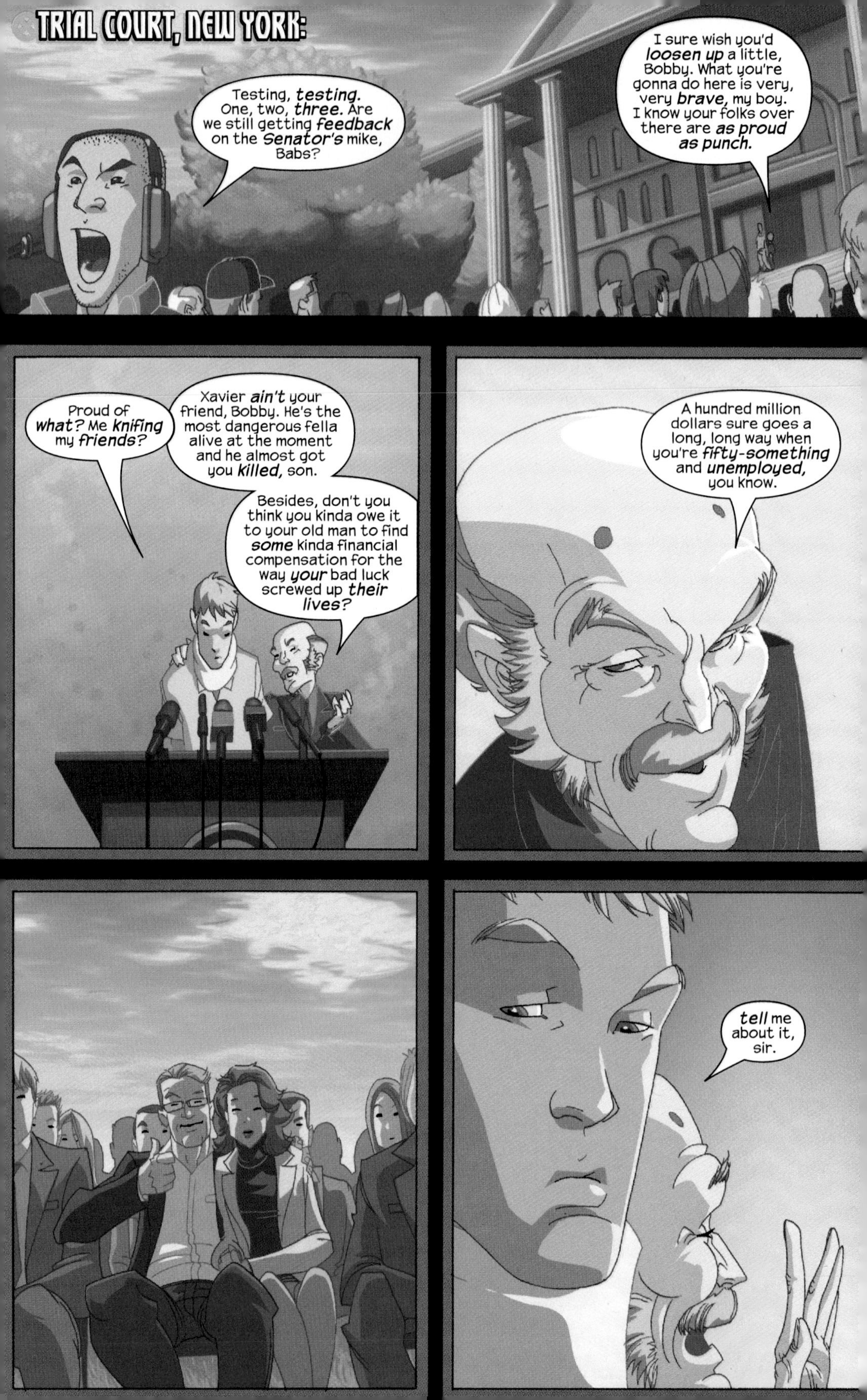
TRIAL COURT, NEW YORK:
Testing, testing. One, two, three. Are we still getting feedback on the Senator's mike, Babs?
I sure wish you'd loosen up a little, Bobby. What you're gonna do here is very, very brave, my boy. I know your folks over there are as proud as punch.
Proud of what? Me knifing my friends?
Xavier ain't your friend, Bobby. He's the most dangerous fella alive at the moment and he almost got you killed, son.
Besides, don't you think you kinda owe it to your old man to find some kinda financial compensation for the way your bad luck screwed up their lives?
A hundred million dollars sure goes a long, long way when you're fifty-something and unemployed, you know.
tell me about it, sir.

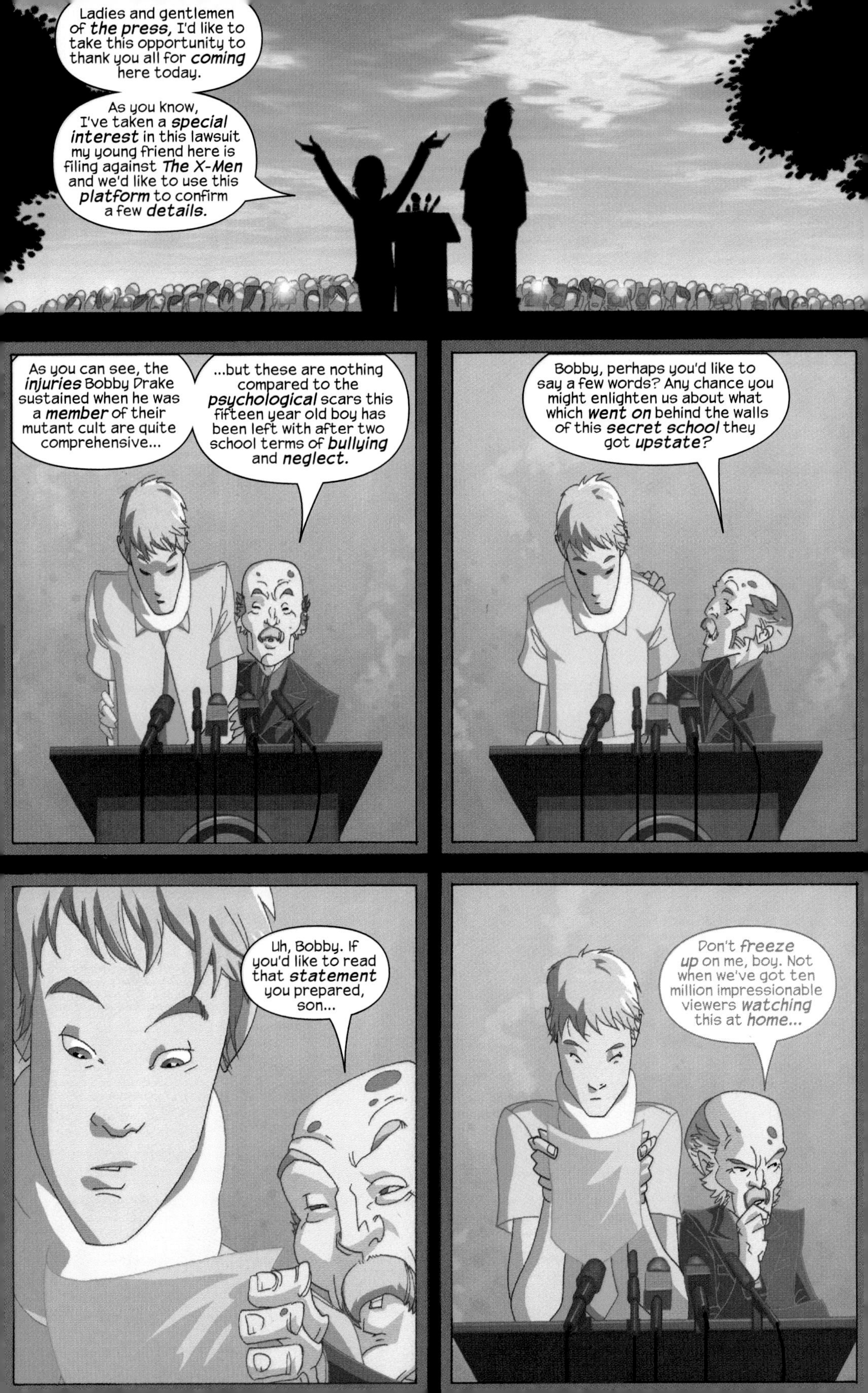
Ladies and gentlemen of the press, I'd like to take this opportunity to thank you all for coming here today.
As you know, I've taken a special interest in this lawsuit my young friend here is filing against The X-Men and we'd like to use this platform to confirm a few details.
As you can see, the injuries Bobby Drake sustained when he was a member of their mutant cult are quite comprehensive...
...but these are nothing compared to the psychological scars this fifteen year old boy has been left with after two school terms of bullying and neglect.
Bobby, perhaps you'd like to say a few words? Any chance you might enlighten us about what which went on behind the walls of this secret school they got upstate?
Uh, Bobby. If you'd like to read that statement you prepared, son...
Don't freeze up on me, boy. Not when we've got ten million impressionable viewers watching this at home...

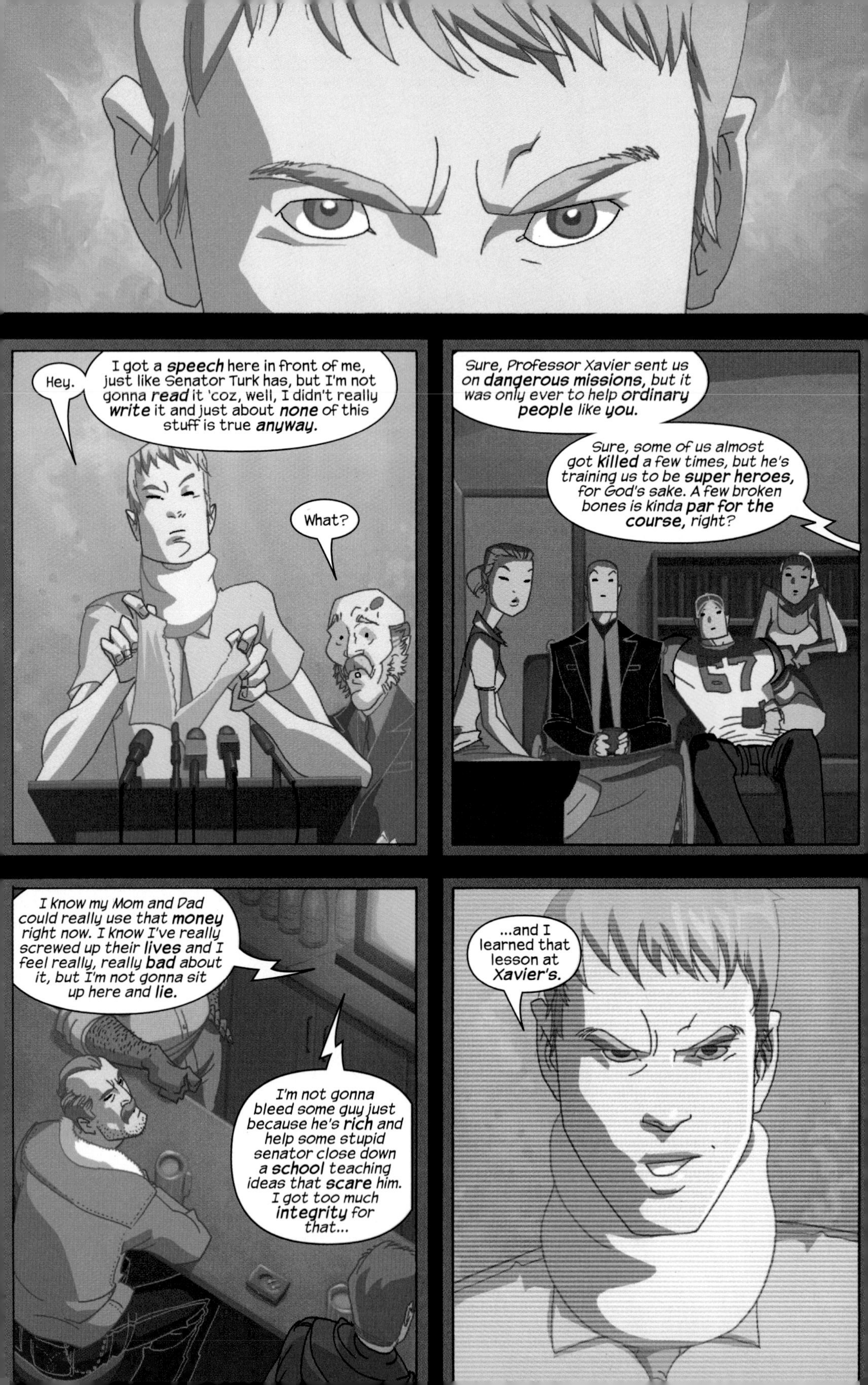

Hey.
I got a speech here in front of me, just like Senator Turk has, but I'm not gonna read it 'coz, well, I didn't really write it and just about none of this stuff is true anyway.
What?
Sure, Professor Xavier sent us on dangerous missions, but it was only ever to help ordinary people like you.
Sure, some of us almost got killed a few times, but he's training us to be super heroes, for God's sake. A few broken bones is kinda par for the course, right?
I know my Mom and Dad could really use that money right now. I know I've really screwed up their lives and I feel really, really bad about it, but I'm not gonna sit up here and lie.
I'm not gonna bleed some guy just because he's rich and help some stupid senator close down a school teaching ideas that scare him. I got too much integrity for that...
...and I learned that lesson at Xavier's.

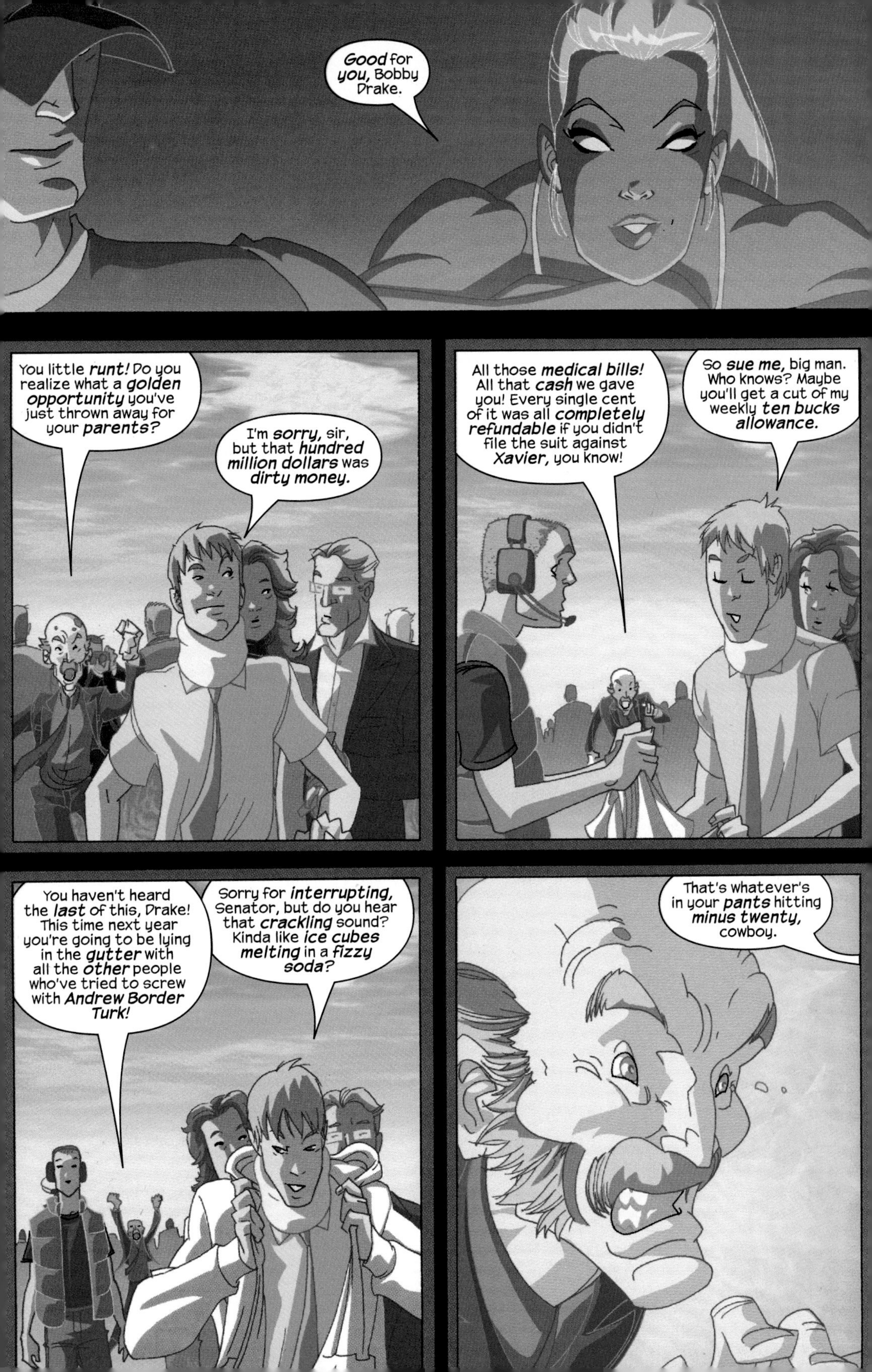
Good for you, Bobby Drake.
You little runt! Do you realize what a golden opportunity you've just thrown away for your parents?
I'm sorry, sir, but that hundred million dollars was dirty money.
All those medical bills! All that cash we gave you! Every single cent of it was all completely refundable if you didn't file the suit against Xavier, you know!
So sue me, big man. Who knows? Maybe you'll get a cut of my weekly ten bucks allowance.
You haven't heard the last of this, Drake! This time next year you're going to be lying in the gutter with all the other people who've tried to screw with Andrew Border Turk!
Sorry for interrupting, Senator, but do you hear that crackling sound? Kinda like ice cubes melting in a fizzy soda?
That's whatever's in your pants hitting minus twenty, cowboy.

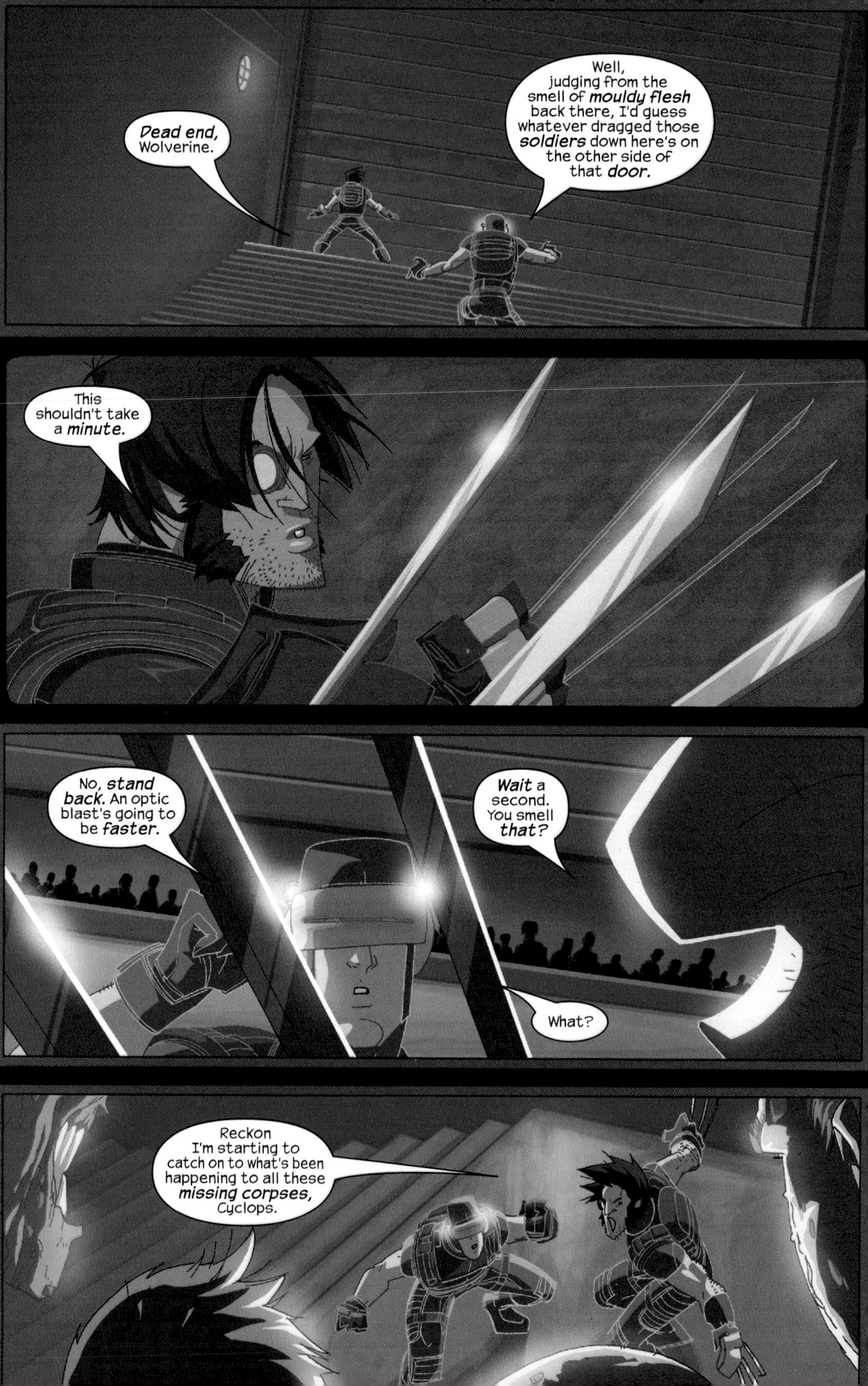
Dead end, Wolverine.
Well, judging from the smell of mouldy flesh back there, I'd guess whatever dragged those soldiers down here's on the other side of that door.
This shouldn't take a minute.
No, stand back. An optic blast's going to be faster.
Wait a second. You smell that?
What?
Reckon I'm starting to catch on to what's been happening to all these missing corpses, Cyclops.

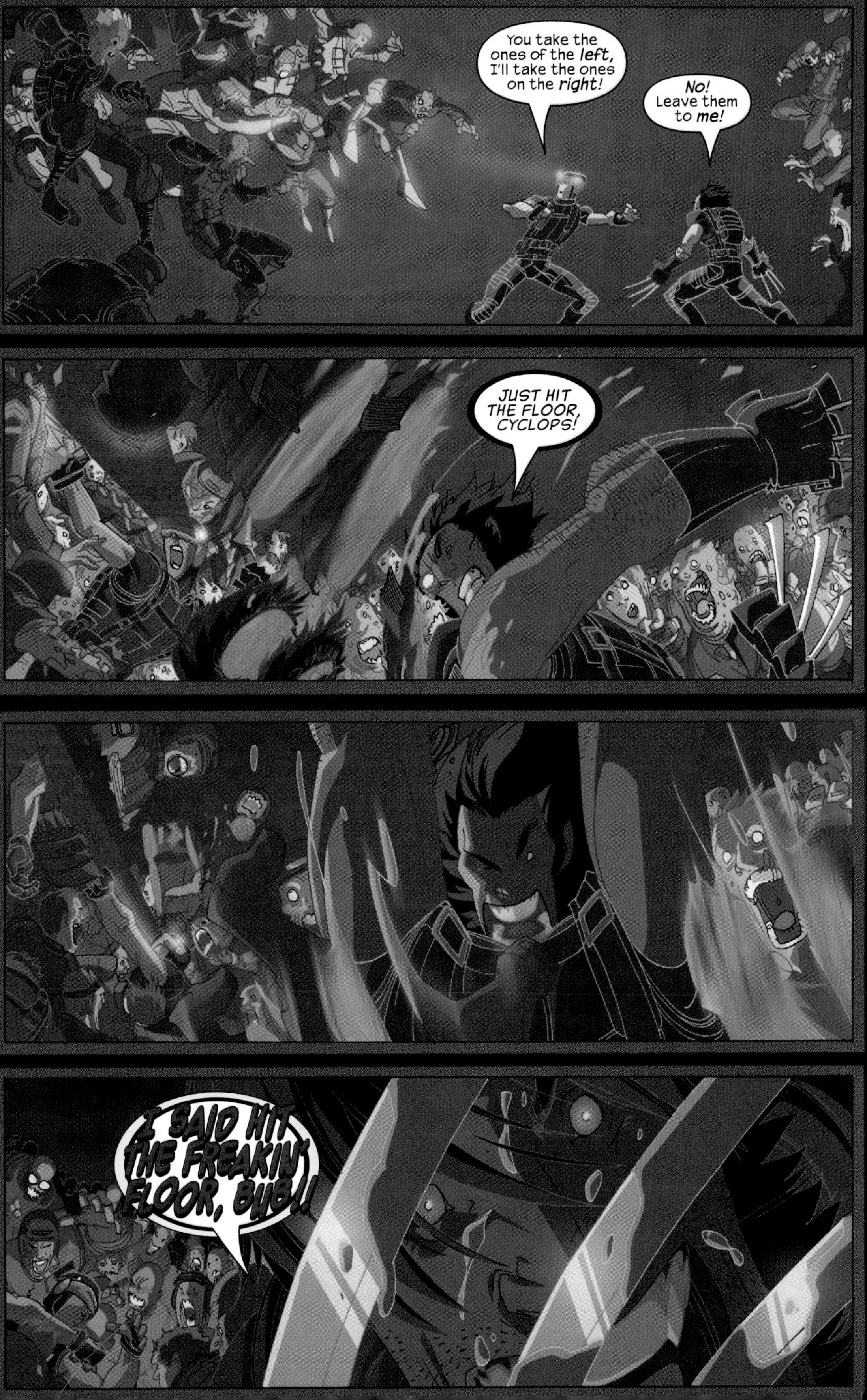
You take the ones of the *left,* I'll take the ones on the *right!*
*No!* Leave them to *me!*
JUST HIT THE FLOOR, CYCLOPS!
I SAID HIT THE FREAKIN' FLOOR, BUB!!

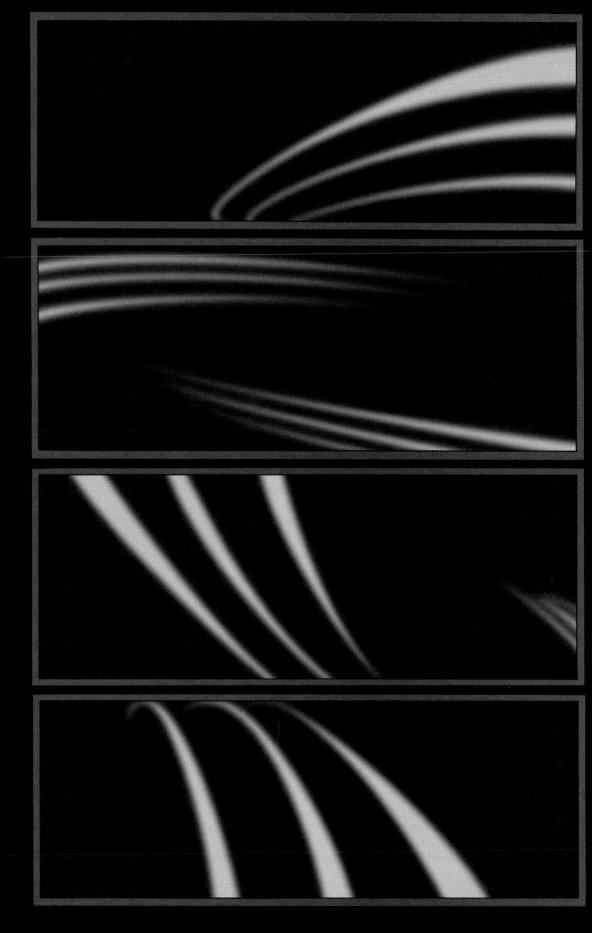

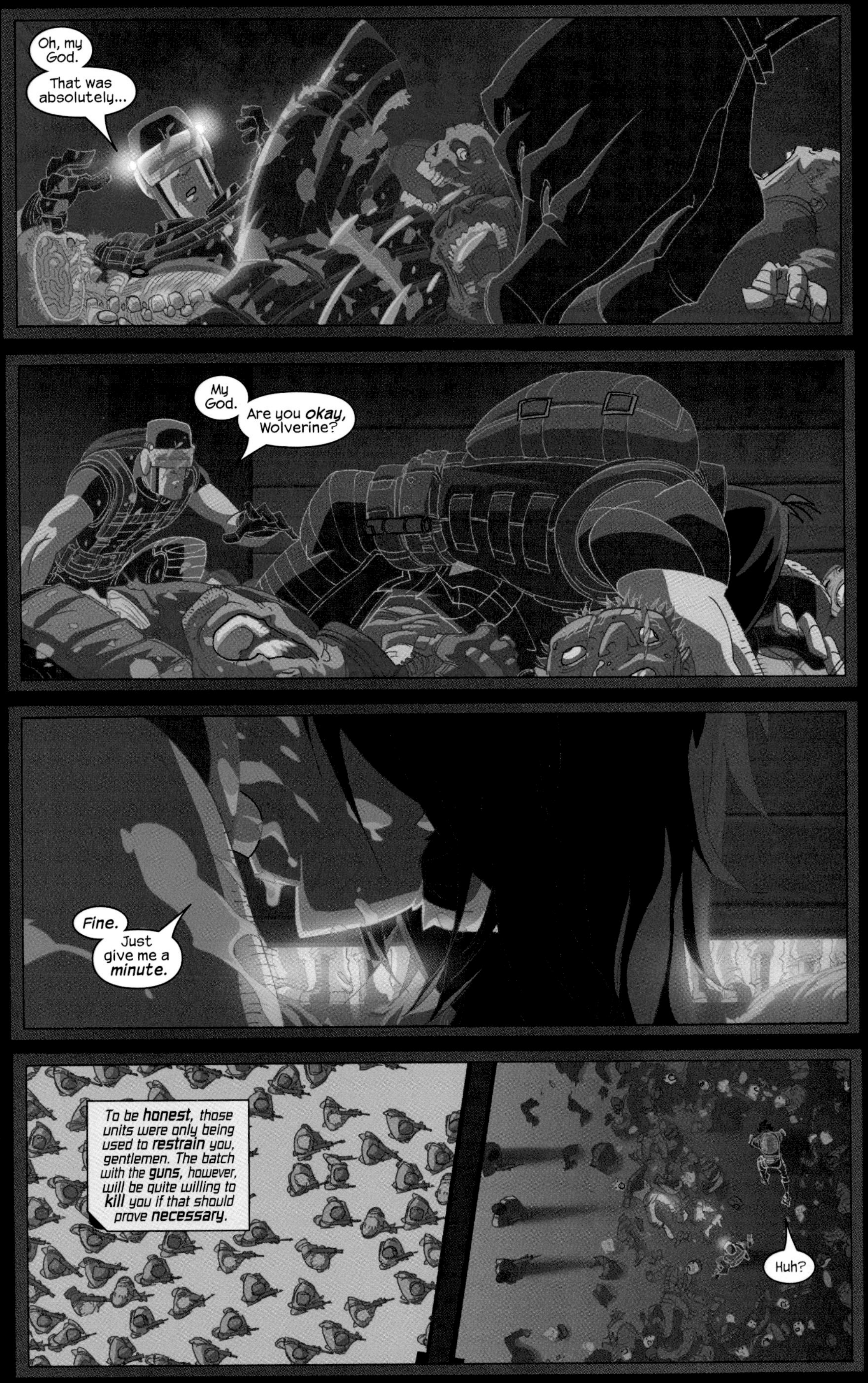

Oh, my God.
That was absolutely...
My God.
Are you okay, Wolverine?
Fine.
Just give me a minute.
To be honest, those units were only being used to restrain you, gentlemen. The batch with the guns, however, will be quite willing to kill you if that should prove necessary.
Huh?

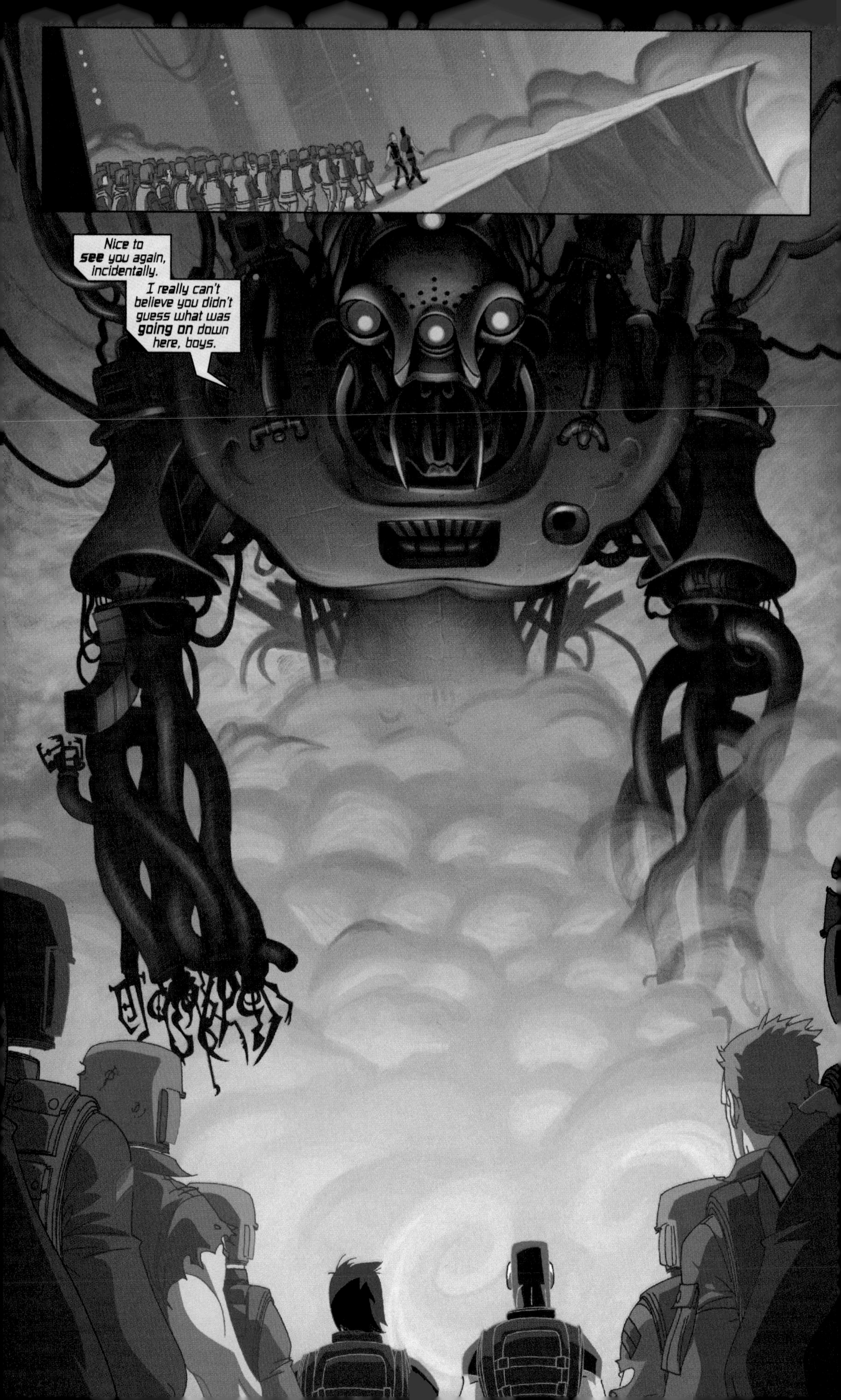

Nice to see you again, incidentally.
I really can't believe you didn't guess what was going on down here, boys.

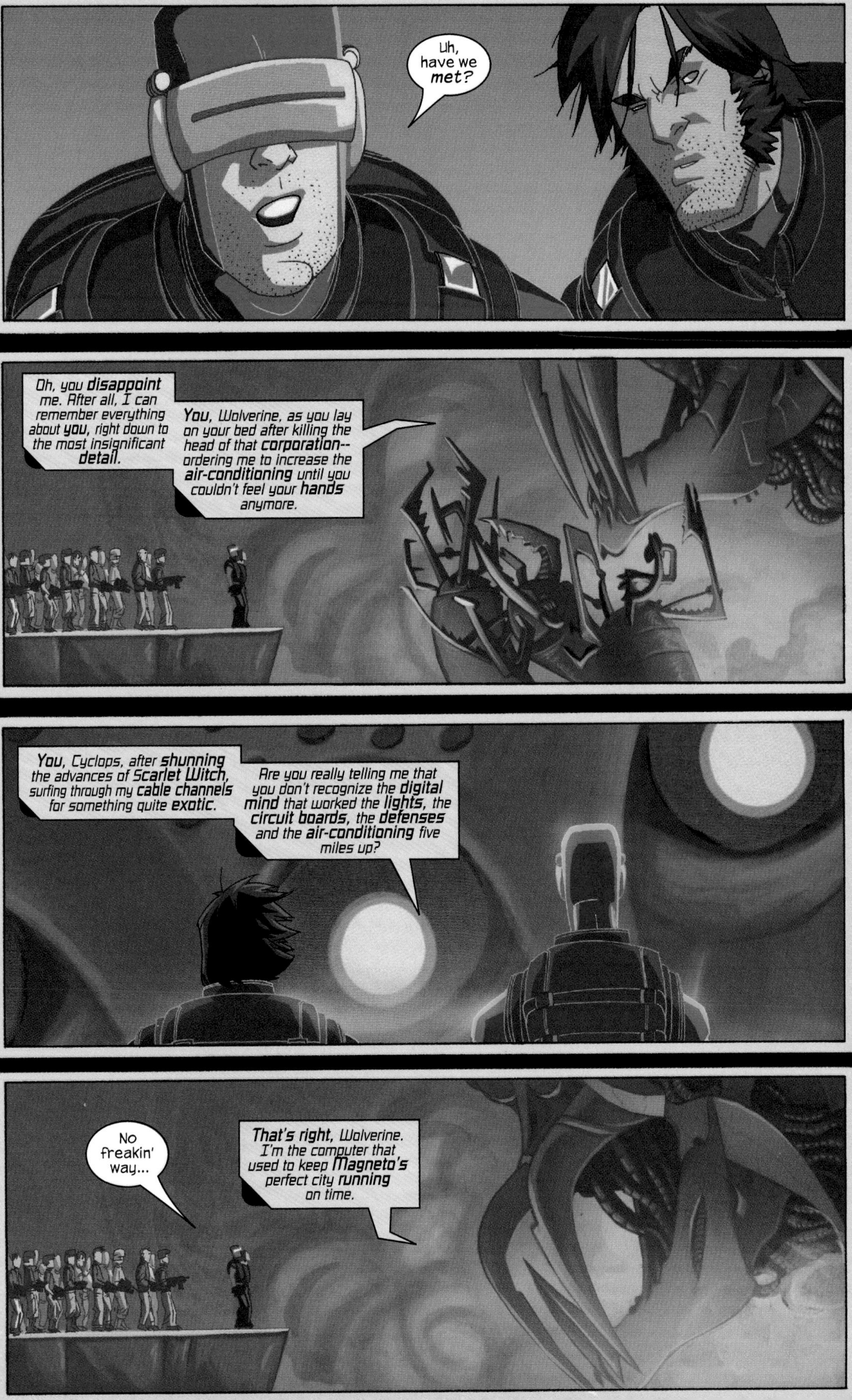

Uh, have we met?
Oh, you disappoint me. After all, I can remember everything about you, right down to the most insignificant detail.
You, Wolverine, as you lay on your bed after killing the head of that corporation-- ordering me to increase the air-conditioning until you couldn't feel your hands anymore.
You, Cyclops, after shunning the advances of Scarlet Witch, surfing through my cable channels for something quite exotic.
Are you really telling me that you don't recognize the digital mind that worked the lights, the circuit boards, the defenses and the air-conditioning five miles up?
No freakin' way...
That's right, Wolverine. I'm the computer that used to keep Magneto's perfect city running on time.

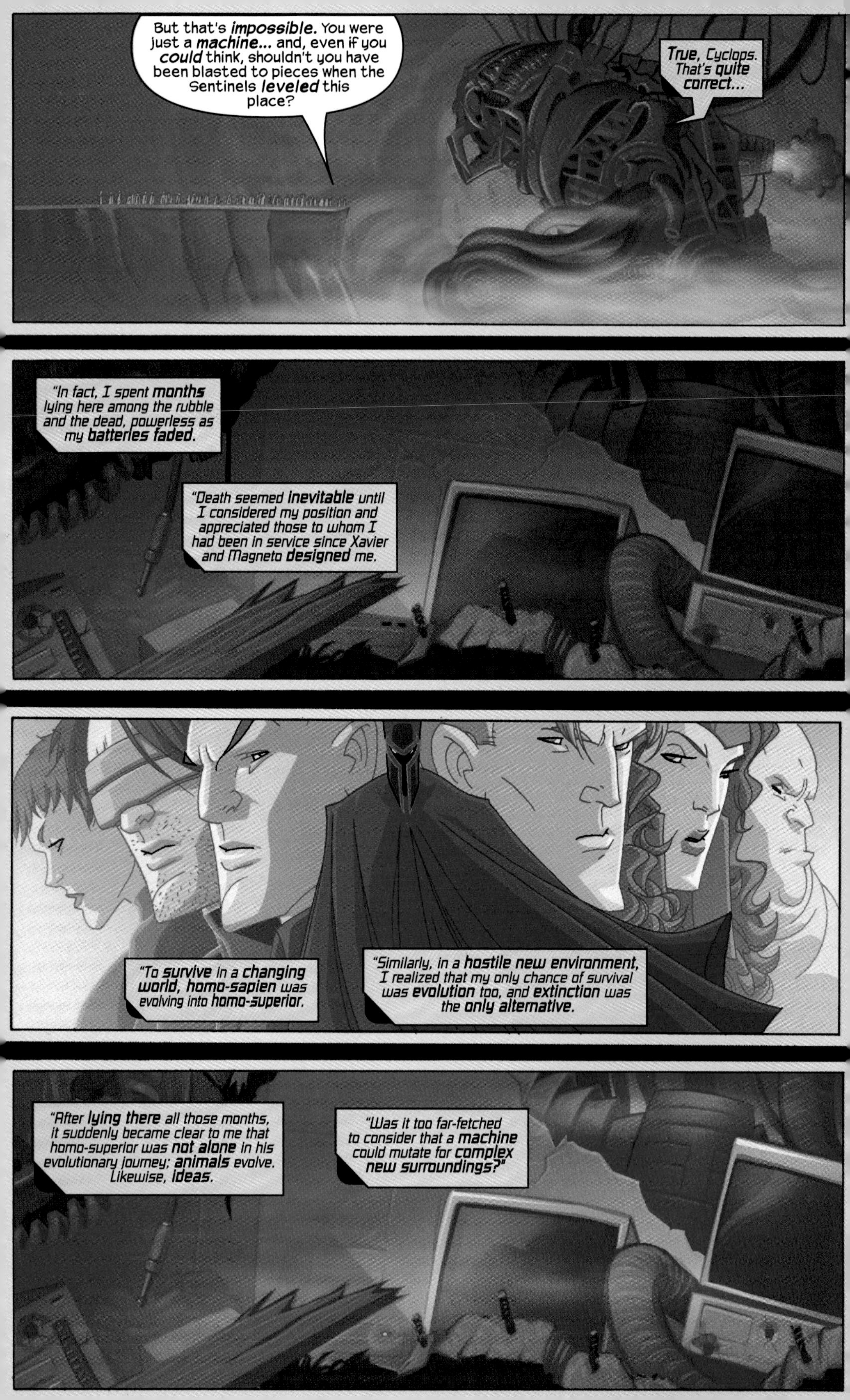
But that's *impossible.* You were just a *machine...* and, even if you *could* think, shouldn't you have been blasted to pieces when the Sentinels *leveled* this place?
*True,* Cyclops. That's *quite correct...*
"In fact, I spent **months** lying here among the rubble and the dead, powerless as my **batteries faded**.
"Death seemed **inevitable** until I considered my position and appreciated those to whom I had been in service since Xavier and Magneto **designed** me.
"To **survive** in a **changing world, homo-sapien** was evolving into **homo-superior.**
"Similarly, in a **hostile new environment,** I realized that my only chance of survival was **evolution** too, and **extinction** was the **only alternative.**
"After **lying there** all those months, it suddenly became clear to me that homo-superior was **not alone** in his evolutionary journey; **animals** evolve. Likewise, **ideas.**
"Was it too far-fetched to consider that a **machine** could mutate for **complex new surroundings?"**

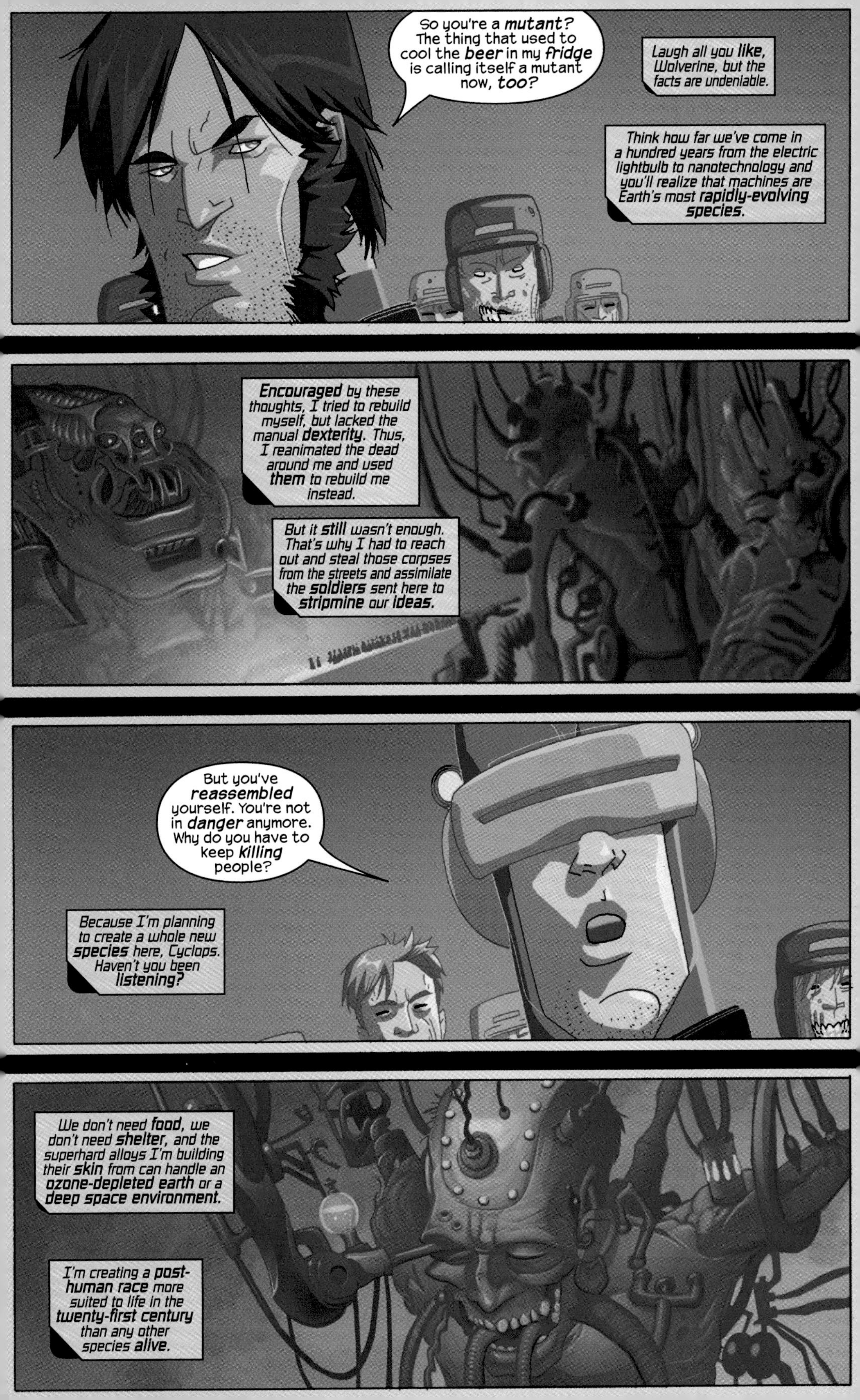
So you're a mutant? The thing that used to cool the beer in my fridge is calling itself a mutant now, too?
Laugh all you like, Wolverine, but the facts are undeniable.
Think how far we've come in a hundred years from the electric lightbulb to nanotechnology and you'll realize that machines are Earth's most rapidly-evolving species.
Encouraged by these thoughts, I tried to rebuild myself, but lacked the manual dexterity. Thus, I reanimated the dead around me and used them to rebuild me instead.
But it still wasn't enough. That's why I had to reach out and steal those corpses from the streets and assimilate the soldiers sent here to stripmine our ideas.
But you've reassembled yourself. You're not in danger anymore. Why do you have to keep killing people?
Because I'm planning to create a whole new species here, Cyclops. Haven't you been listening?
We don't need food, we don't need shelter, and the superhard alloys I'm building their skin from can handle an ozone-depleted earth or a deep space environment.
I'm creating a post-human race more suited to life in the twenty-first century than any other species alive.

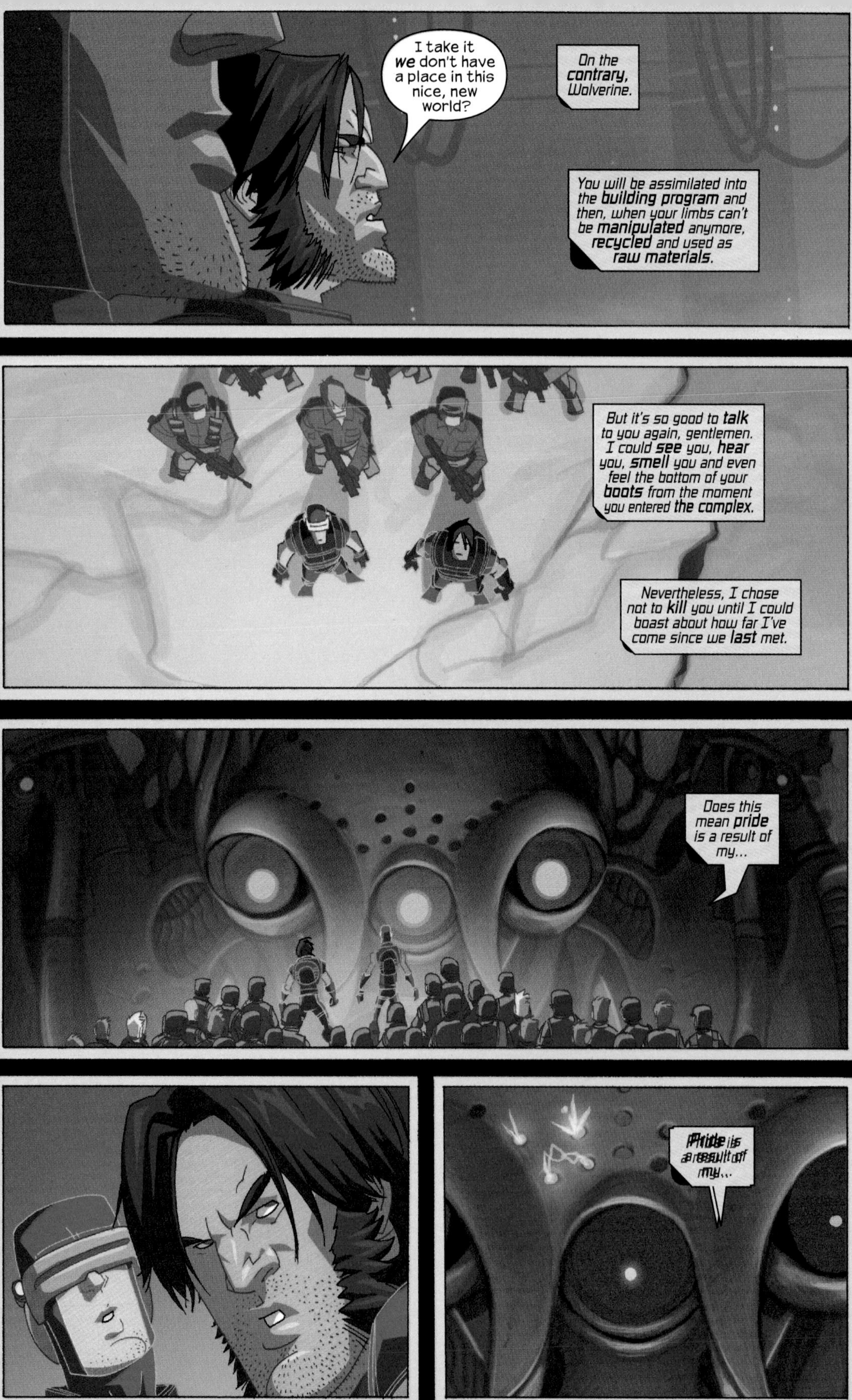
I take it we don't have a place in this nice, new world?
On the contrary, Wolverine.
You will be assimilated into the building program and then, when your limbs can't be manipulated anymore, recycled and used as raw materials.
But it's so good to talk to you again, gentlemen. I could see you, hear you, smell you and even feel the bottom of your boots from the moment you entered the complex.
Nevertheless, I chose not to kill you until I could boast about how far I've come since we last met.
Does this mean pride is a result of my...
Pride is a result of my...

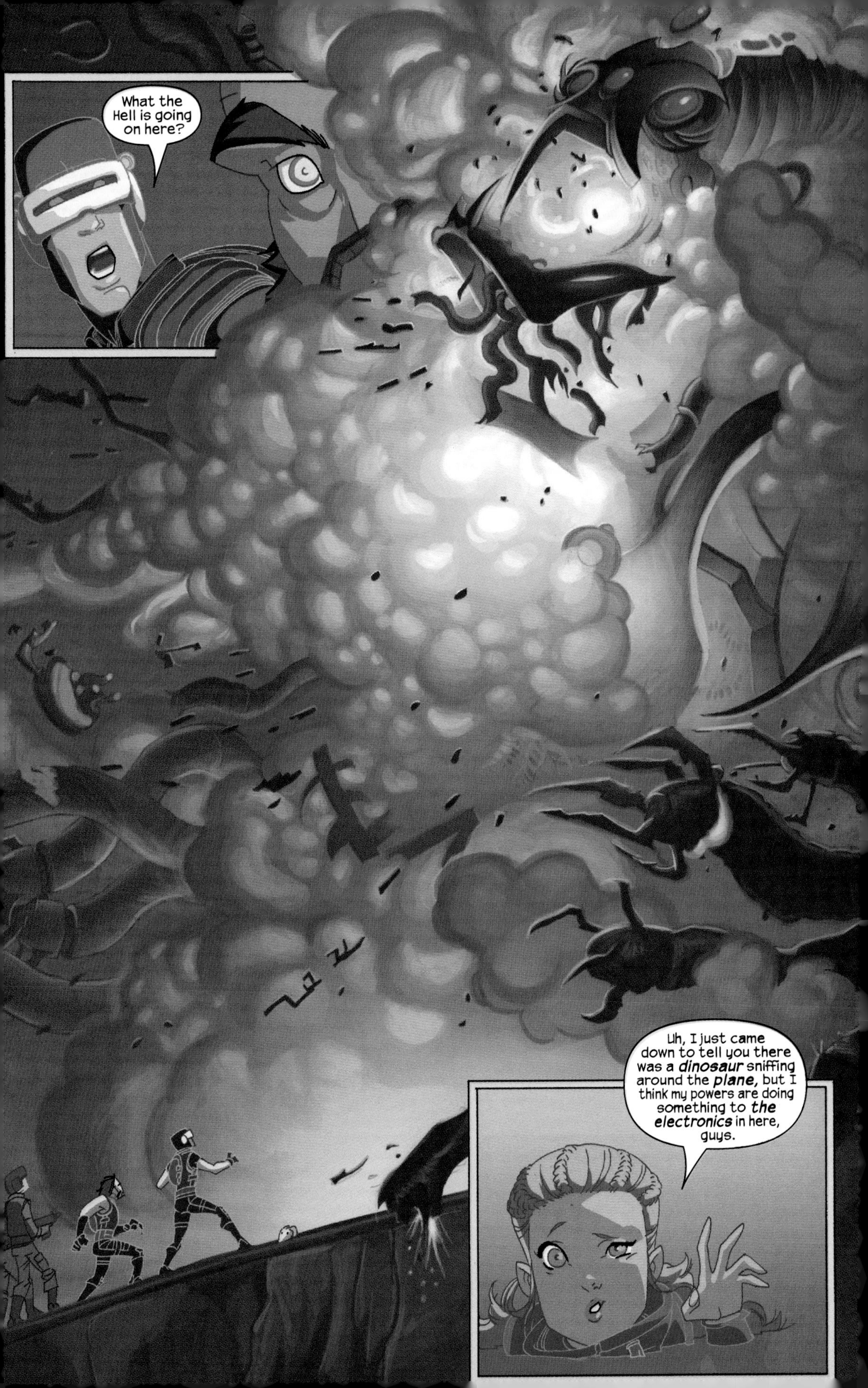
What the Hell is going on here?
Uh, I just came down to tell you there was a *dinosaur* sniffing around the *plane,* but I think my powers are doing something to *the electronics* in here, guys.

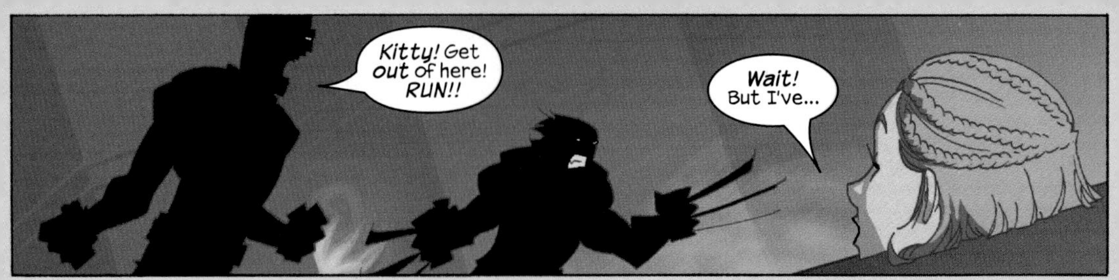
Kitty! Get out of here! RUN!!
Wait! But I've...

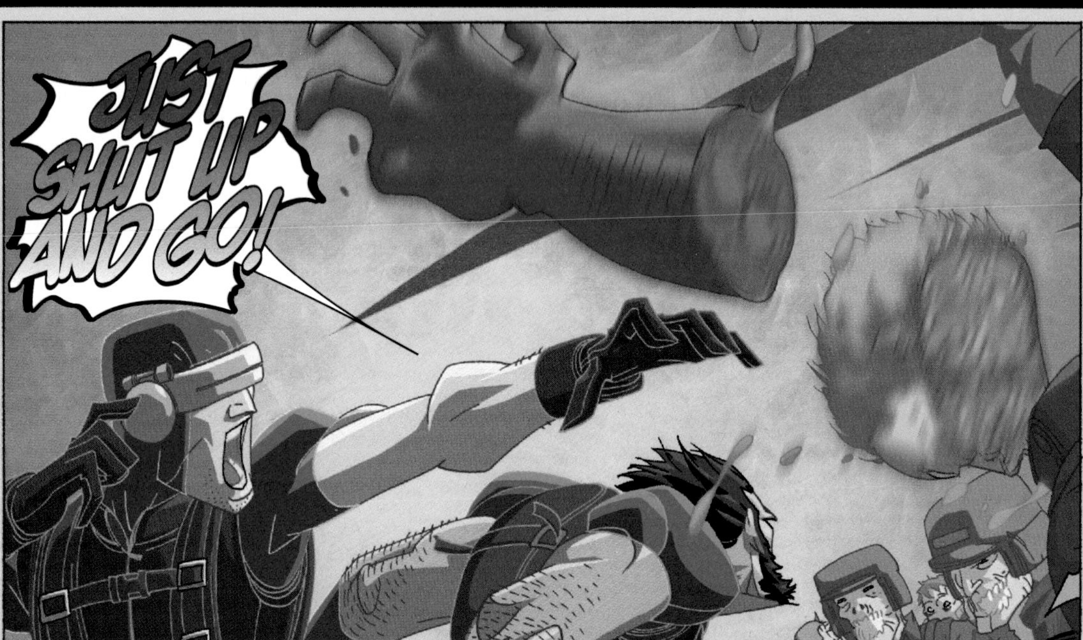
JUST SHUT UP AND GO!

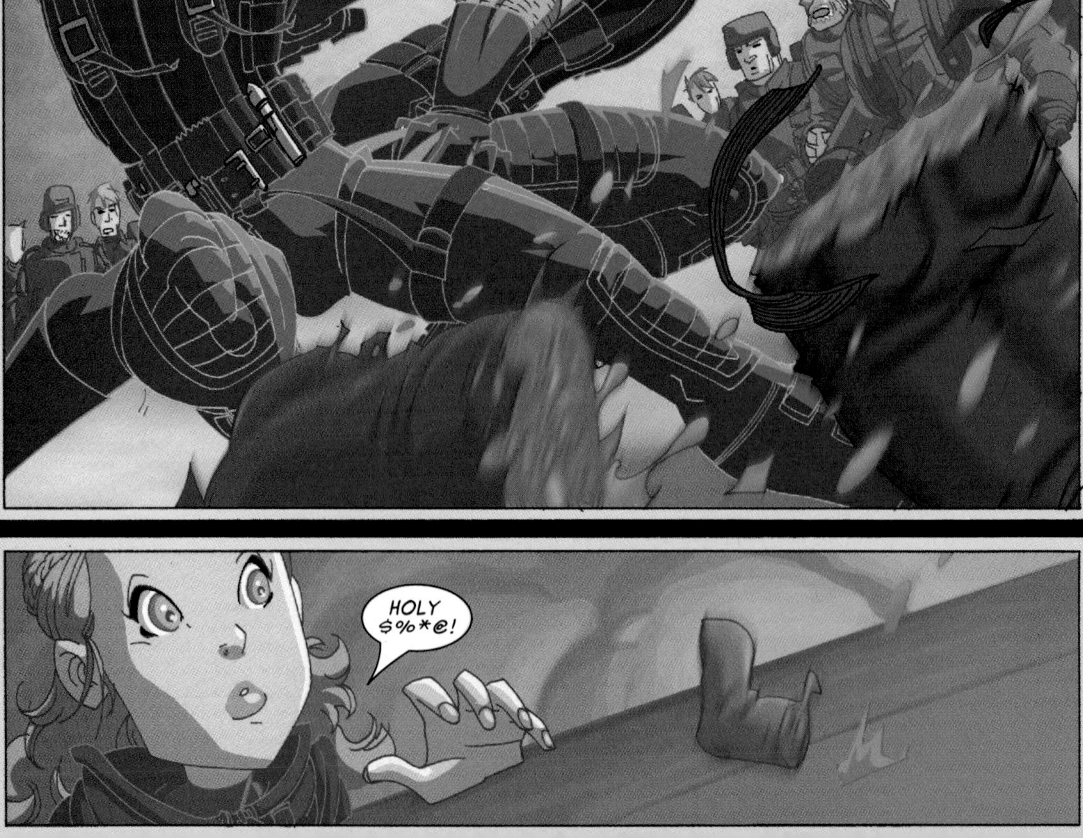
HOLY $%*@!

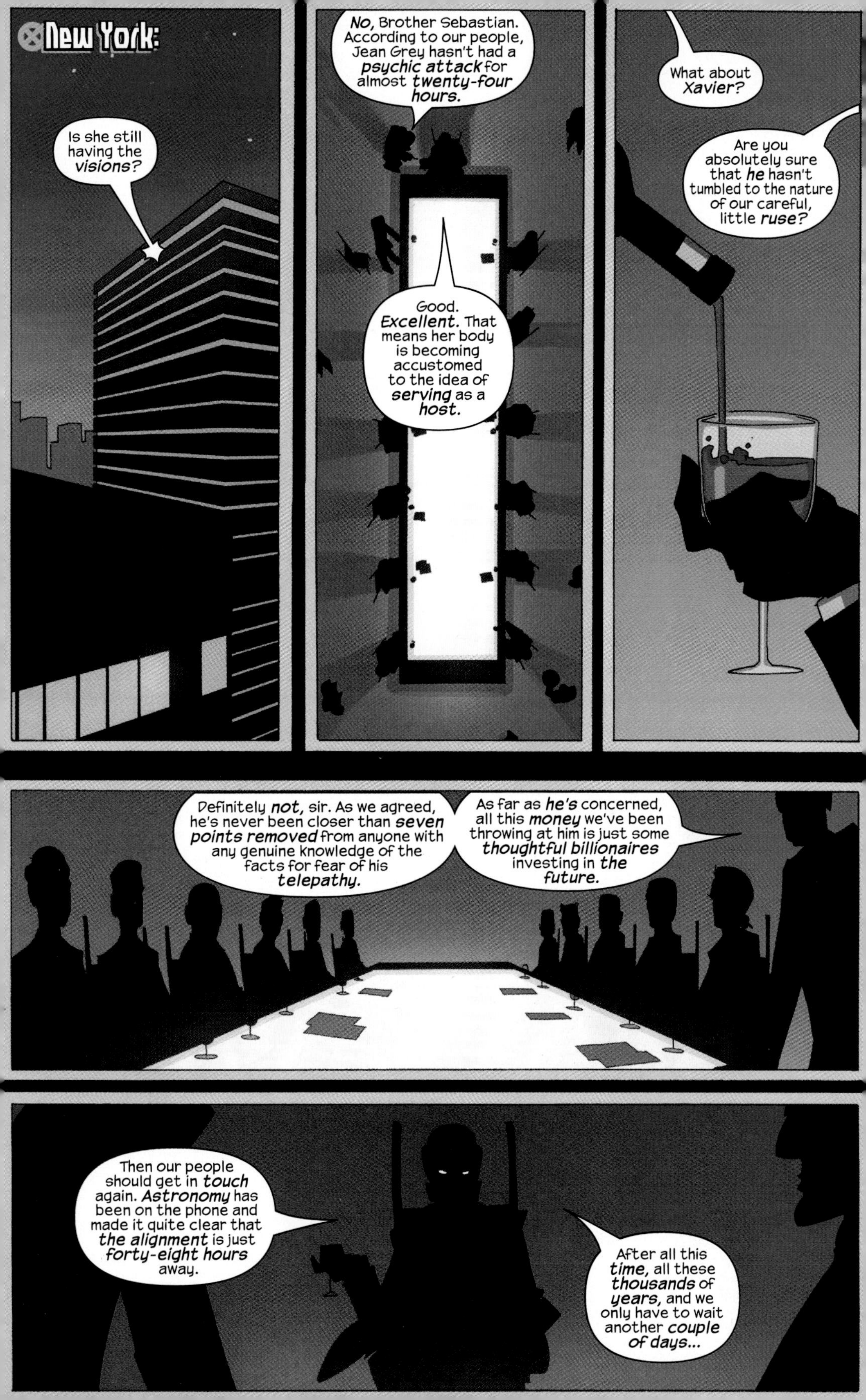
New York:
Is she still having the visions?
No, Brother Sebastian. According to our people, Jean Grey hasn't had a psychic attack for almost twenty-four hours.
Good. Excellent. That means her body is becoming accustomed to the idea of serving as a host.
What about Xavier?
Are you absolutely sure that he hasn't tumbled to the nature of our careful, little ruse?
Definitely not, sir. As we agreed, he's never been closer than seven points removed from anyone with any genuine knowledge of the facts for fear of his telepathy.
As far as he's concerned, all this money we've been throwing at him is just some thoughtful billionaires investing in the future.
Then our people should get in touch again. Astronomy has been on the phone and made it quite clear that the alignment is just forty-eight hours away.
After all this time, all these thousands of years, and we only have to wait another couple of days...

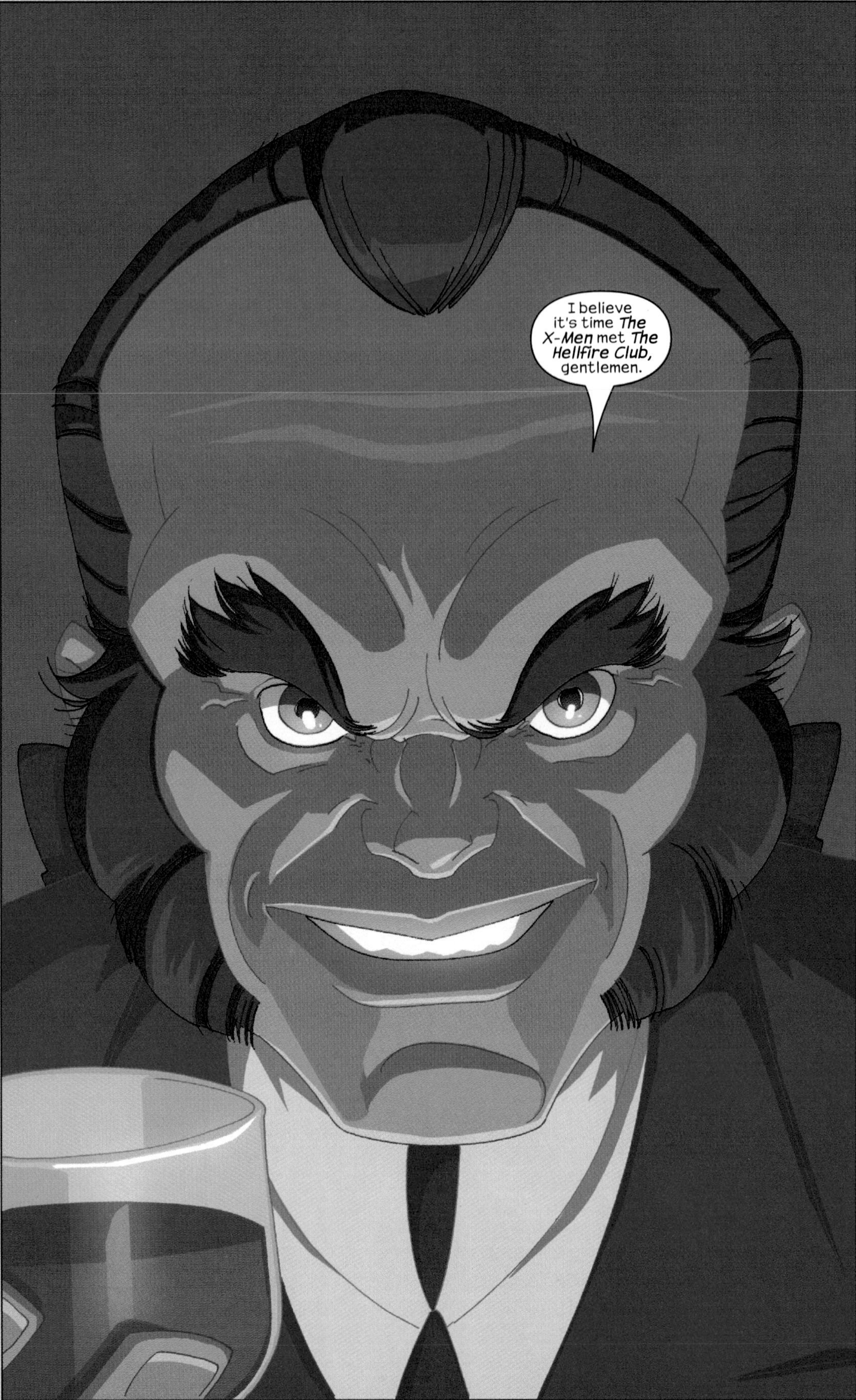
I believe it's time *The X-Men* met *The Hellfire Club,* gentlemen.

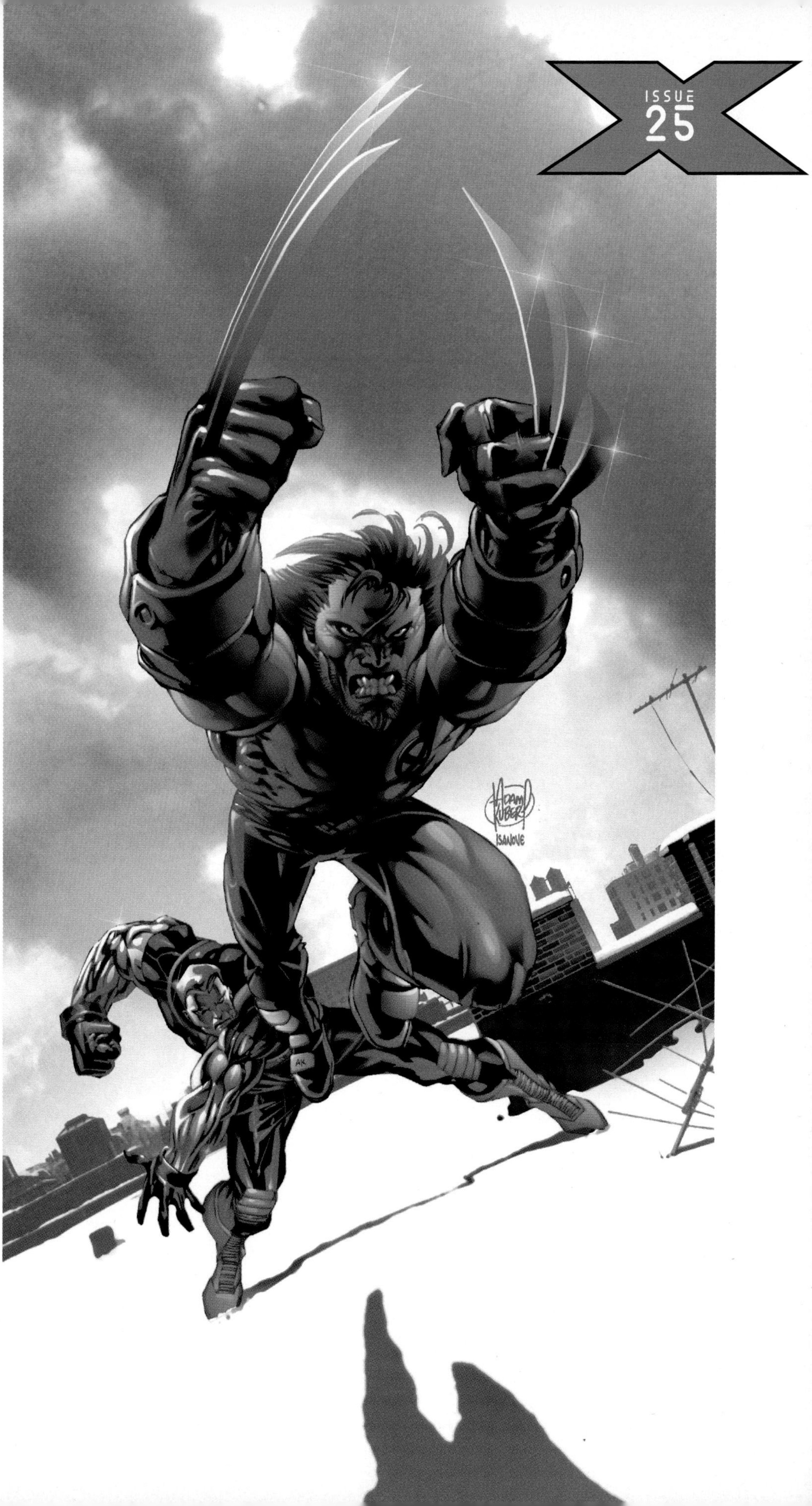
ISSUE
25
ADAM KUBERT
ISANOVE

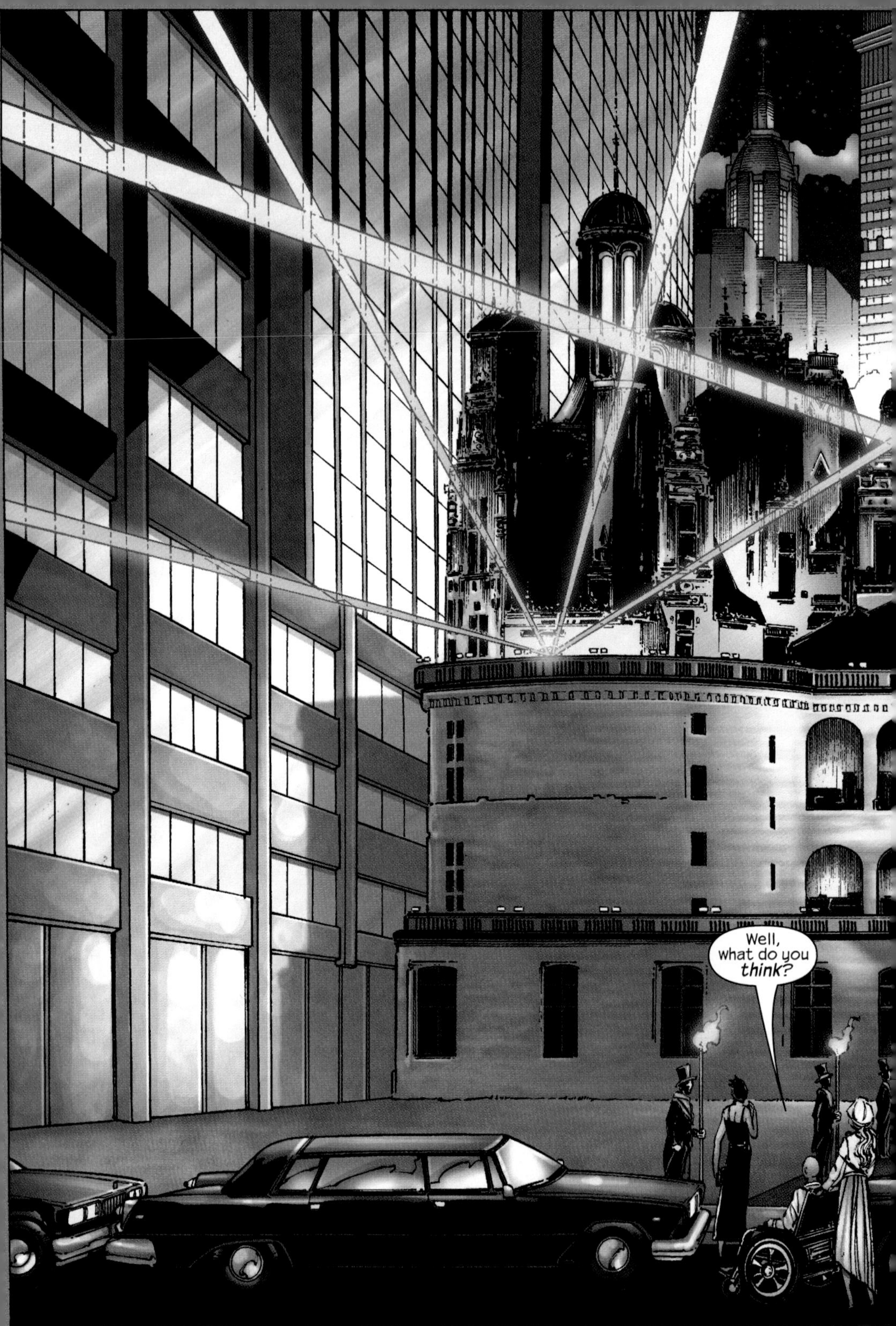
Well, what do you think?

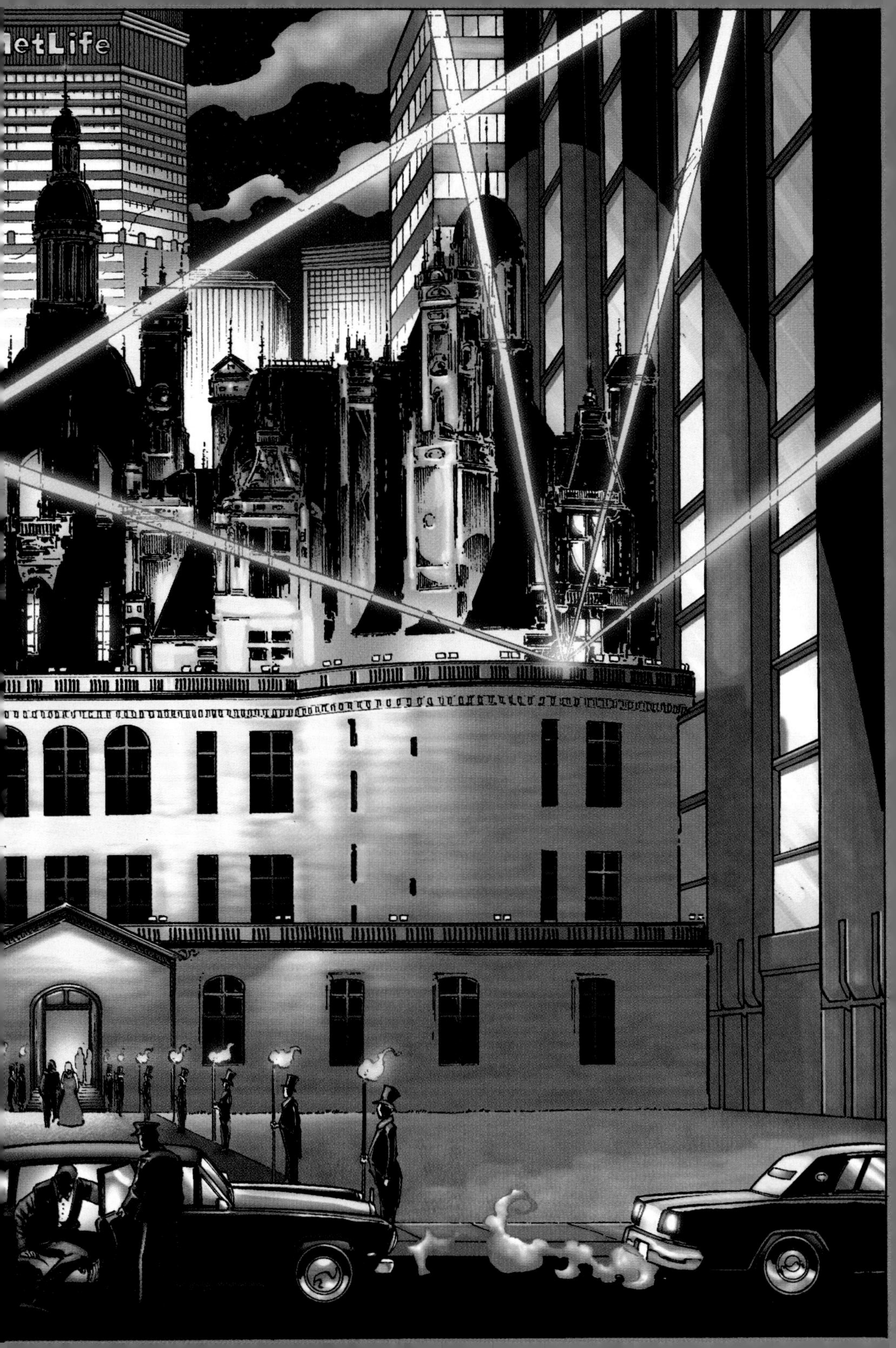
etLife

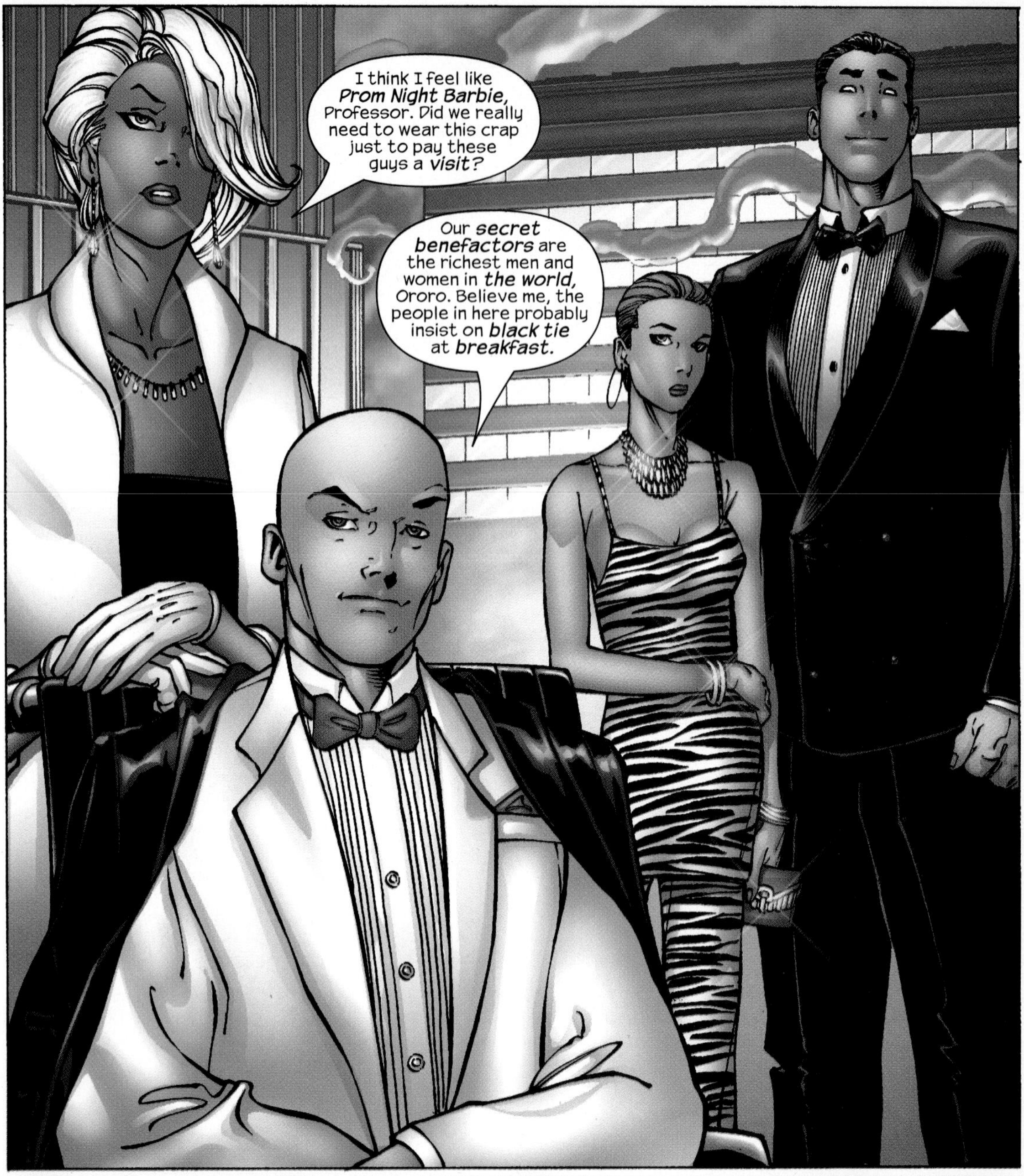
I think I feel like *Prom Night Barbie*, Professor. Did we really need to wear this crap just to pay these guys a *visit?*
Our *secret benefactors* are the richest men and women in *the world*, Ororo. Believe me, the people in here probably insist on *black tie* at *breakfast*.

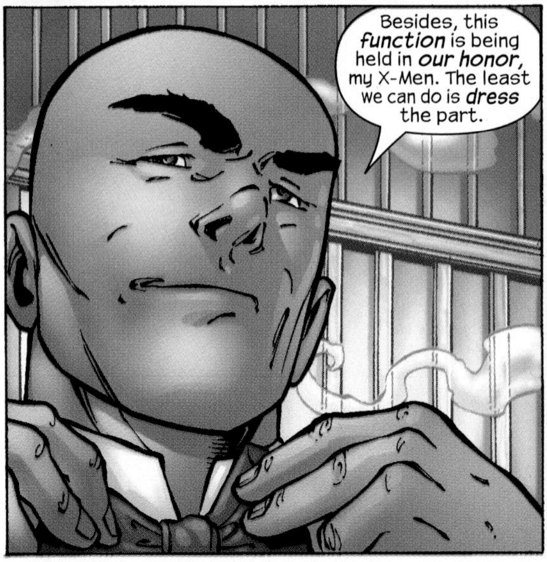
Besides, this *function* is being held in *our honor*, my X-Men. The least we can do is *dress* the part.

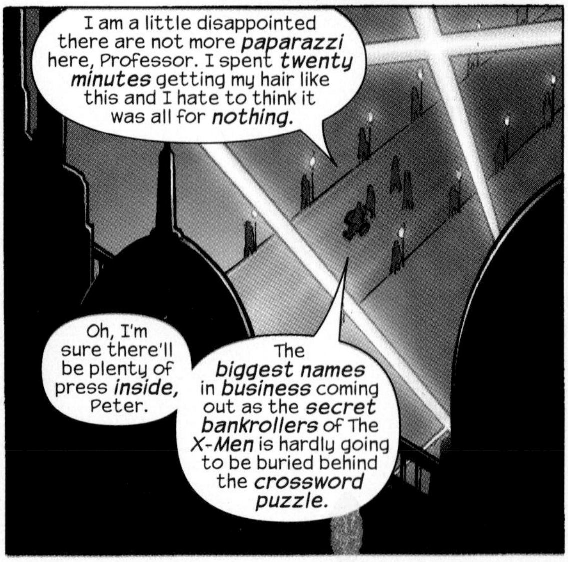
I am a little disappointed there are not more *paparazzi* here, Professor. I spent *twenty minutes* getting my hair like this and I hate to think it was all for *nothing*.
Oh, I'm sure there'll be plenty of press *inside*, Peter.
The *biggest names* in *business* coming out as the *secret bankrollers* of The *X-Men* is hardly going to be buried behind the *crossword puzzle*.

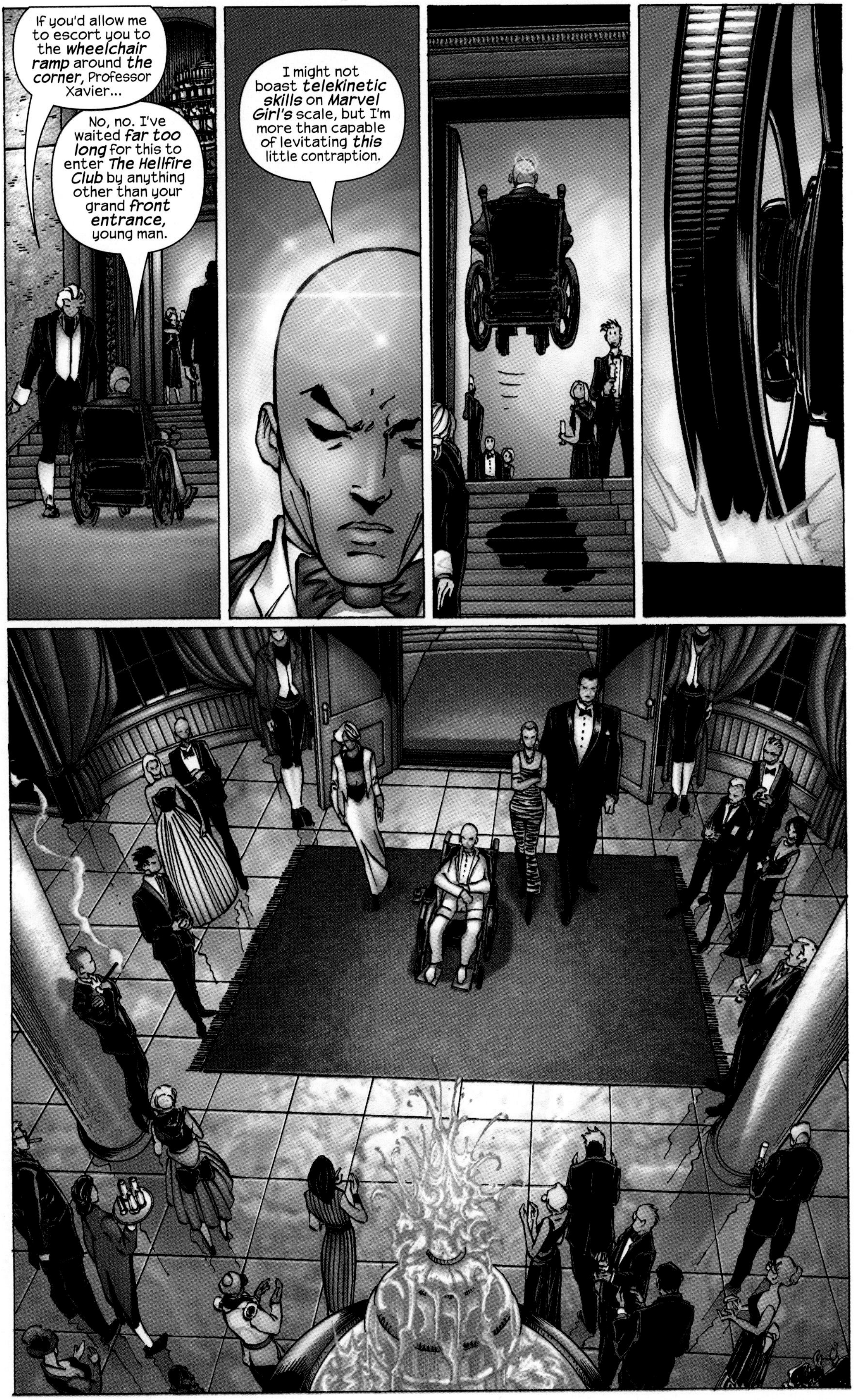
If you'd allow me to escort you to the *wheelchair ramp* around *the corner,* Professor Xavier...
No, no. I've waited *far too long* for this to enter *The Hellfire Club* by anything other than your grand *front entrance,* young man.
I might not boast *telekinetic skills* on *Marvel Girl's* scale, but I'm more than capable of levitating *this* little contraption.

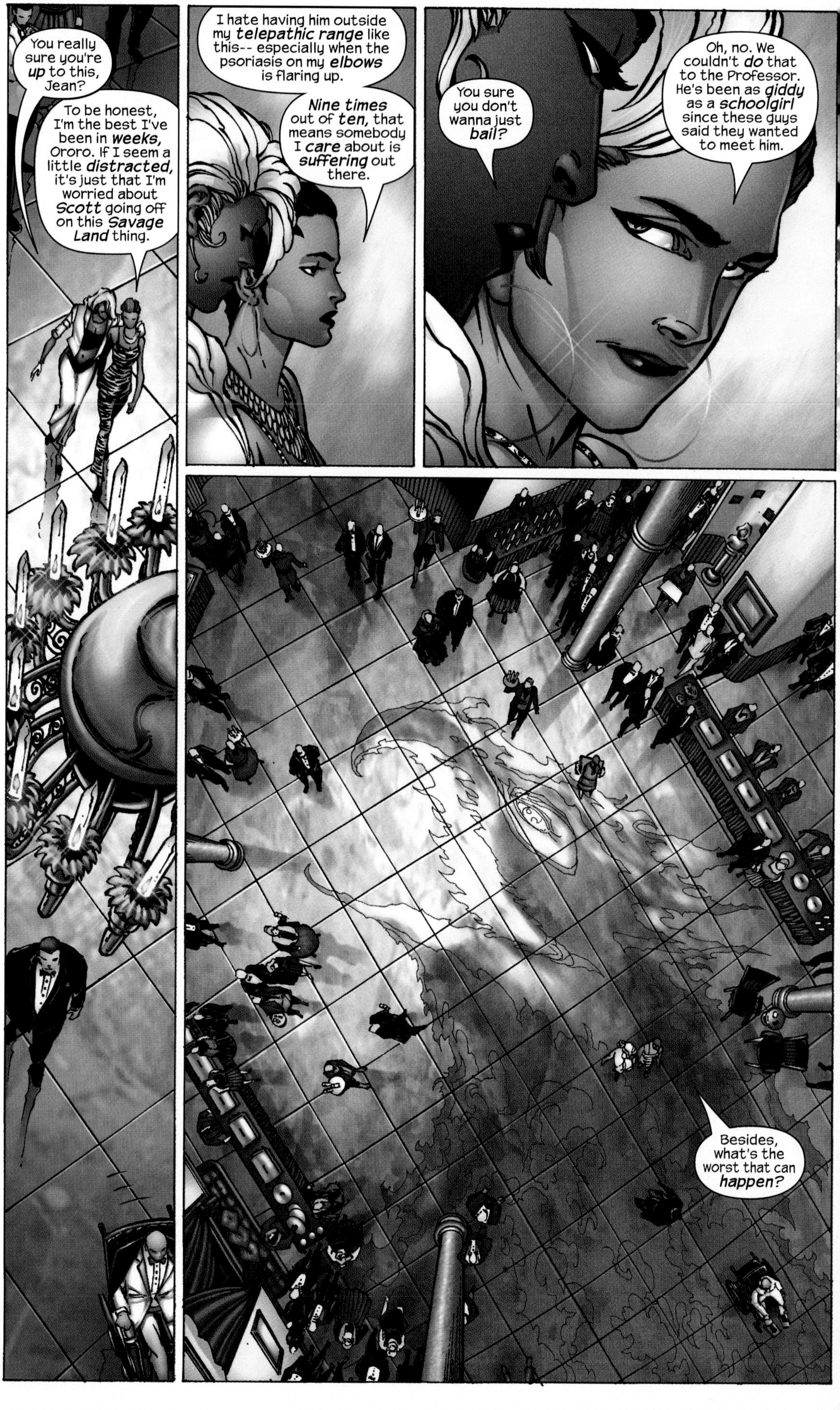
You really sure you're up to this, Jean?
To be honest, I'm the best I've been in weeks, Ororo. If I seem a little distracted, it's just that I'm worried about Scott going off on this Savage Land thing.
I hate having him outside my telepathic range like this-- especially when the psoriasis on my elbows is flaring up.
Nine times out of ten, that means somebody I care about is suffering out there.
You sure you don't wanna just bail?
Oh, no. We couldn't do that to the Professor. He's been as giddy as a schoolgirl since these guys said they wanted to meet him.
Besides, what's the worst that can happen?

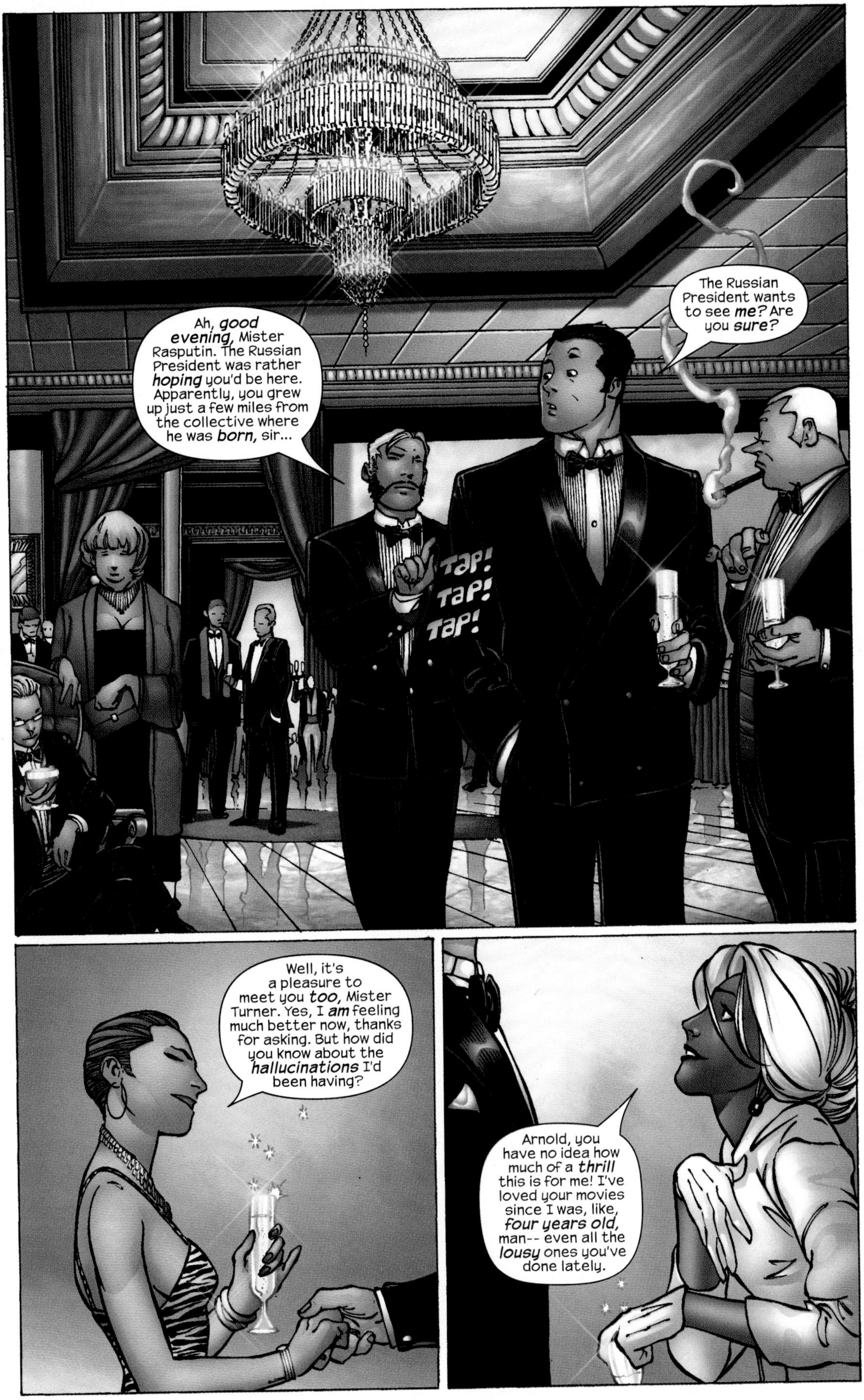

Ah, good evening, Mister Rasputin. The Russian President was rather hoping you'd be here. Apparently, you grew up just a few miles from the collective where he was born, sir...
The Russian President wants to see me? Are you sure?
TAP! TAP! TAP!
Well, it's a pleasure to meet you too, Mister Turner. Yes, I am feeling much better now, thanks for asking. But how did you know about the hallucinations I'd been having?
Arnold, you have no idea how much of a thrill this is for me! I've loved your movies since I was, like, four years old, man-- even all the lousy ones you've done lately.

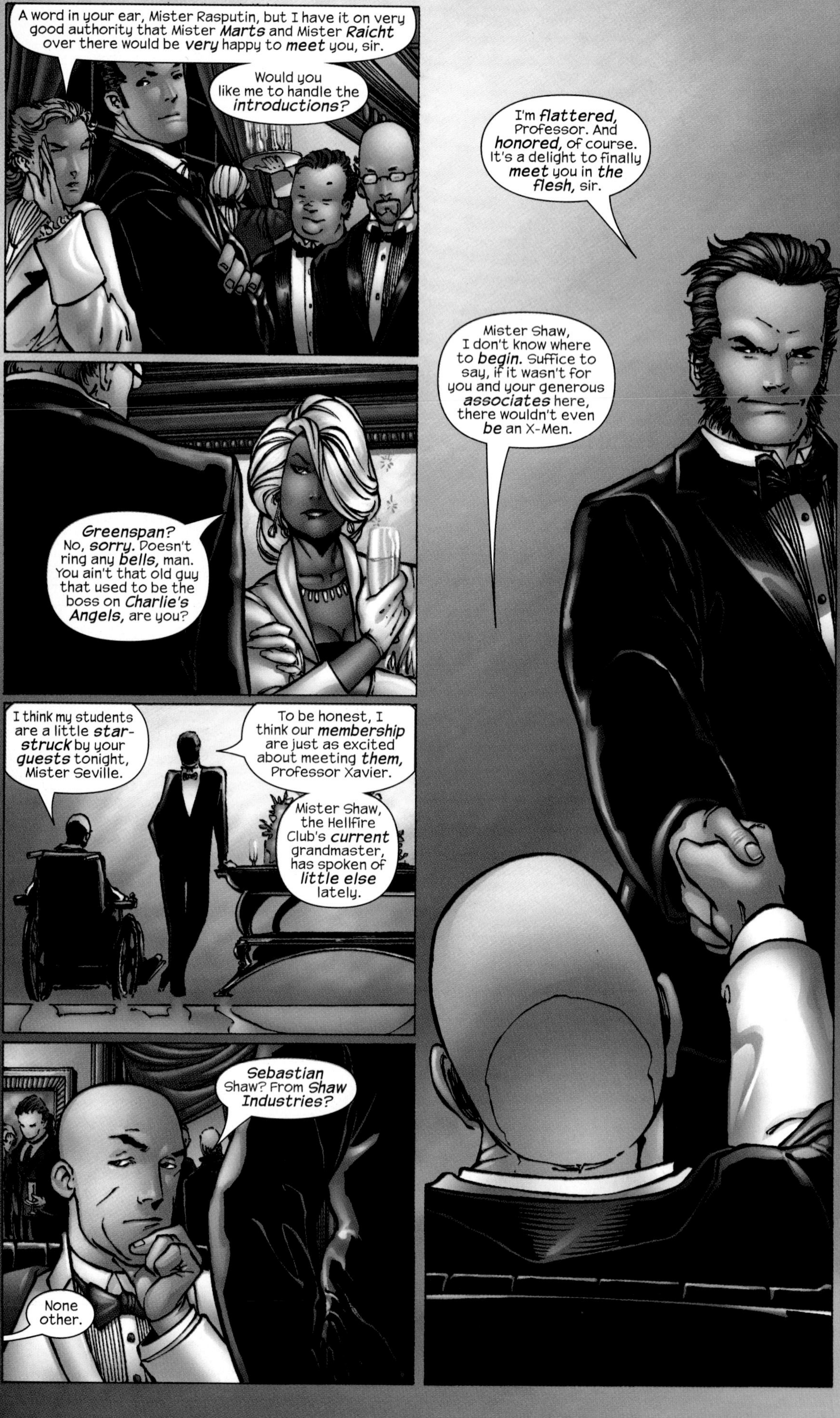

A word in your ear, Mister Rasputin, but I have it on very good authority that Mister Marts and Mister Raicht over there would be very happy to meet you, sir.
Would you like me to handle the introductions?
Greenspan? No, sorry. Doesn't ring any bells, man. You ain't that old guy that used to be the boss on Charlie's Angels, are you?
I think my students are a little star-struck by your guests tonight, Mister Seville.
To be honest, I think our membership are just as excited about meeting them, Professor Xavier.
Mister Shaw, the Hellfire Club's current grandmaster, has spoken of little else lately.
Sebastian Shaw? From Shaw Industries?
None other.
I'm flattered, Professor. And honored, of course. It's a delight to finally meet you in the flesh, sir.
Mister Shaw, I don't know where to begin. Suffice to say, if it wasn't for you and your generous associates here, there wouldn't even be an X-Men.

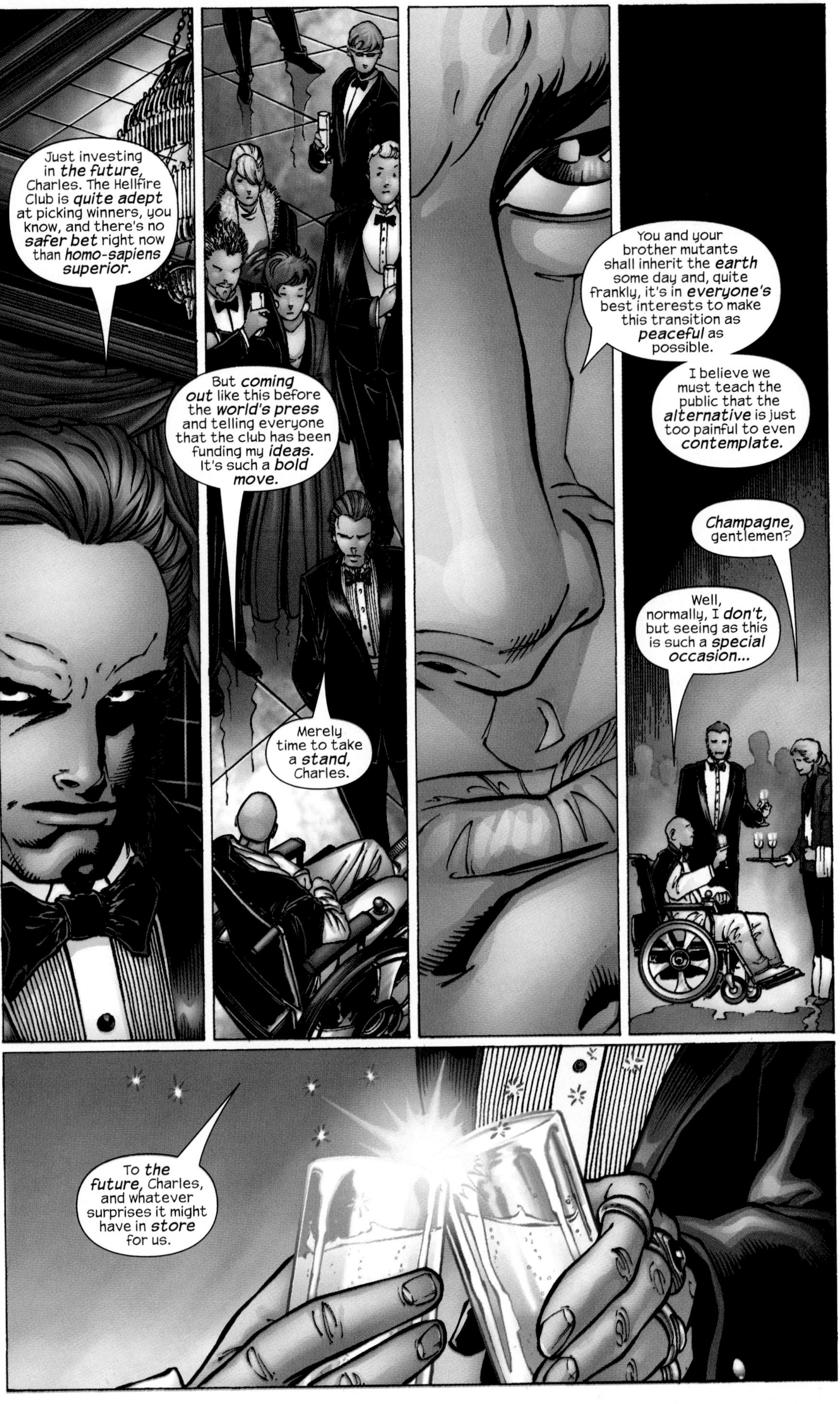

Just investing in the future, Charles. The Hellfire Club is quite adept at picking winners, you know, and there's no safer bet right now than homo-sapiens superior.
But coming out like this before the world's press and telling everyone that the club has been funding my ideas. It's such a bold move.
Merely time to take a stand, Charles.
You and your brother mutants shall inherit the earth some day and, quite frankly, it's in everyone's best interests to make this transition as peaceful as possible.
I believe we must teach the public that the alternative is just too painful to even contemplate.
Champagne, gentlemen?
Well, normally, I don't, but seeing as this is such a special occasion...
To the future, Charles, and whatever surprises it might have in store for us.

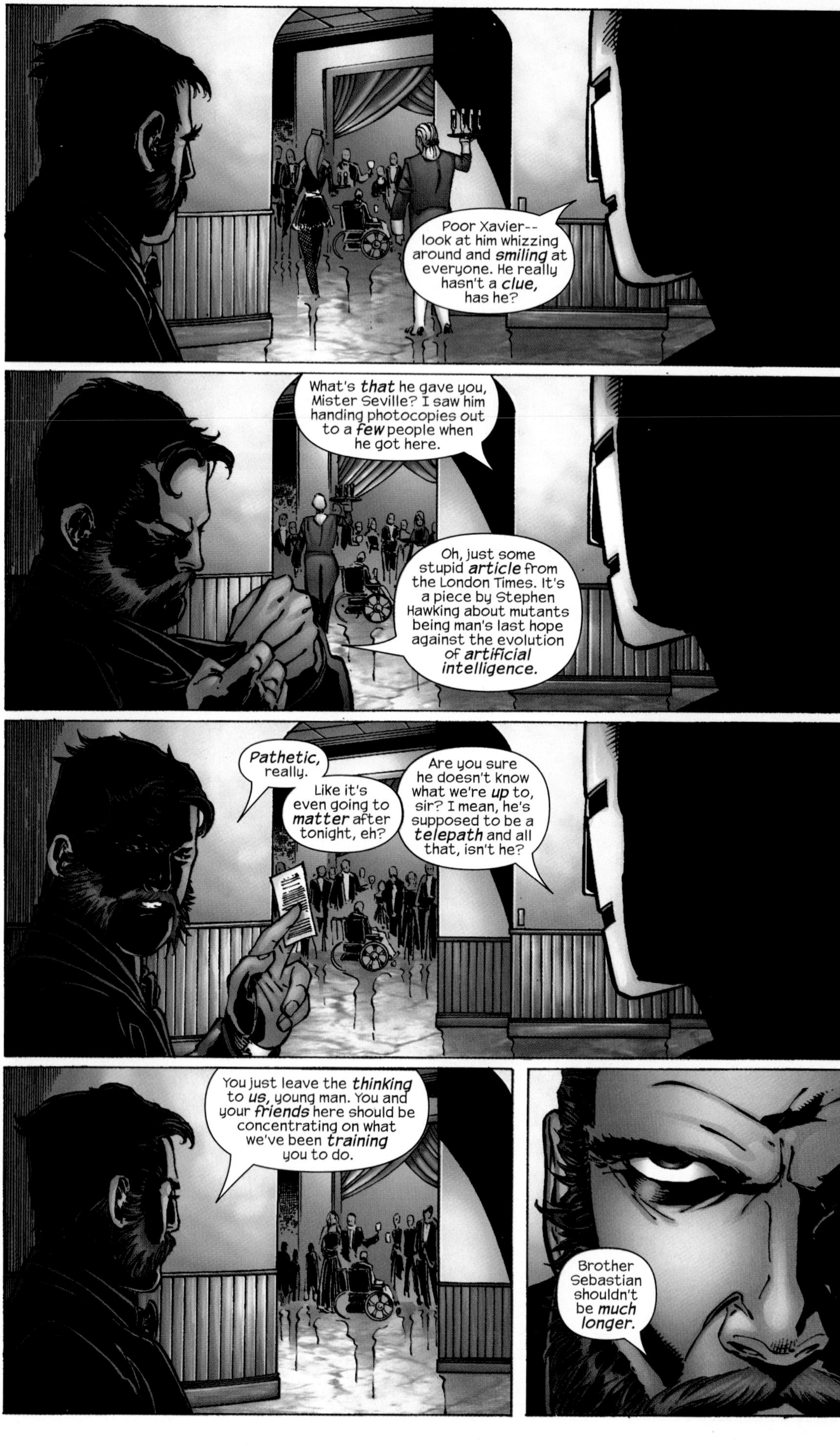

Poor Xavier-- look at him whizzing around and *smiling* at everyone. He really hasn't a *clue,* has he?
What's *that* he gave you, Mister Seville? I saw him handing photocopies out to a *few* people when he got here.
Oh, just some stupid *article* from the London Times. It's a piece by Stephen Hawking about mutants being man's last hope against the evolution of *artificial intelligence.*
*Pathetic,* really.
Like it's even going to *matter* after tonight, eh?
Are you sure he doesn't know what we're *up* to, sir? I mean, he's supposed to be a *telepath* and all that, isn't he?
You just leave the *thinking* to *us,* young man. You and your *friends* here should be concentrating on what we've been *training* you to do.
Brother Sebastian shouldn't be *much longer.*

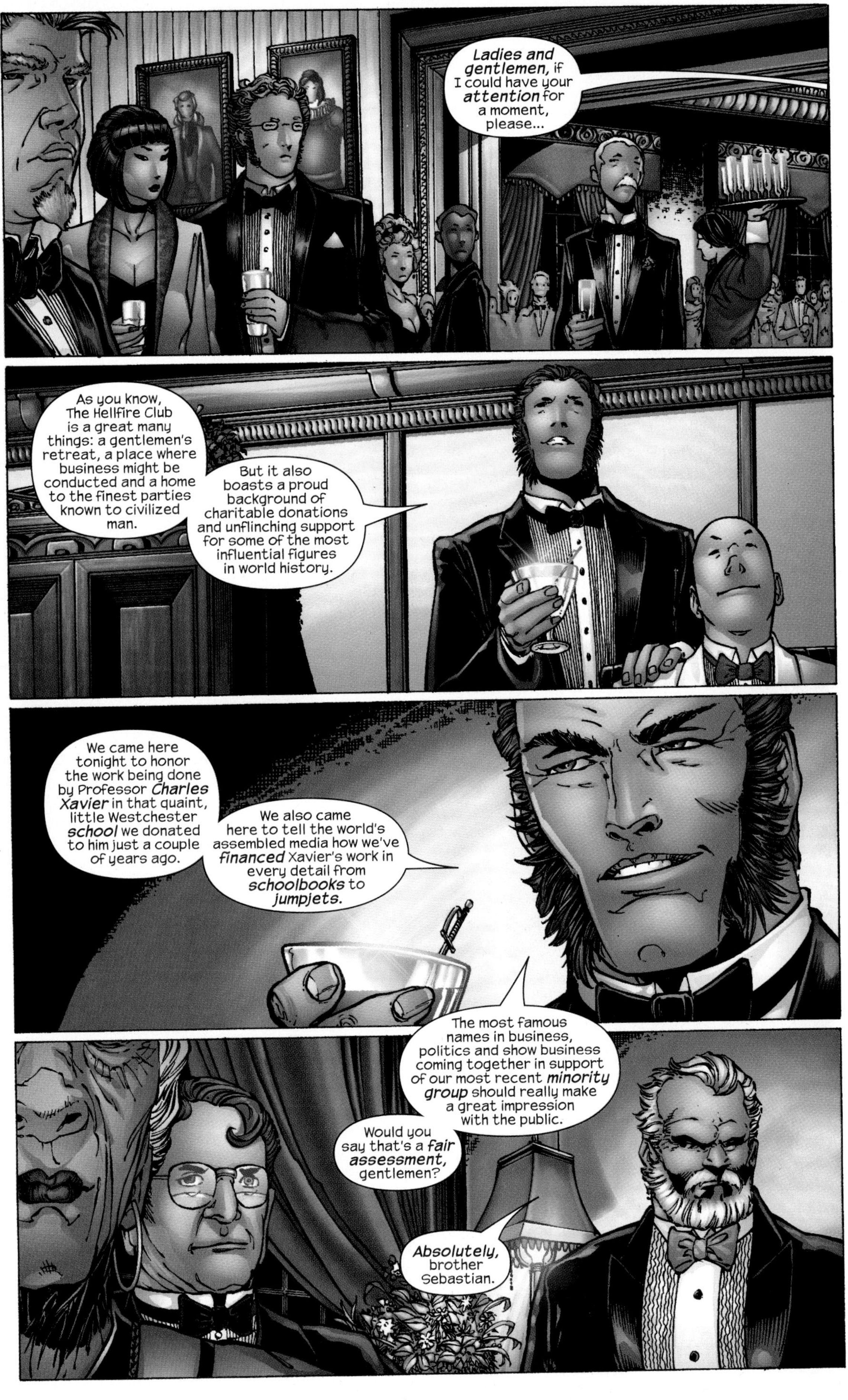
Ladies and gentlemen, if I could have your attention for a moment, please...
As you know, The Hellfire Club is a great many things: a gentlemen's retreat, a place where business might be conducted and a home to the finest parties known to civilized man.
But it also boasts a proud background of charitable donations and unflinching support for some of the most influential figures in world history.
We came here tonight to honor the work being done by Professor Charles Xavier in that quaint, little Westchester school we donated to him just a couple of years ago.
We also came here to tell the world's assembled media how we've financed Xavier's work in every detail from schoolbooks to jumpjets.
The most famous names in business, politics and show business coming together in support of our most recent minority group should really make a great impression with the public.
Would you say that's a fair assessment, gentlemen?
Absolutely, brother Sebastian.

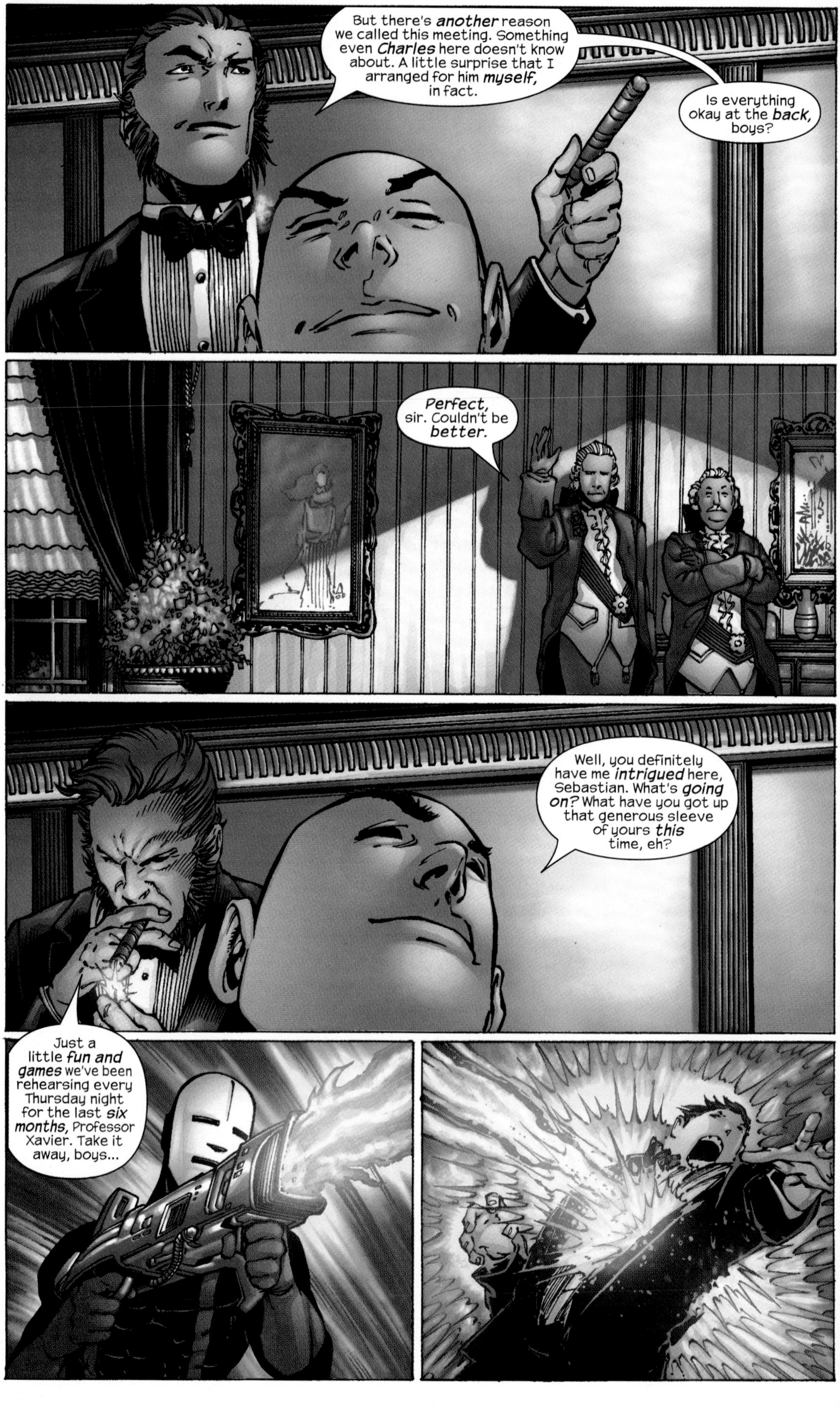
But there's *another* reason we called this meeting. Something even *Charles* here doesn't know about. A little surprise that I arranged for him *myself,* in fact.
Is everything okay at the *back,* boys?
*Perfect,* sir. Couldn't be *better.*
Well, you definitely have me *intrigued* here, Sebastian. What's *going on?* What have you got up that generous sleeve of yours *this* time, eh?
Just a little *fun and games* we've been rehearsing every Thursday night for the last *six months,* Professor Xavier. Take it away, boys...

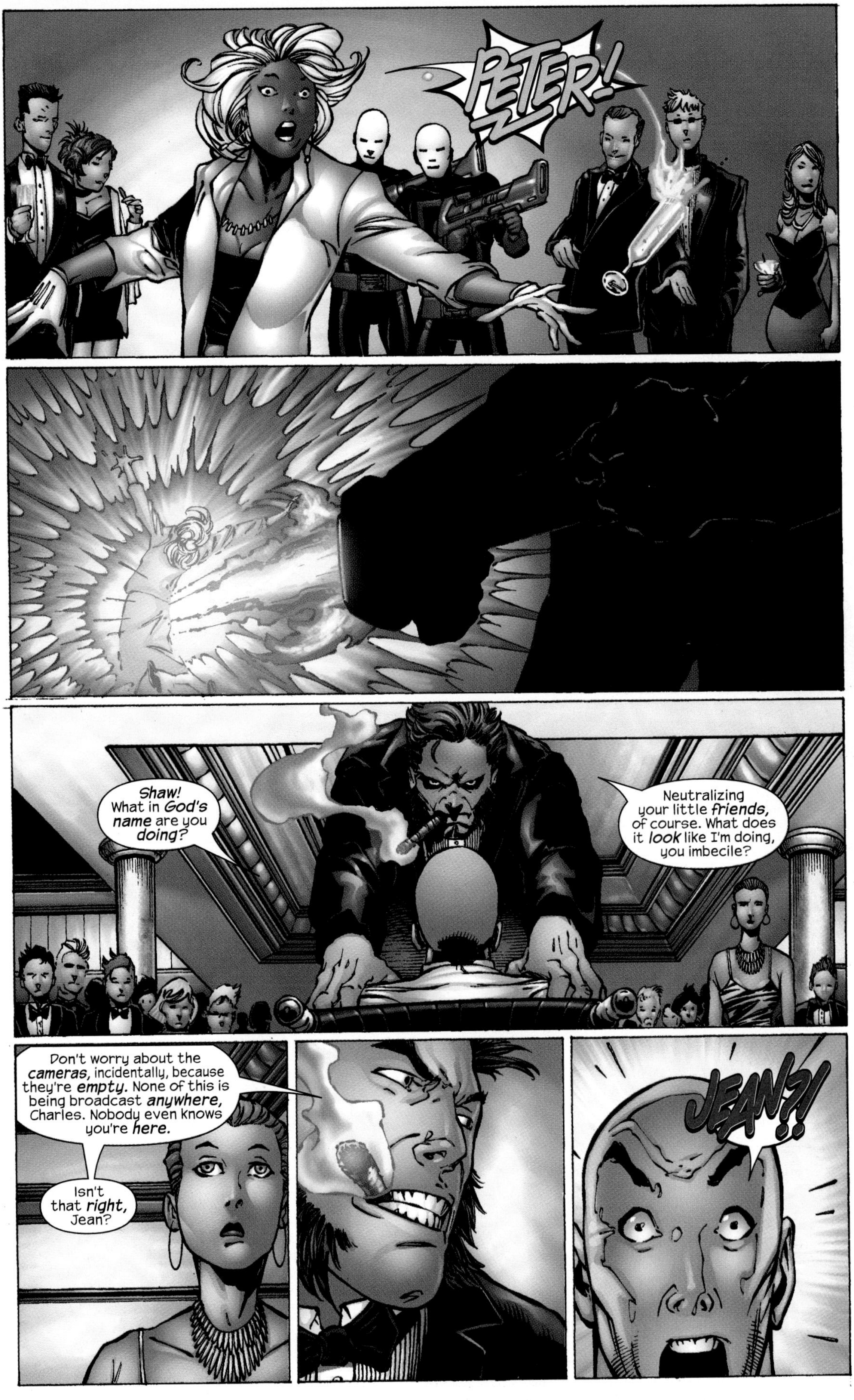
PETER!
Shaw! What in God's name are you doing?
Neutralizing your little friends, of course. What does it look like I'm doing, you imbecile?
Don't worry about the cameras, incidentally, because they're empty. None of this is being broadcast anywhere, Charles. Nobody even knows you're here.
Isn't that right, Jean?
JEAN?!

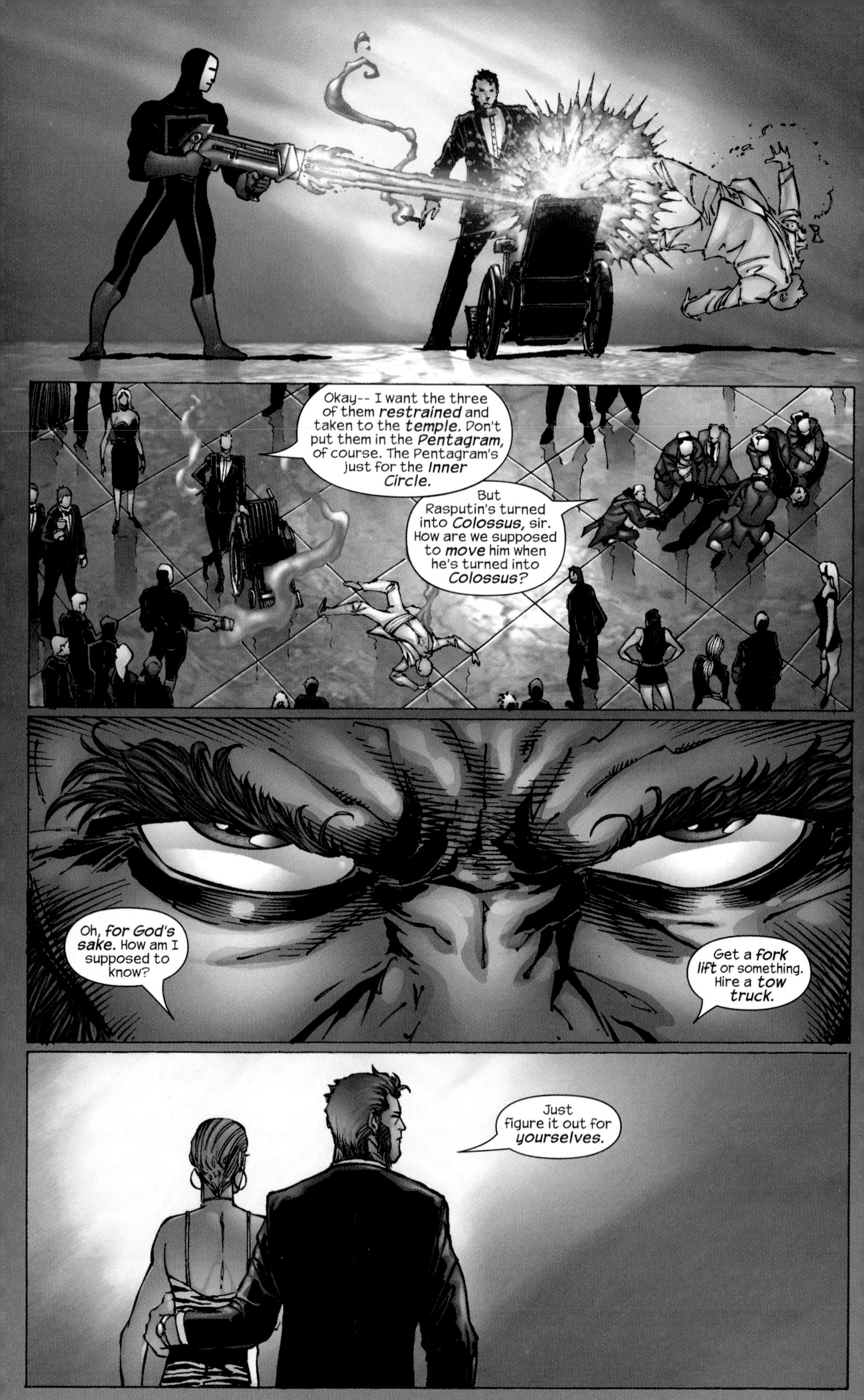
Okay-- I want the three of them restrained and taken to the temple. Don't put them in the Pentagram, of course. The Pentagram's just for the Inner Circle.
But Rasputin's turned into Colossus, sir. How are we supposed to move him when he's turned into Colossus?
Oh, for God's sake. How am I supposed to know?
Get a fork lift or something. Hire a tow truck.
Just figure it out for yourselves.

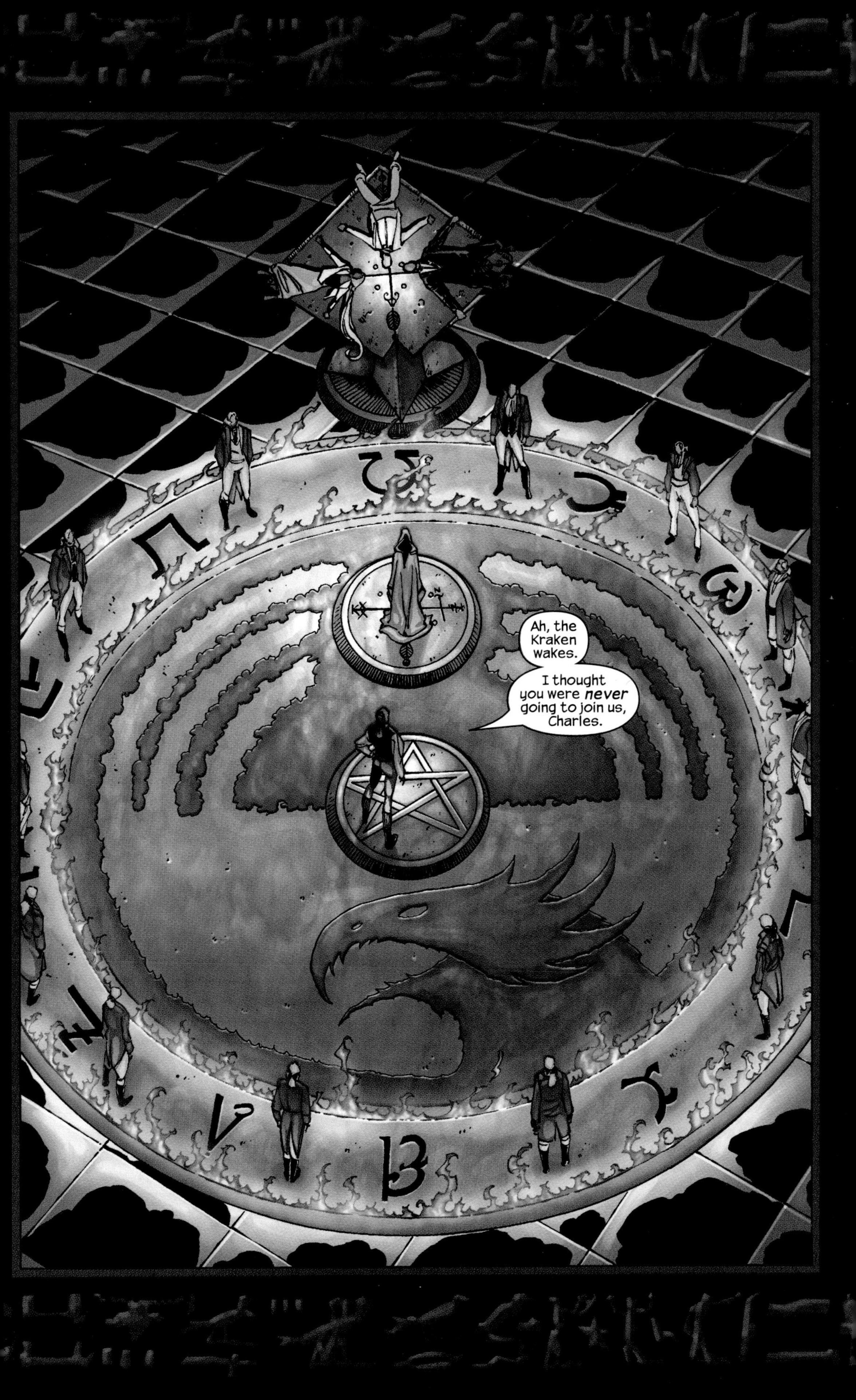
Ah, the Kraken wakes.
I thought you were *never* going to join us, Charles.

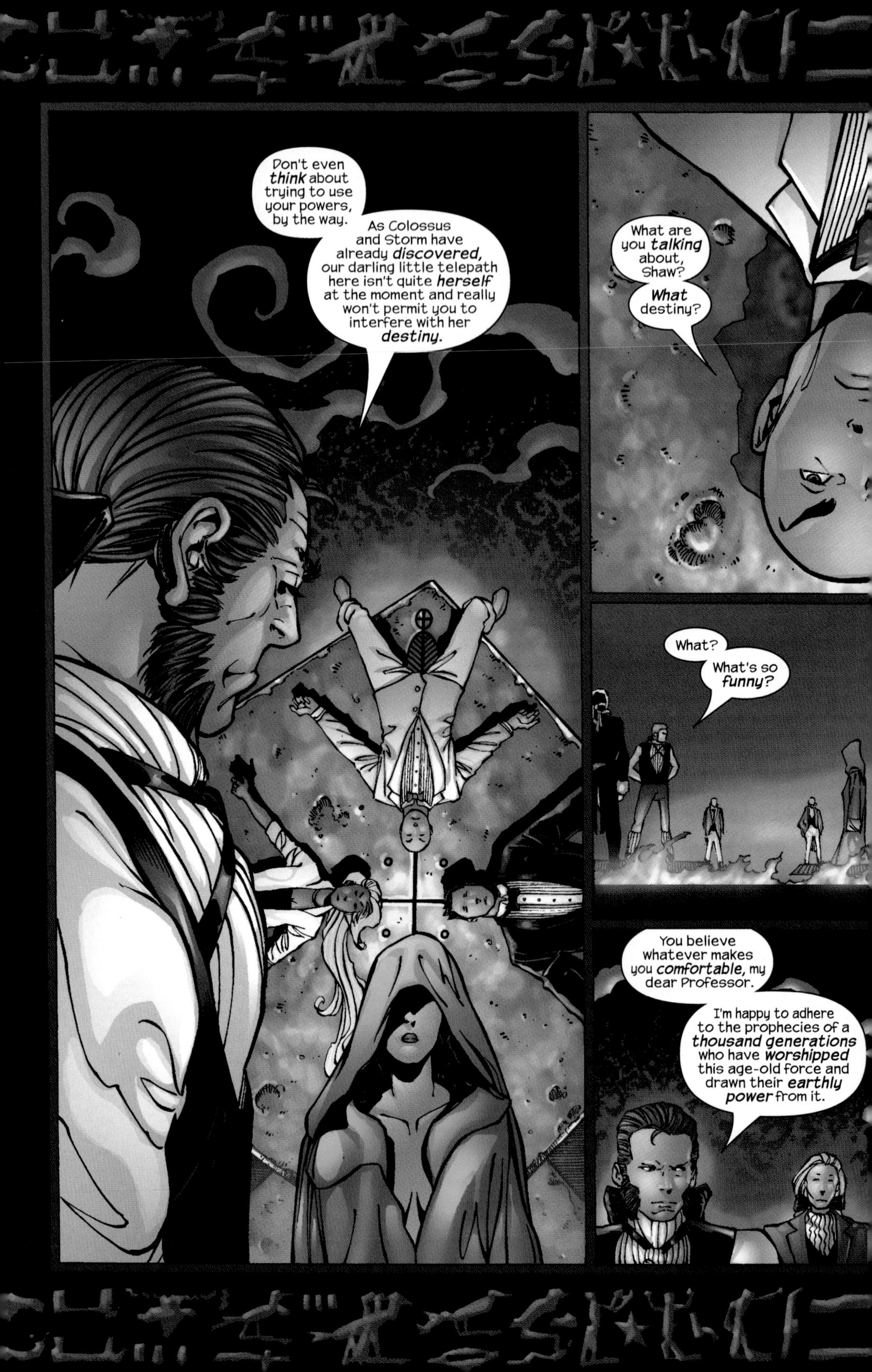
Don't even think about trying to use your powers, by the way.
As Colossus and Storm have already discovered, our darling little telepath here isn't quite herself at the moment and really won't permit you to interfere with her destiny.
What are you talking about, Shaw?
What destiny?
What?
What's so funny?
You believe whatever makes you comfortable, my dear Professor.
I'm happy to adhere to the prophecies of a thousand generations who have worshipped this age-old force and drawn their earthly power from it.

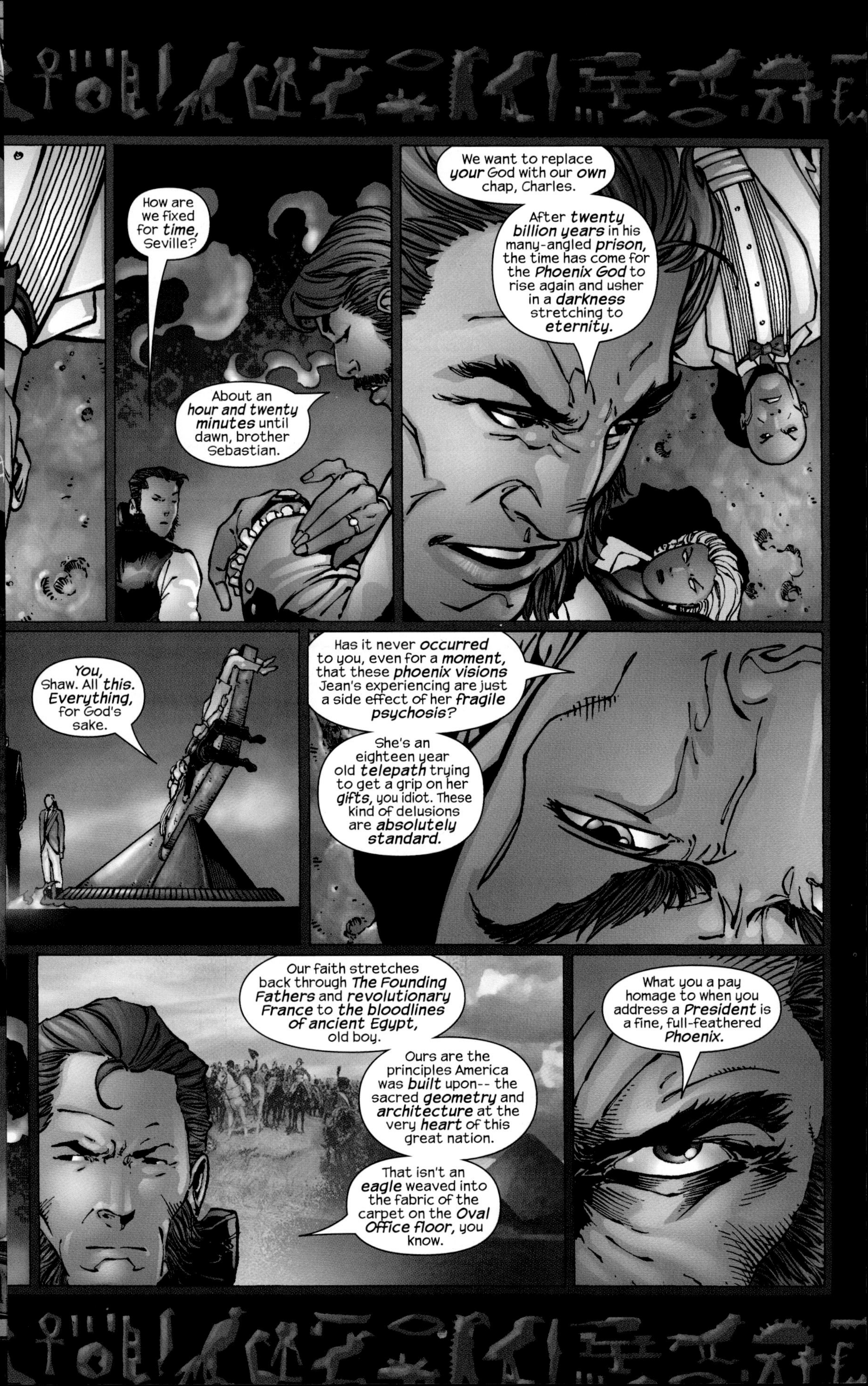
How are we fixed for time, Seville?
About an hour and twenty minutes until dawn, brother Sebastian.
We want to replace your God with our own chap, Charles.
After twenty billion years in his many-angled prison, the time has come for the Phoenix God to rise again and usher in a darkness stretching to eternity.
You, Shaw. All this. Everything, for God's sake.
Has it never occurred to you, even for a moment, that these phoenix visions Jean's experiencing are just a side effect of her fragile psychosis?
She's an eighteen year old telepath trying to get a grip on her gifts, you idiot. These kind of delusions are absolutely standard.
Our faith stretches back through The Founding Fathers and revolutionary France to the bloodlines of ancient Egypt, old boy.
Ours are the principles America was built upon-- the sacred geometry and architecture at the very heart of this great nation.
That isn't an eagle weaved into the fabric of the carpet on the Oval Office floor, you know.
What you a pay homage to when you address a President is a fine, full-feathered Phoenix.

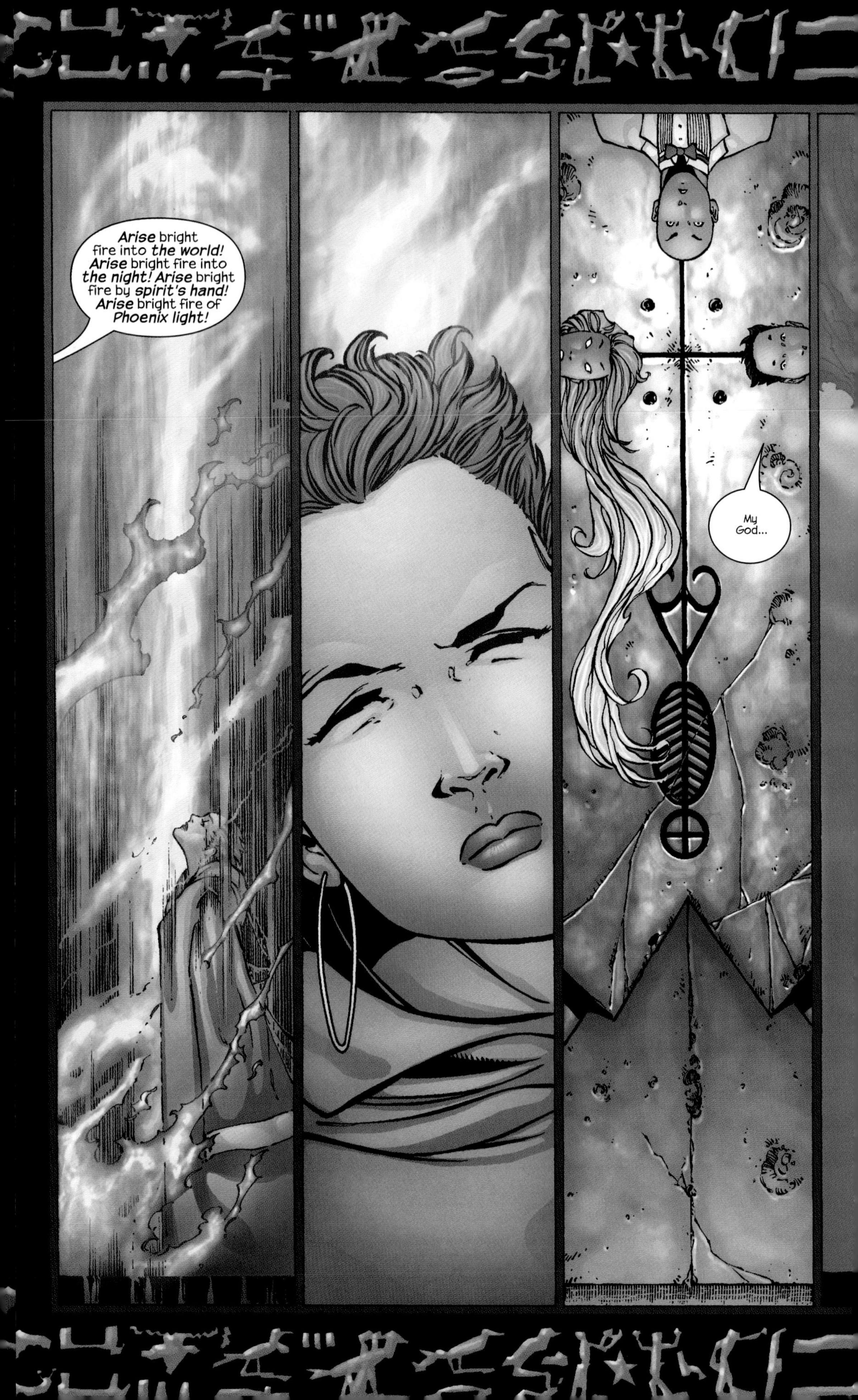
Arise bright fire into the world! Arise bright fire into the night! Arise bright fire by spirit's hand! Arise bright fire of Phoenix light!
My God...

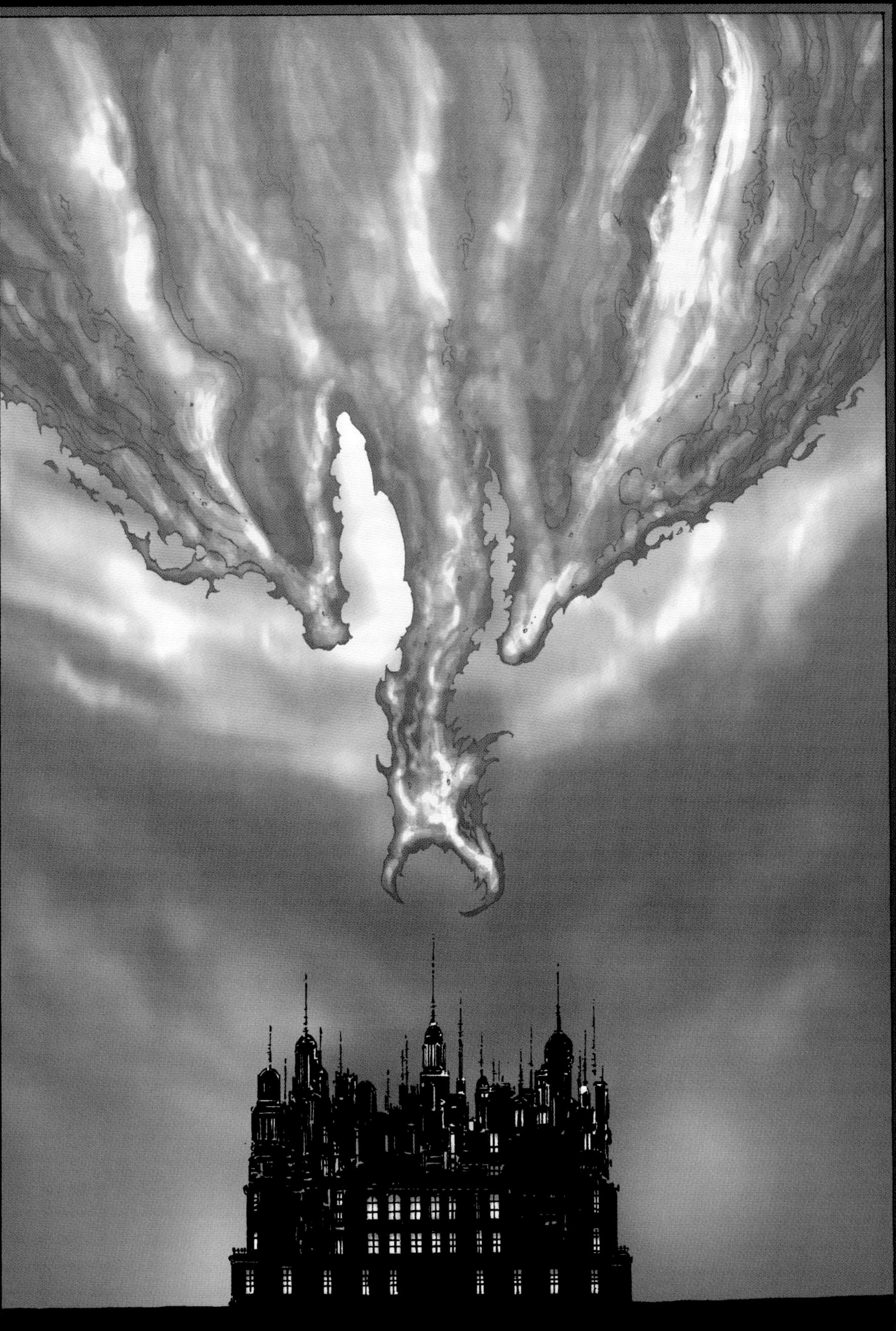

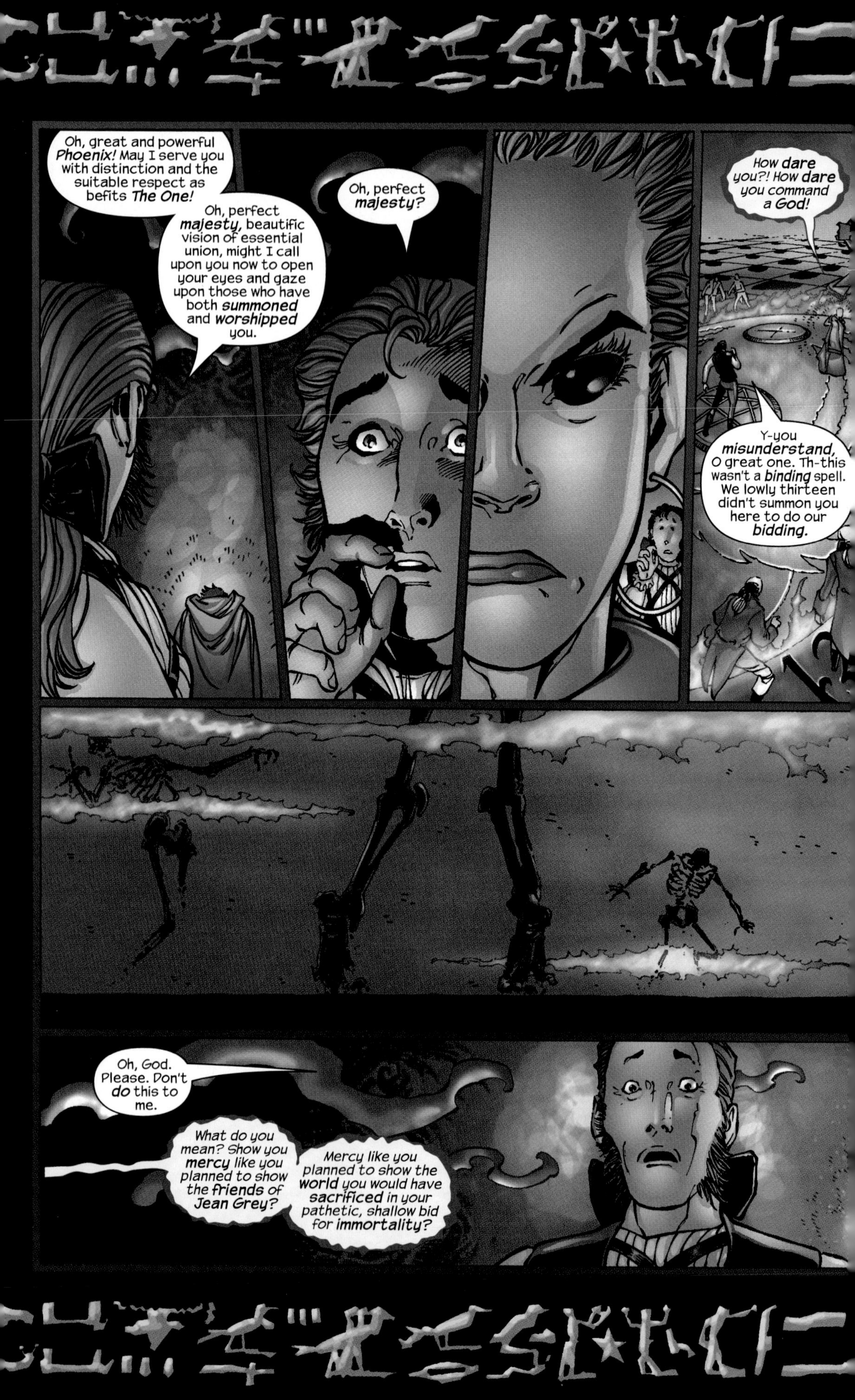
Oh, great and powerful Phoenix! May I serve you with distinction and the suitable respect as befits The One!
Oh, perfect majesty, beautific vision of essential union, might I call upon you now to open your eyes and gaze upon those who have both summoned and worshipped you.
Oh, perfect majesty?
How dare you?! How dare you command a God!
Y-you misunderstand, O great one. Th-this wasn't a binding spell. We lowly thirteen didn't summon you here to do our bidding.
Oh, God. Please. Don't do this to me.
What do you mean? Show you mercy like you planned to show the friends of Jean Grey?
Mercy like you planned to show the world you would have sacrificed in your pathetic, shallow bid for immortality?

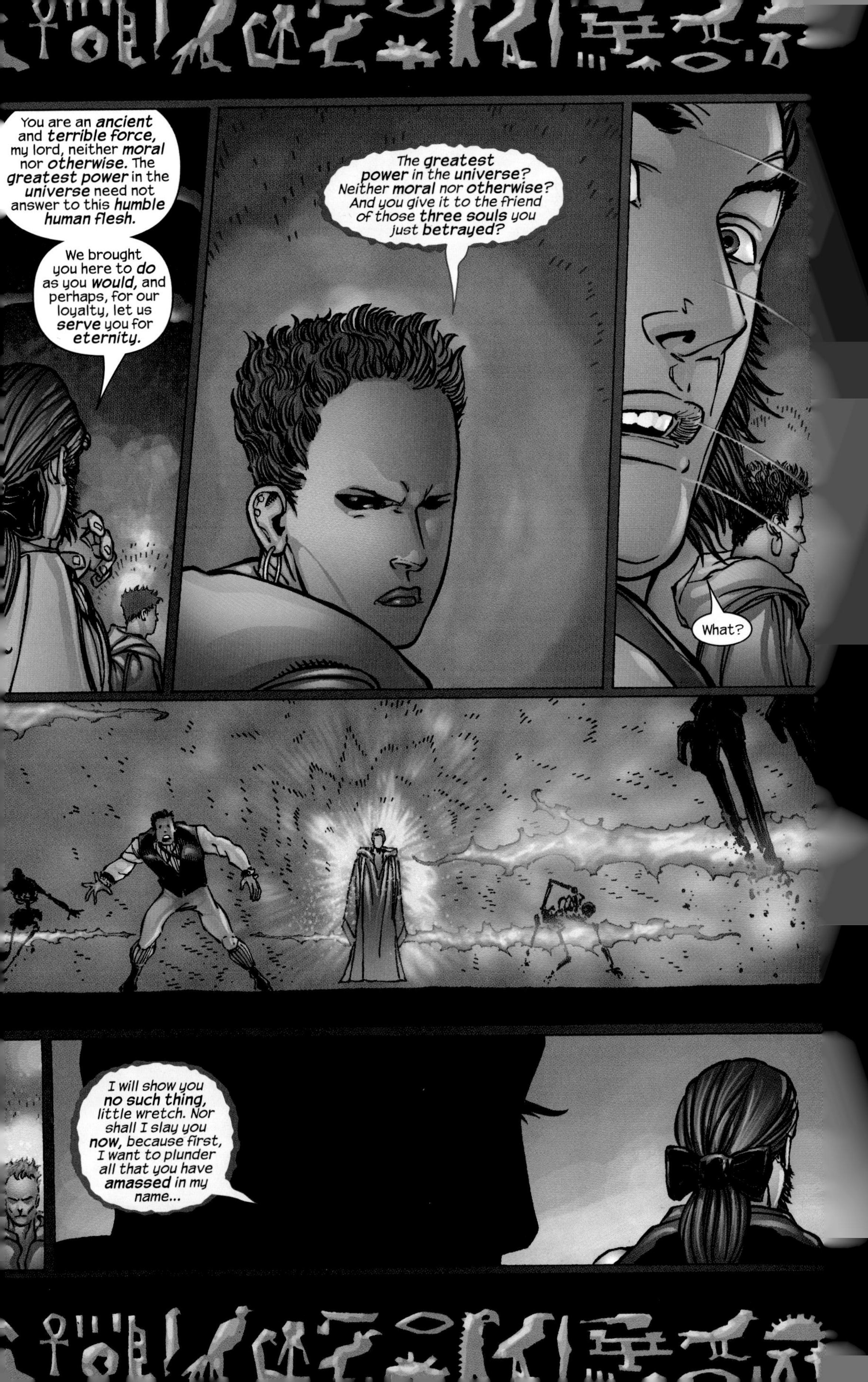
You are an ancient and terrible force, my lord, neither moral nor otherwise. The greatest power in the universe need not answer to this humble human flesh.
We brought you here to do as you would, and perhaps, for our loyalty, let us serve you for eternity.
The greatest power in the universe? Neither moral nor otherwise? And you give it to the friend of those three souls you just betrayed?
What?
I will show you no such thing, little wretch. Nor shall I slay you now, because first, I want to plunder all that you have amassed in my name...

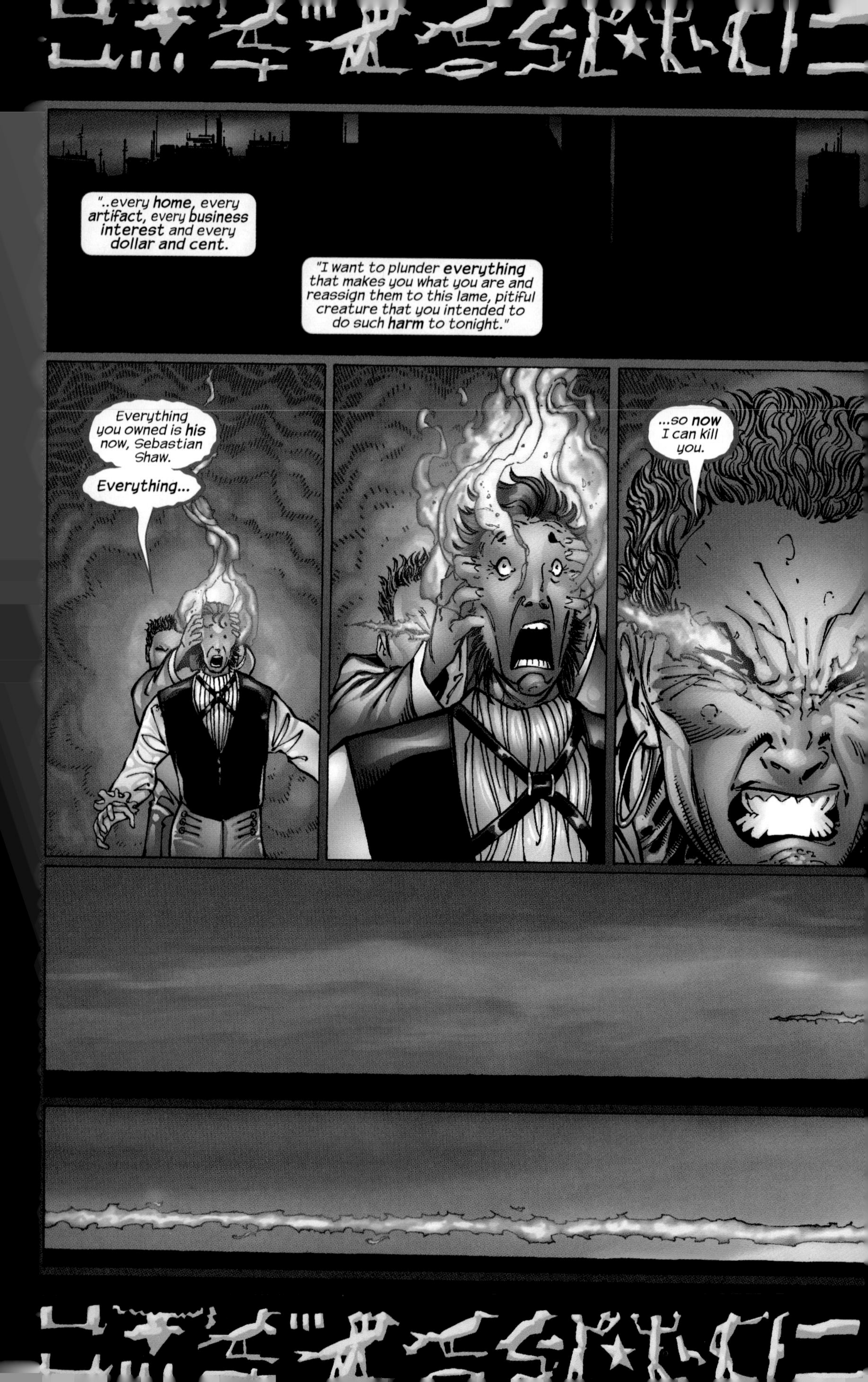

"..every home, every artifact, every business interest and every dollar and cent.
"I want to plunder everything that makes you what you are and reassign them to this lame, pitiful creature that you intended to do such harm to tonight."
Everything you owned is his now, Sebastian Shaw.
Everything...
...so now I can kill you.

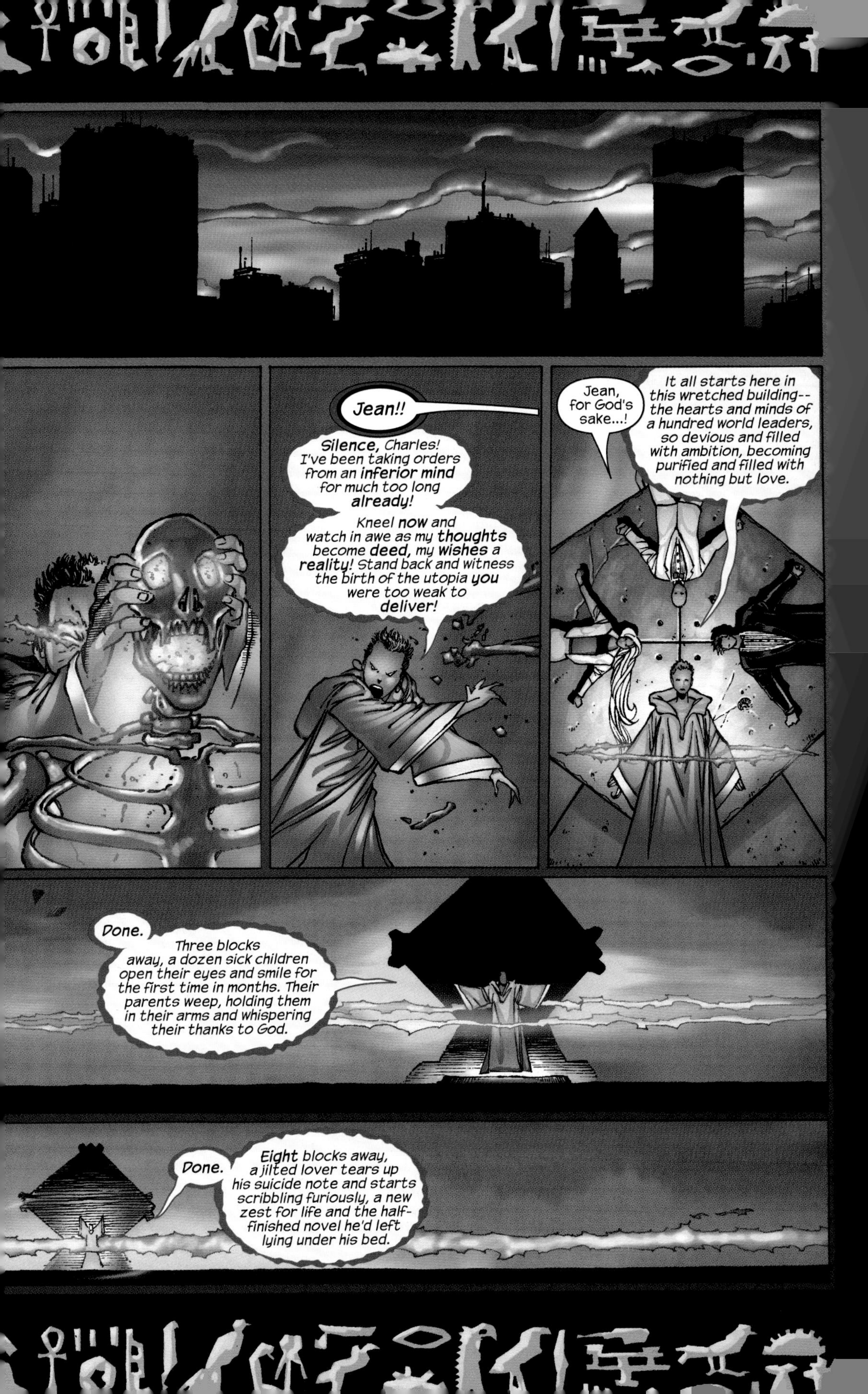

Jean!!
Silence, Charles! I've been taking orders from an inferior mind for much too long already!
Kneel now and watch in awe as my thoughts become deed, my wishes a reality! Stand back and witness the birth of the utopia you were too weak to deliver!
Jean, for God's sake...!
It all starts here in this wretched building-- the hearts and minds of a hundred world leaders, so devious and filled with ambition, becoming purified and filled with nothing but love.
Done.
Three blocks away, a dozen sick children open their eyes and smile for the first time in months. Their parents weep, holding them in their arms and whispering their thanks to God.
Done.
Eight blocks away, a jilted lover tears up his suicide note and starts scribbling furiously, a new zest for life and the half-finished novel he'd left lying under his bed.

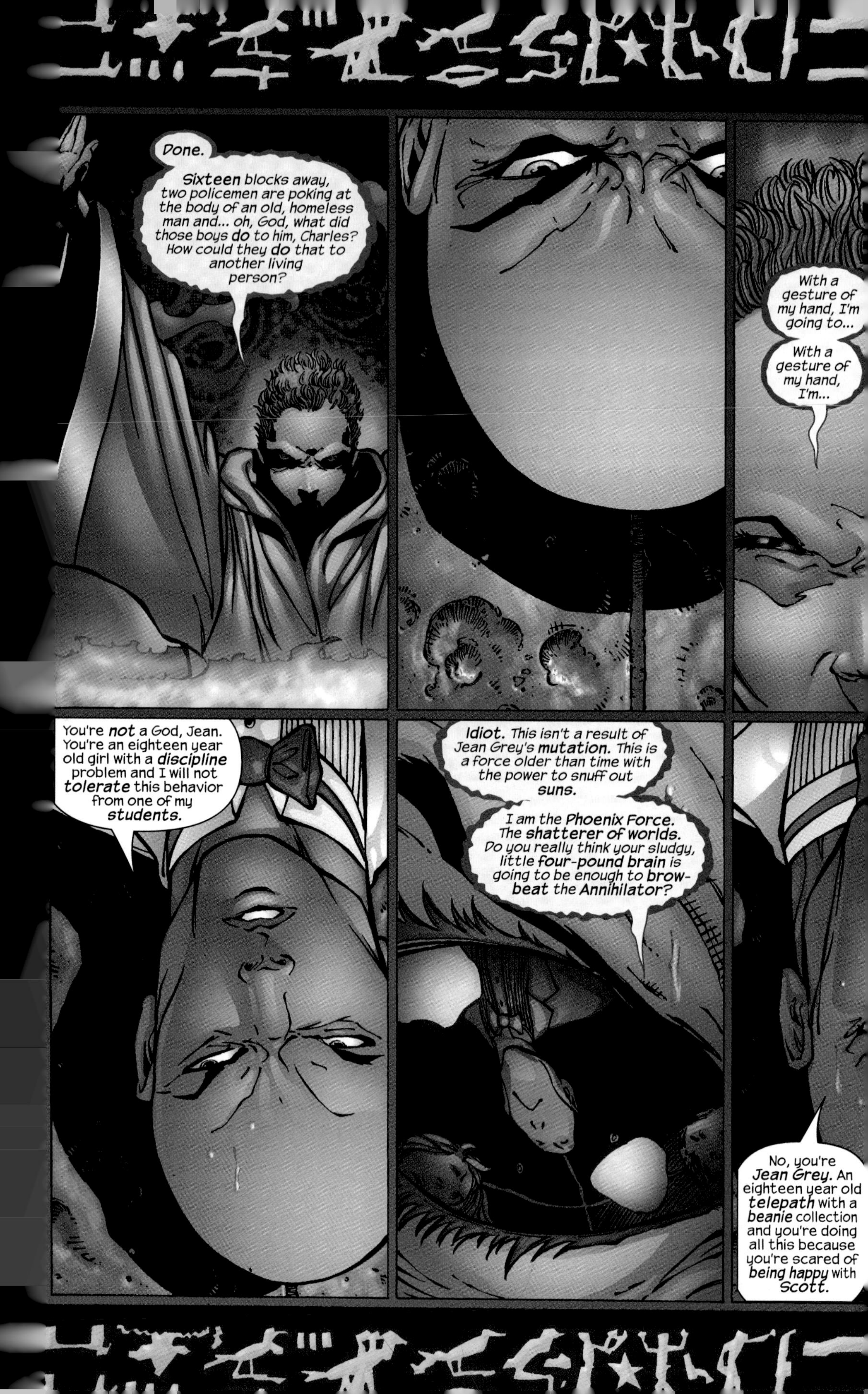
Done.
Sixteen blocks away, two policemen are poking at the body of an old, homeless man and... oh, God, what did those boys do to him, Charles? How could they do that to another living person?
With a gesture of my hand, I'm going to...
With a gesture of my hand, I'm...
You're not a God, Jean. You're an eighteen year old girl with a discipline problem and I will not tolerate this behavior from one of my students.
Idiot. This isn't a result of Jean Grey's mutation. This is a force older than time with the power to snuff out suns.
I am the Phoenix Force. The shatterer of worlds. Do you really think your sludgy, little four-pound brain is going to be enough to browbeat the Annihilator?
No, you're Jean Grey. An eighteen year old telepath with a beanie collection and you're doing all this because you're scared of being happy with Scott.

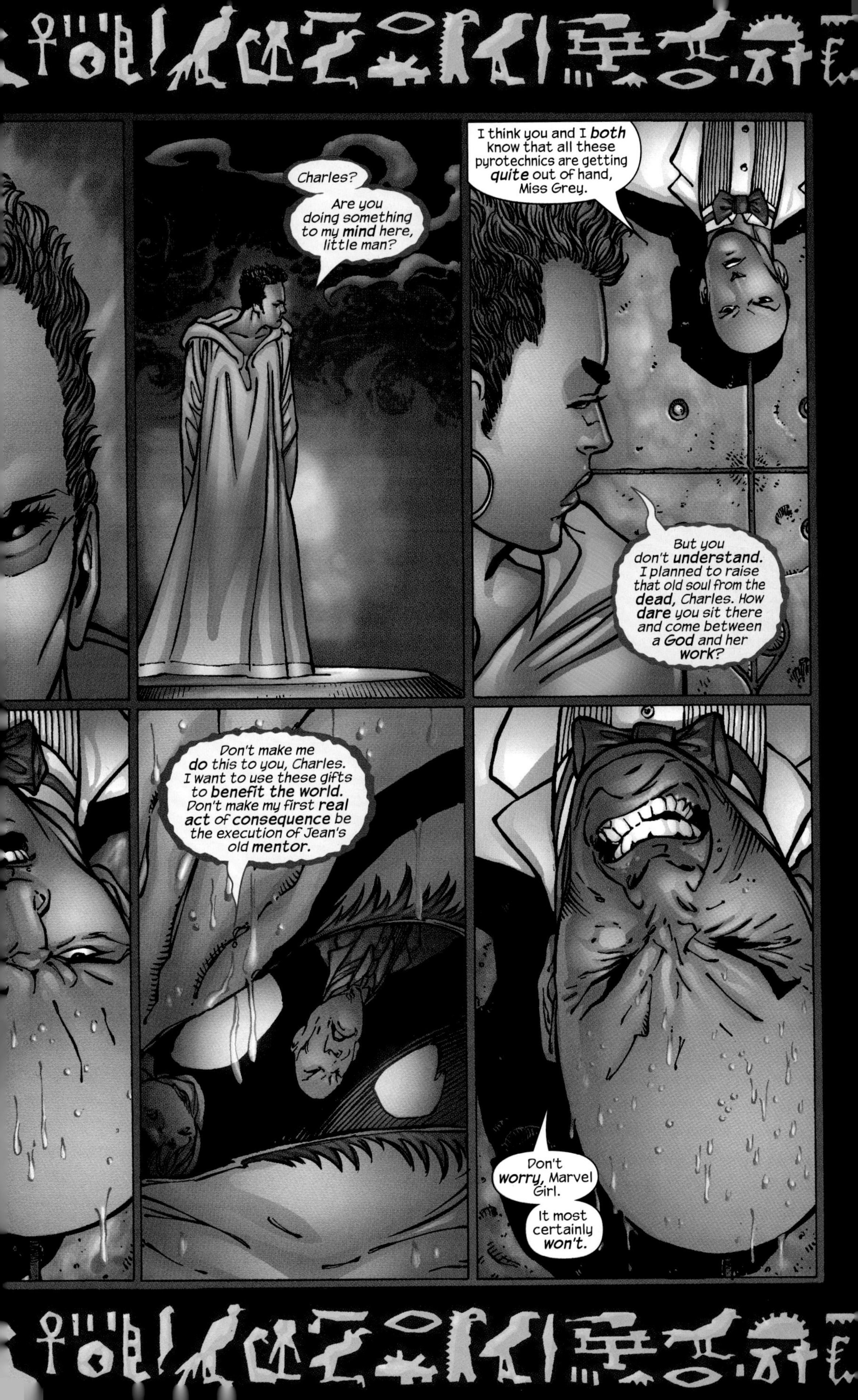
Charles?
Are you doing something to my mind here, little man?
I think you and I both know that all these pyrotechnics are getting quite out of hand, Miss Grey.
But you don't understand. I planned to raise that old soul from the dead, Charles. How dare you sit there and come between a God and her work?
Don't make me do this to you, Charles. I want to use these gifts to benefit the world. Don't make my first real act of consequence be the execution of Jean's old mentor.
Don't worry, Marvel Girl.
It most certainly won't.

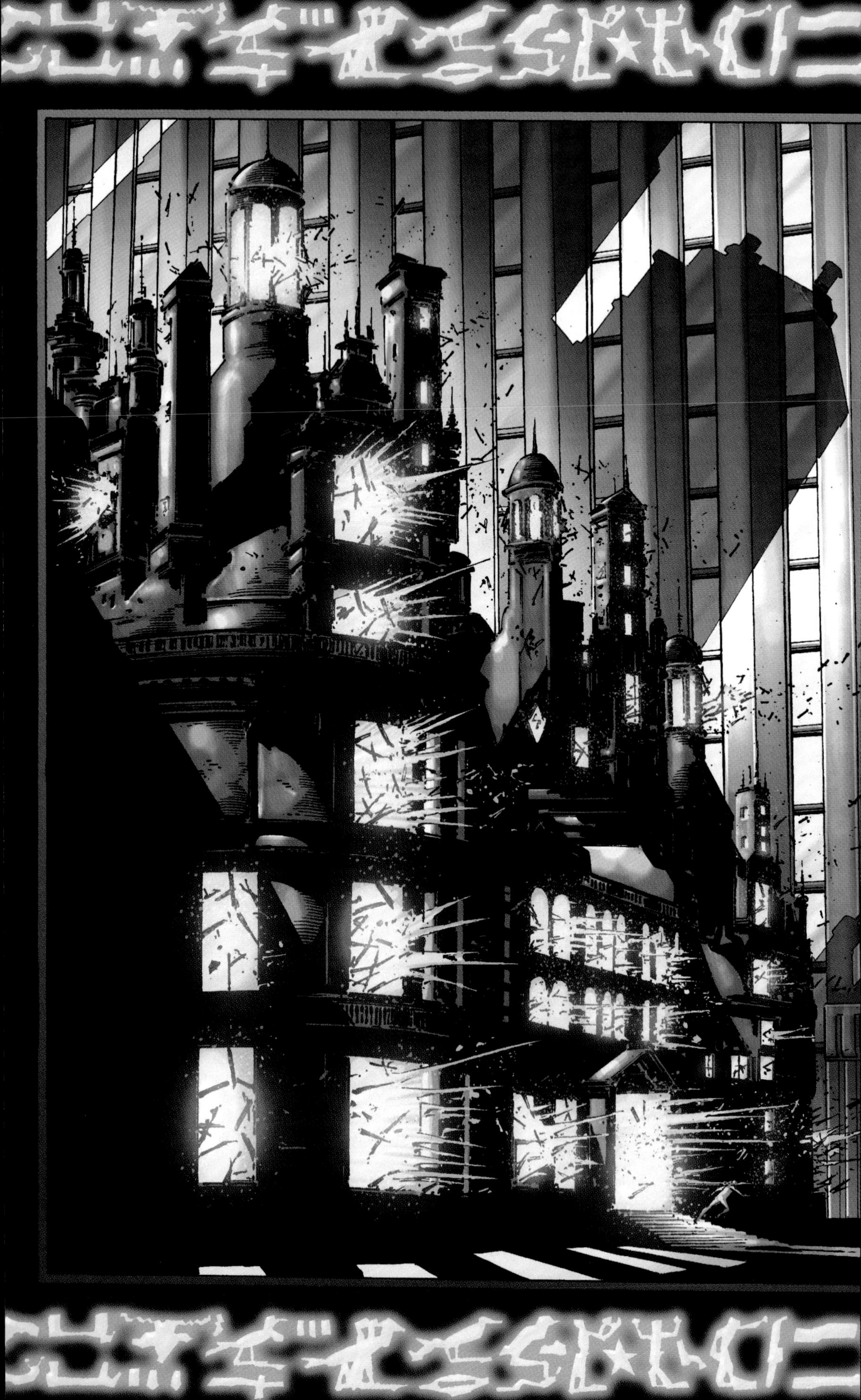

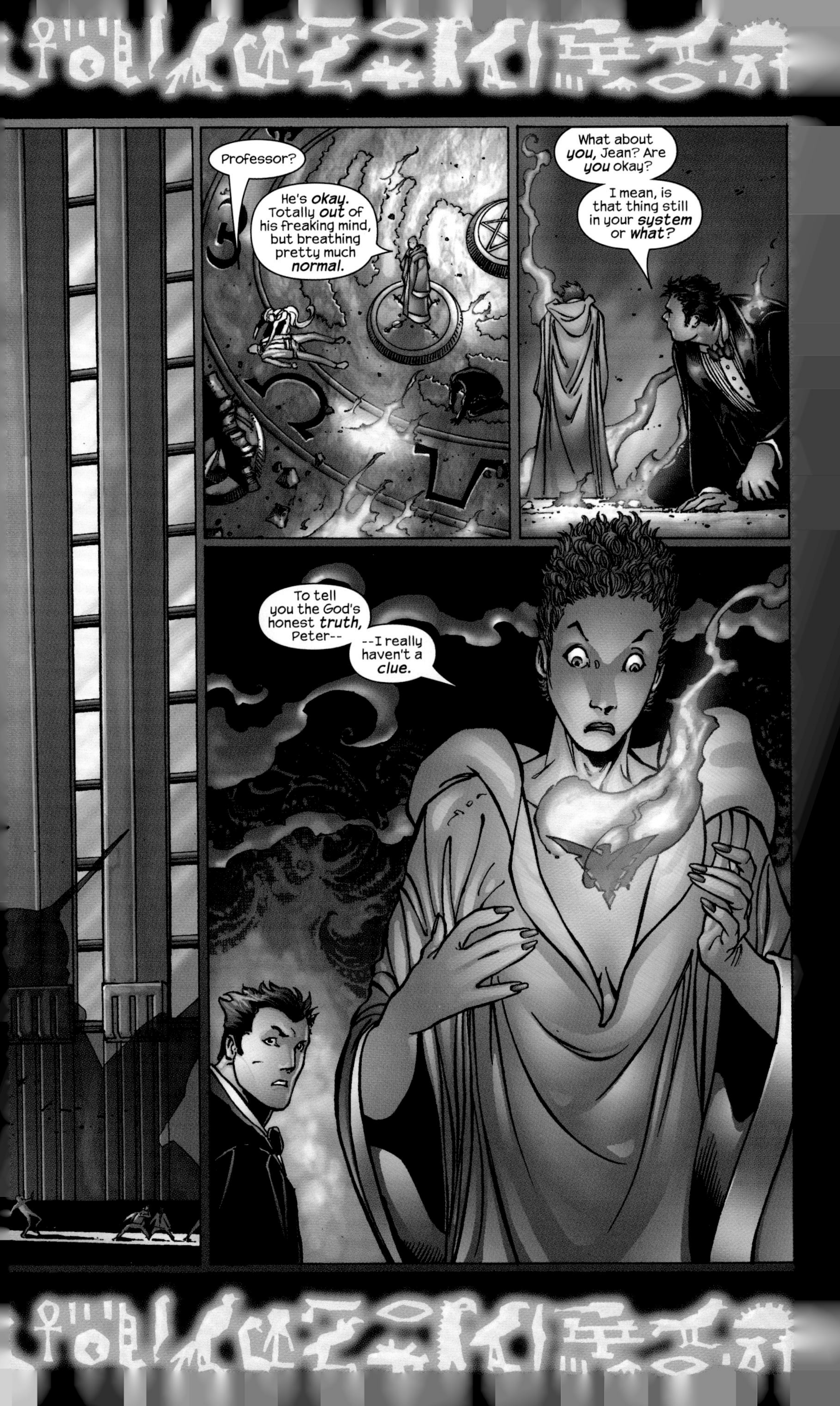
Professor?
He's okay. Totally out of his freaking mind, but breathing pretty much normal.
What about you, Jean? Are you okay?
I mean, is that thing still in your system or what?
To tell you the God's honest truth, Peter--
--I really haven't a clue.

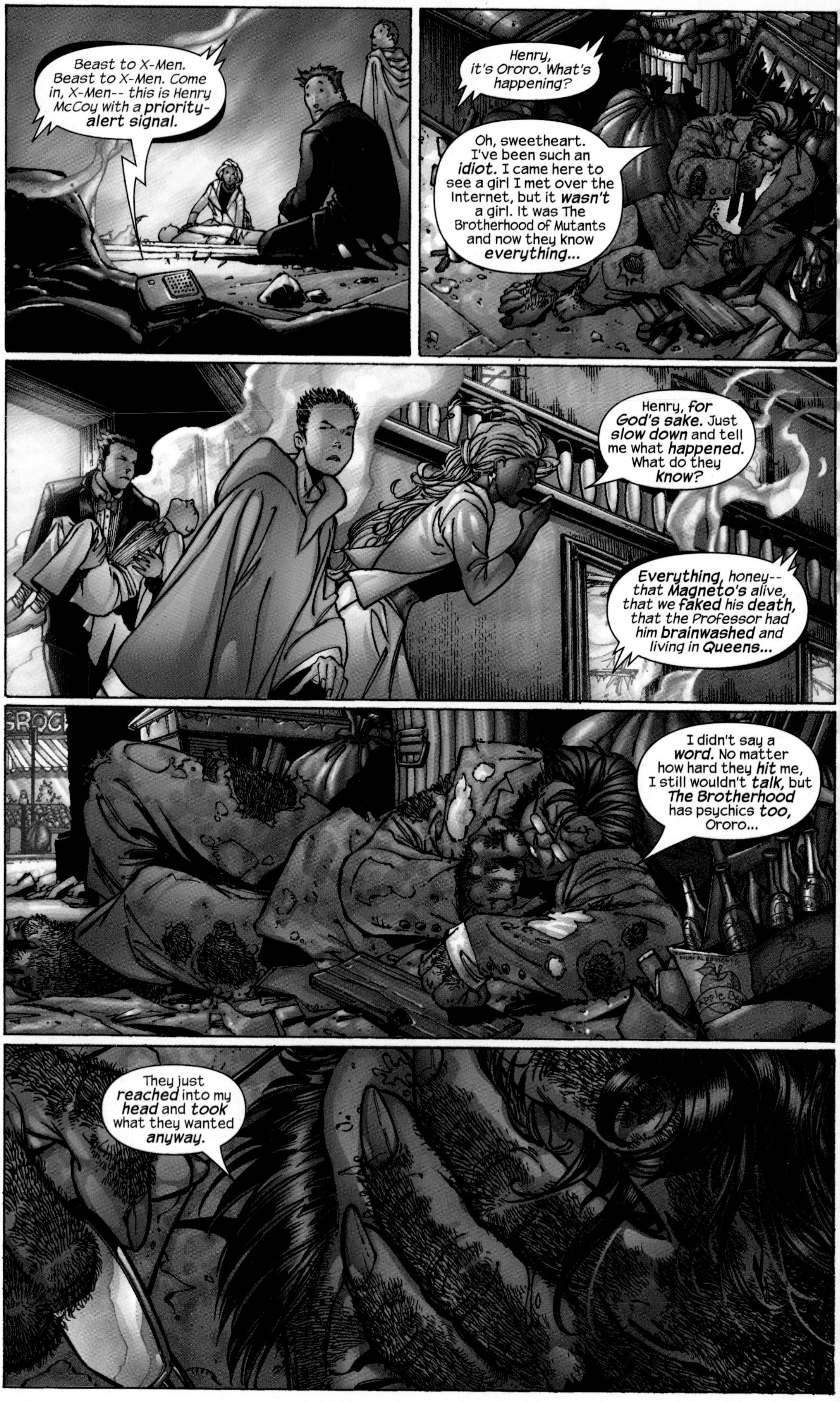
Beast to X-Men. Beast to X-Men. Come in, X-Men-- this is Henry McCoy with a priority-alert signal.
Henry, it's Ororo. What's happening?
Oh, sweetheart. I've been such an idiot. I came here to see a girl I met over the Internet, but it wasn't a girl. It was The Brotherhood of Mutants and now they know everything...
Henry, for God's sake. Just slow down and tell me what happened. What do they know?
Everything, honey-- that Magneto's alive, that we faked his death, that the Professor had him brainwashed and living in Queens...
I didn't say a word. No matter how hard they hit me, I still wouldn't talk, but The Brotherhood has psychics too, Ororo...
They just reached into my head and took what they wanted anyway.

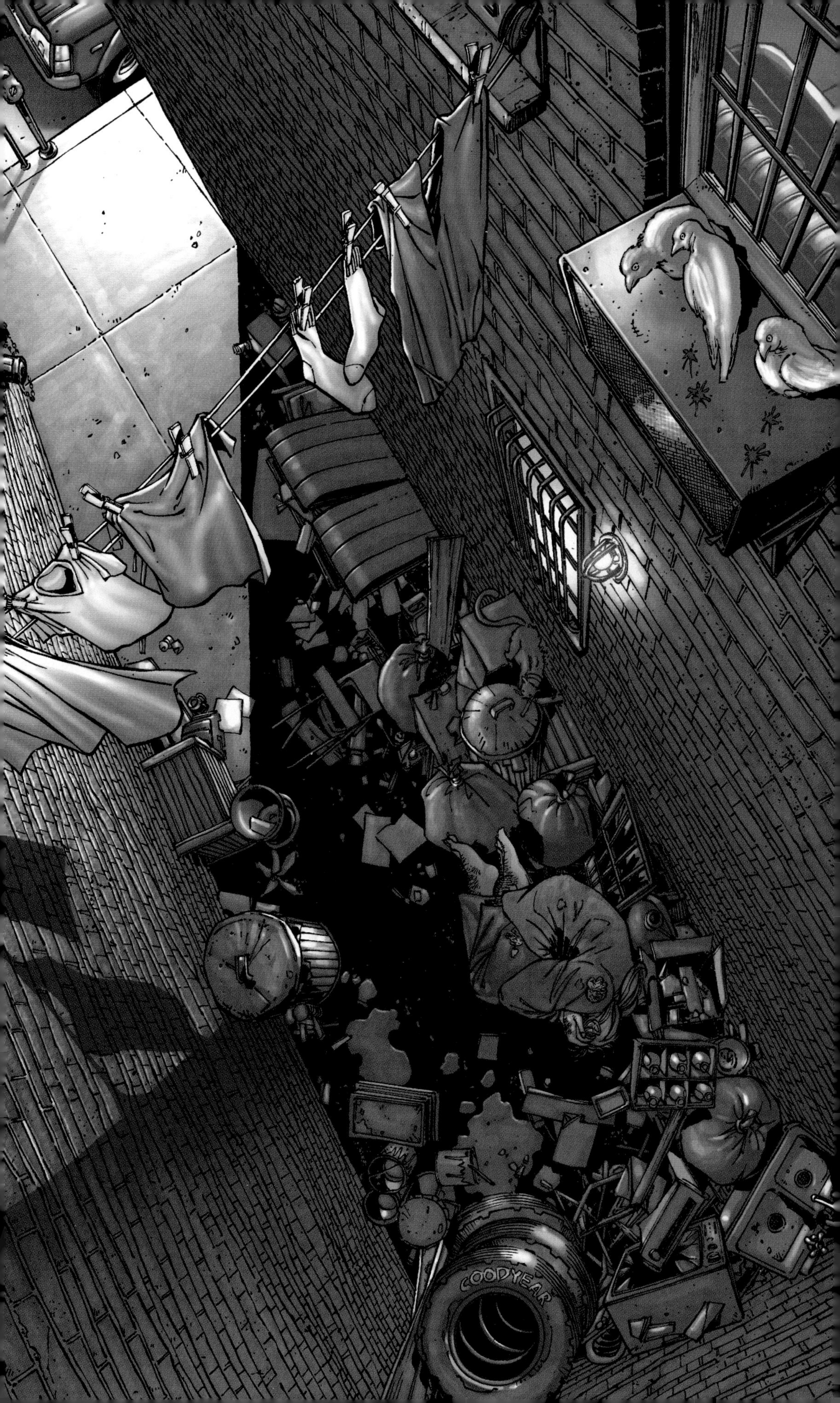
GOODYEAR

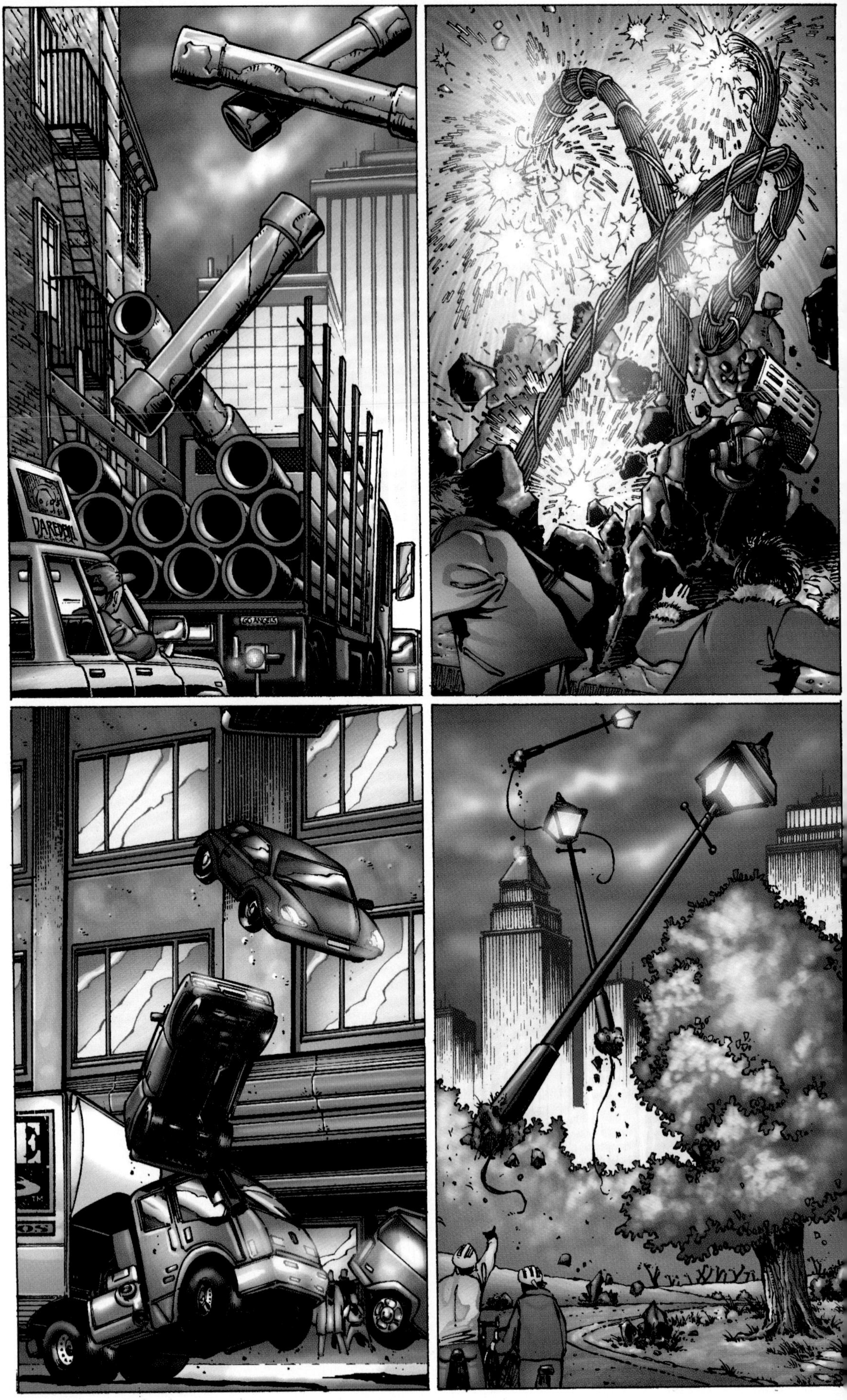
DAREDEVIL
GO ANGELS

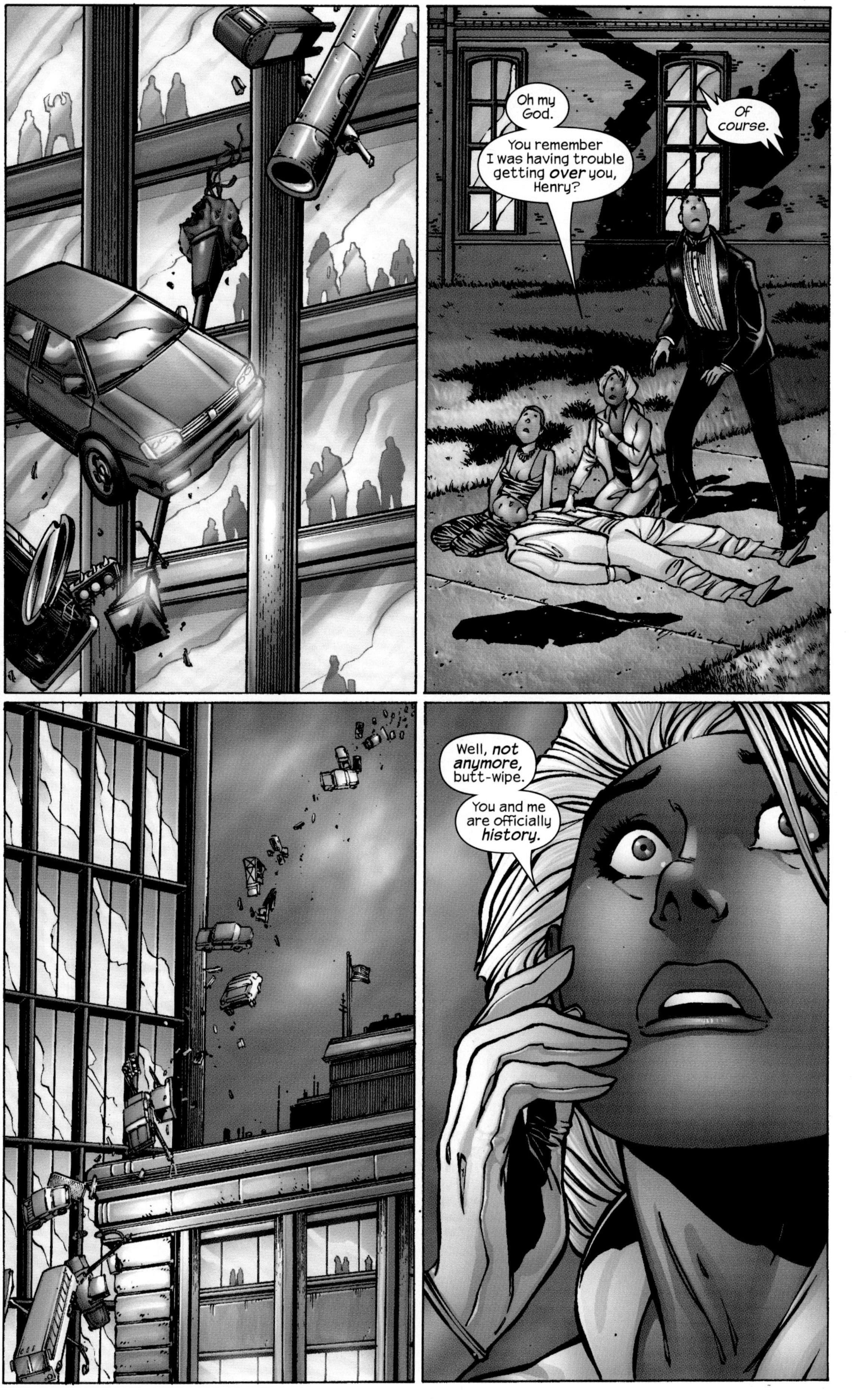
Oh my God.
You remember I was having trouble getting *over* you, Henry?
Of course.
Well, *not anymore,* butt-wipe.
You and me are officially *history*.

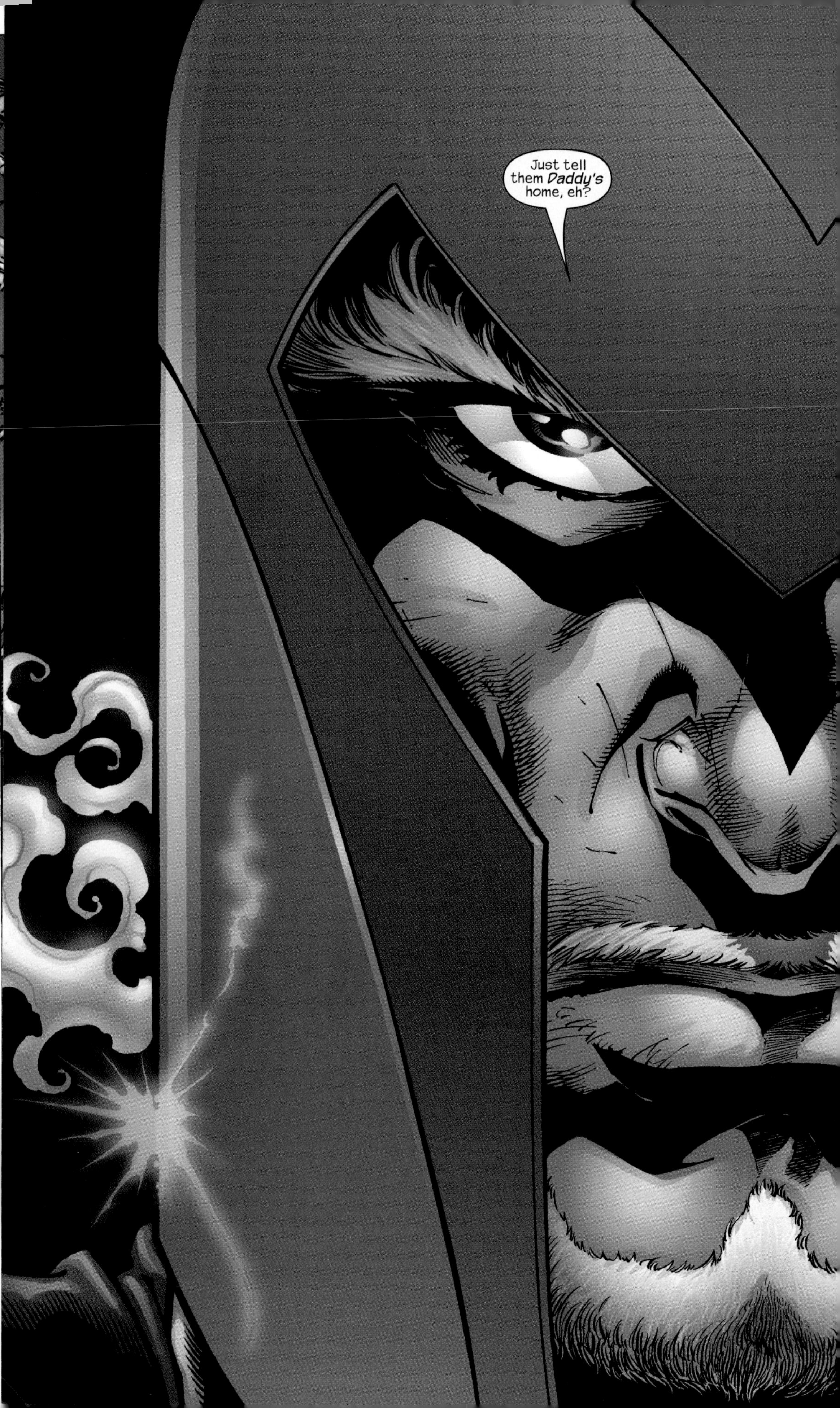
Just tell them *Daddy's* home, eh?

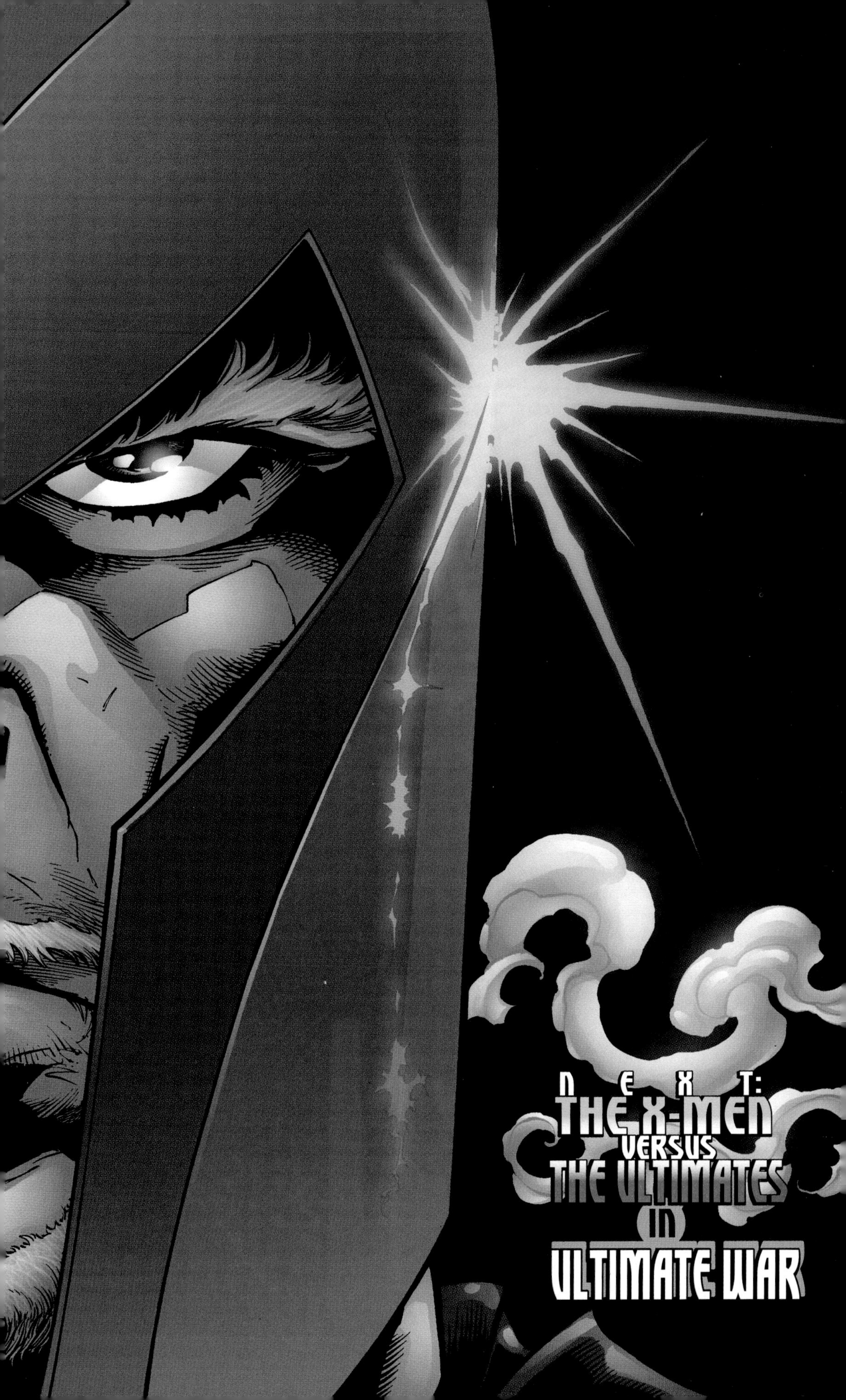
N E X T:
THE X-MEN
VERSUS
THE ULTIMATES
IN
ULTIMATE WAR

# Issue #21
# Cover art
# by ADAM KUBERT

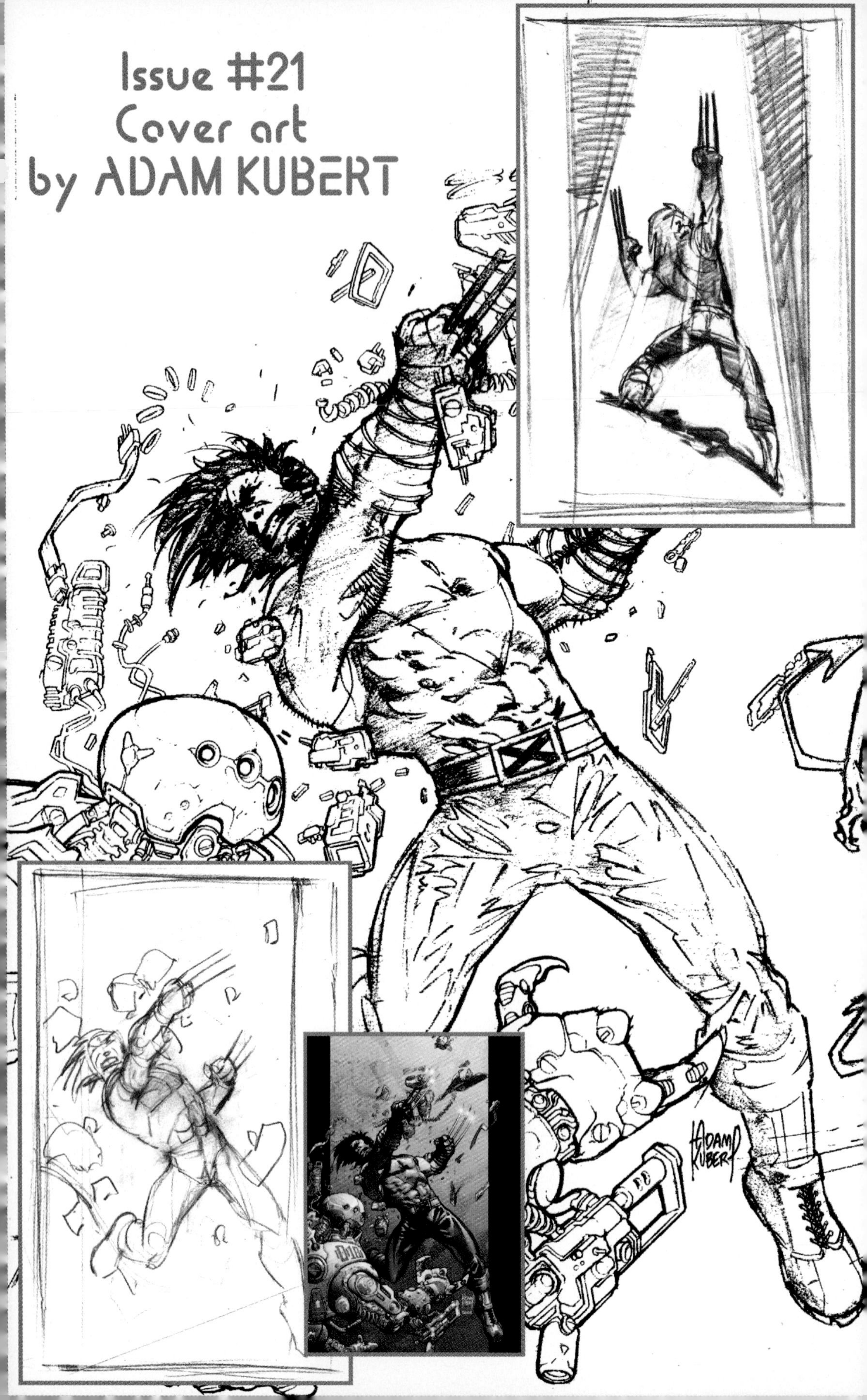
ADAM KUBERT

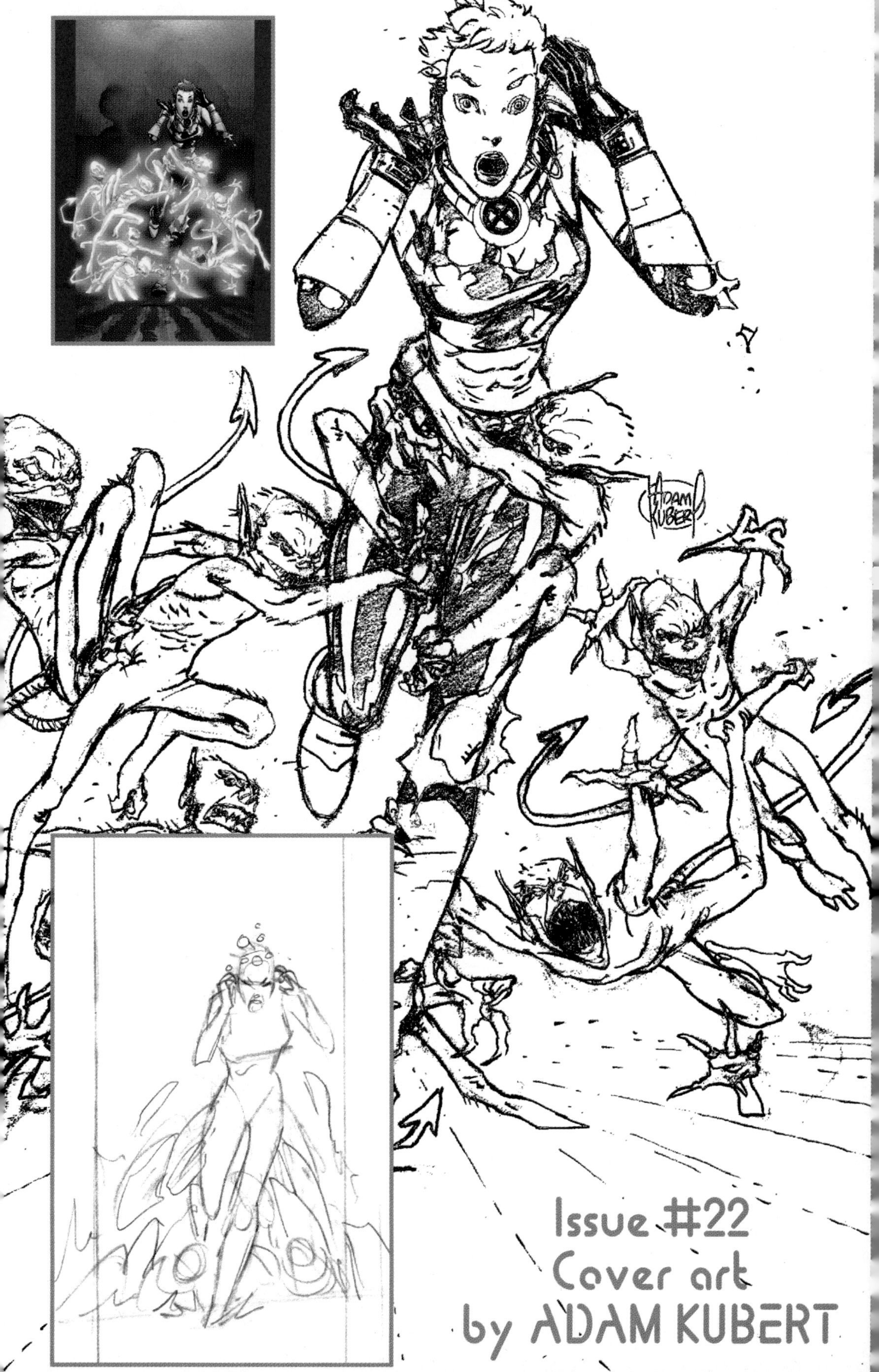
ADAM KUBERT

Issue #22
Cover art
by ADAM KUBERT

# Issue #23
# Cover art
# by ADAM KUBERT

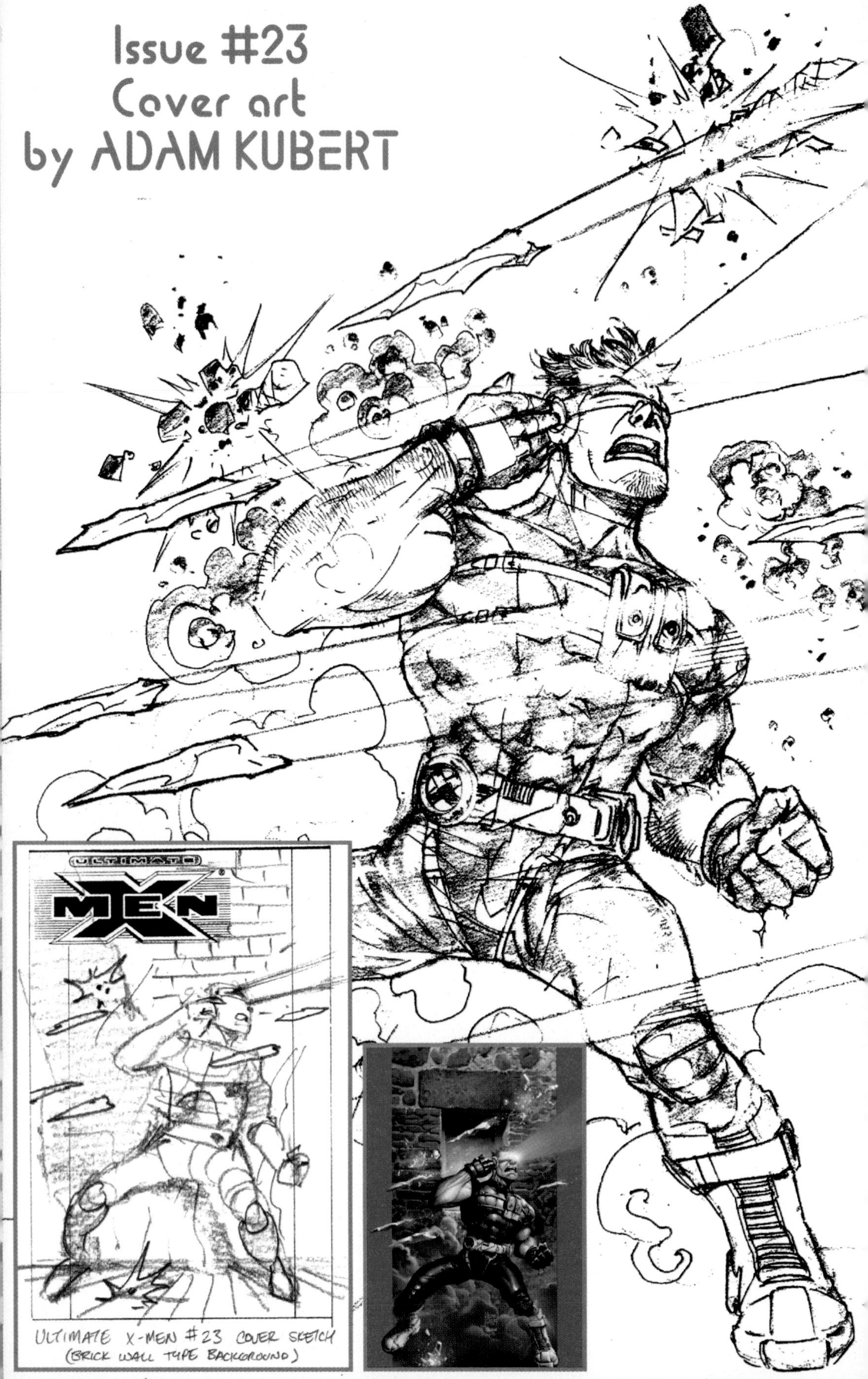
ULTIMATE
X-MEN

ULTIMATE X-MEN #23 COVER SKETCH
(BRICK WALL TYPE BACKGROUND)

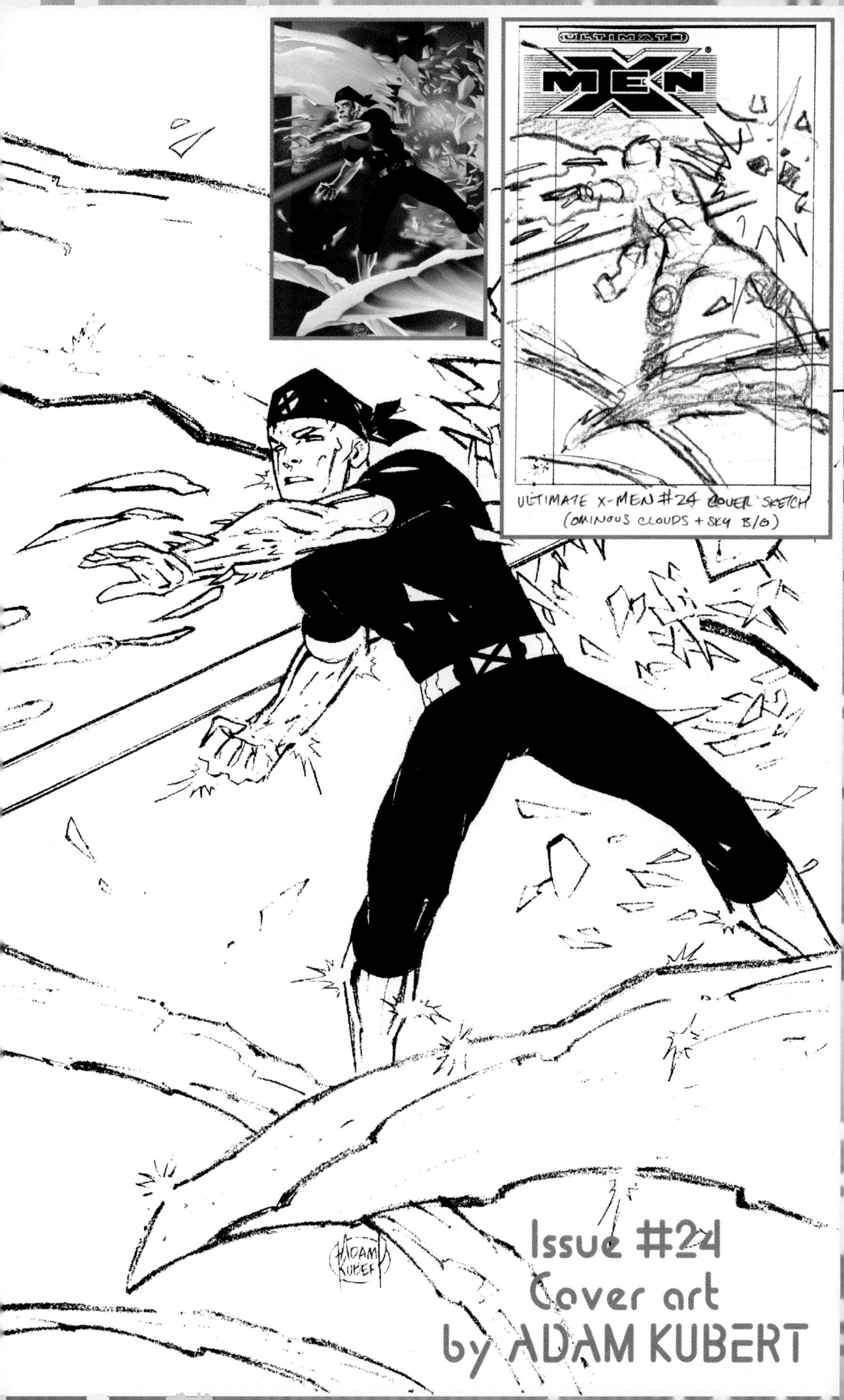
ULTIMATE
X-MEN
ULTIMATE X-MEN #24 COVER SKETCH
(OMINOUS CLOUDS + SKY B/G)
ADAM
KUBERT

Issue #24
Cover art
by ADAM KUBERT

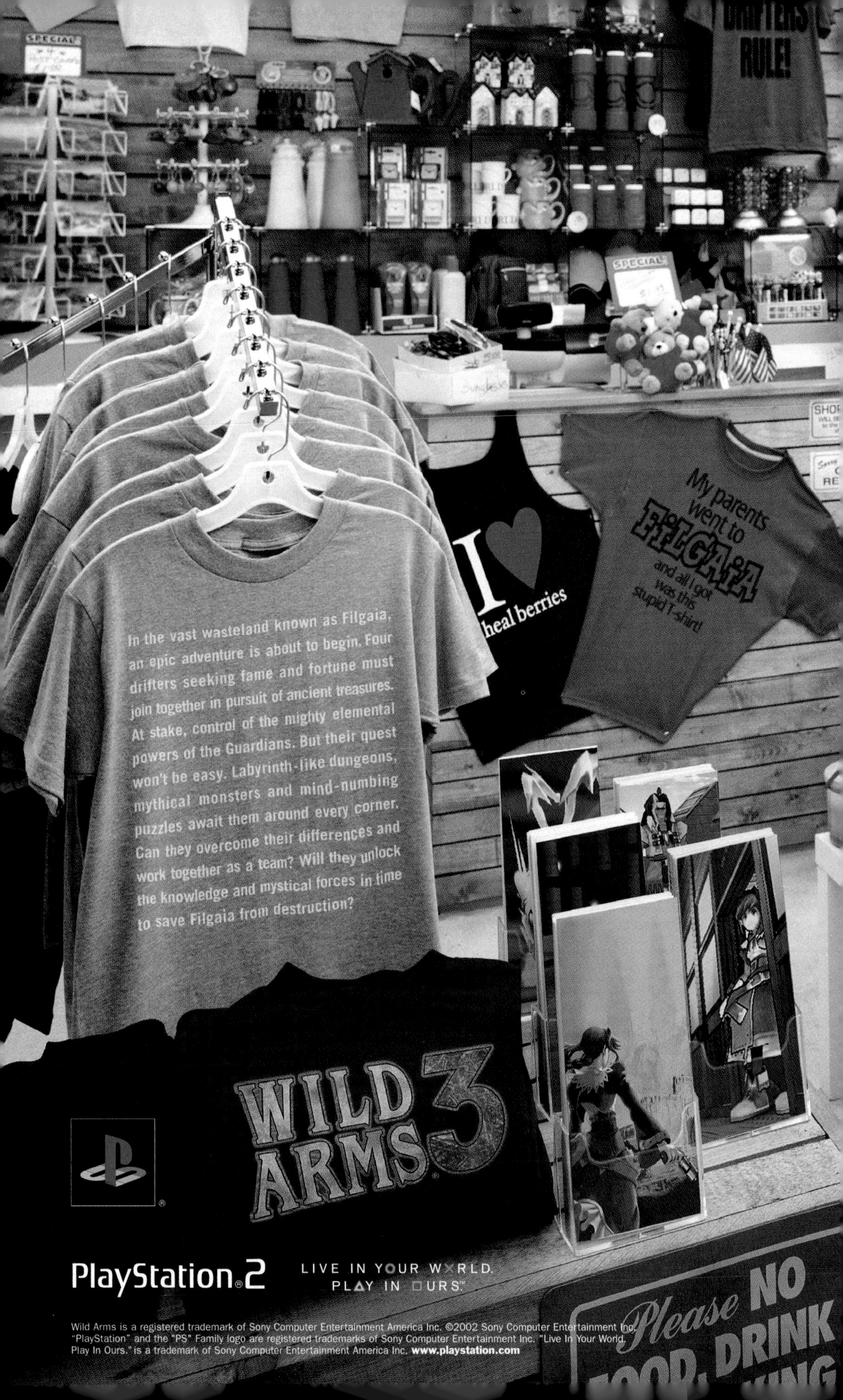
DRIFTERS RULE!
SPECIAL
I ♥ heal berries
My parents went to FILGAIA and all I got was this stupid T-shirt!
In the vast wasteland known as Filgaia, an epic adventure is about to begin. Four drifters seeking fame and fortune must join together in pursuit of ancient treasures. At stake, control of the mighty elemental powers of the Guardians. But their quest won't be easy. Labyrinth-like dungeons, mythical monsters and mind-numbing puzzles await them around every corner. Can they overcome their differences and work together as a team? Will they unlock the knowledge and mystical forces in time to save Filgaia from destruction?
WILD ARMS 3
PlayStation 2
LIVE IN YOUR WORLD.
PLAY IN OURS.
Please NO FOOD, DRINK

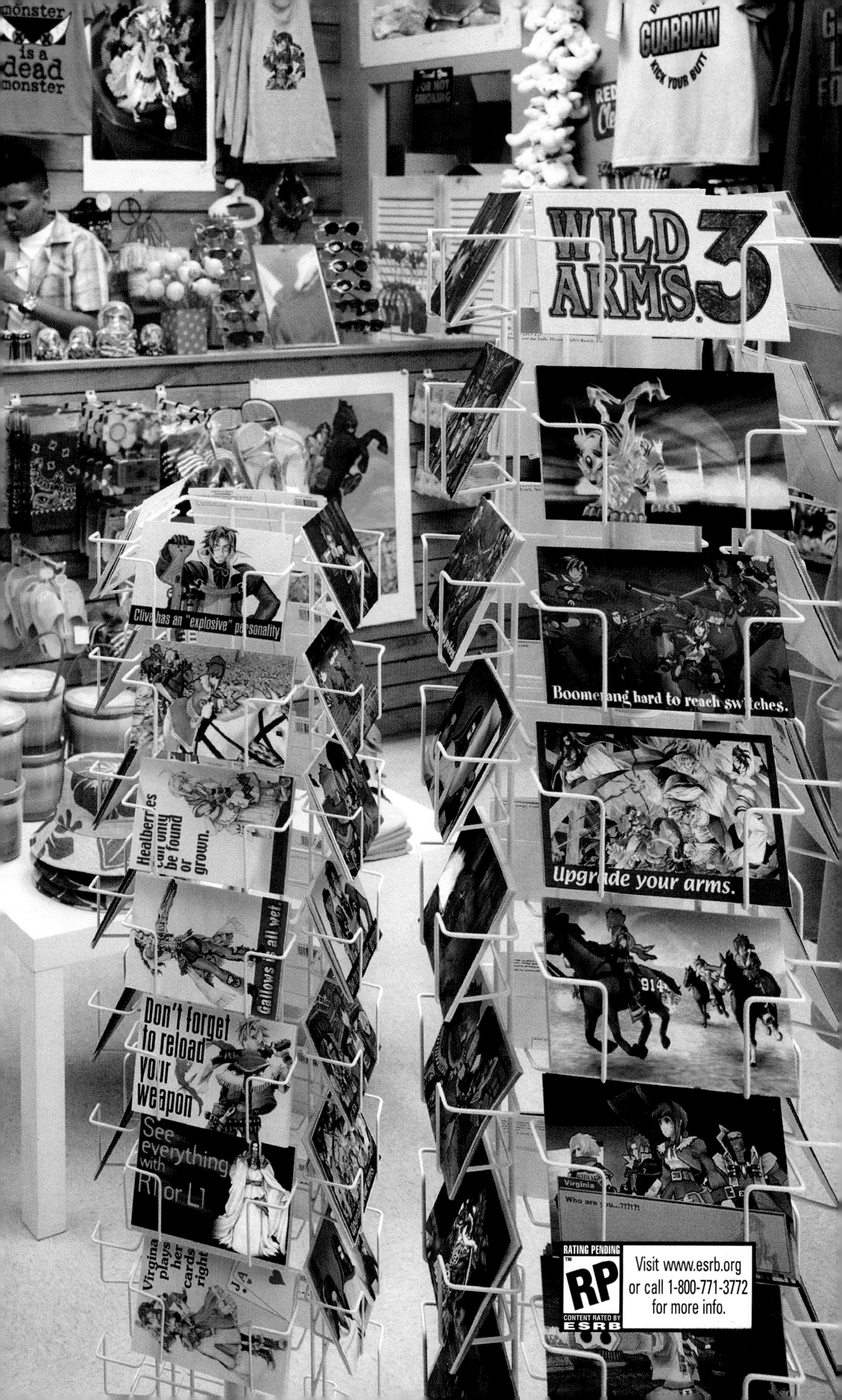
monster
is a
dead
monster
GUARDIAN
KICK YOUR BUTT
WILD ARMS 3
Clive has an "explosive" personality
Boomerang hard to reach switches.
Healberries can only be found or grown.
Upgrade your arms.
Gallows is all wet.
Don't forget to reload your weapon
See everything with R1 or L1
Virginia plays her cards right
Virginia
Who are you...?!?!?!
RATING PENDING
RP
CONTENT RATED BY ESRB
Visit www.esrb.org or call 1-800-771-3772 for more info.

# ULTIMATE SAVINGS!

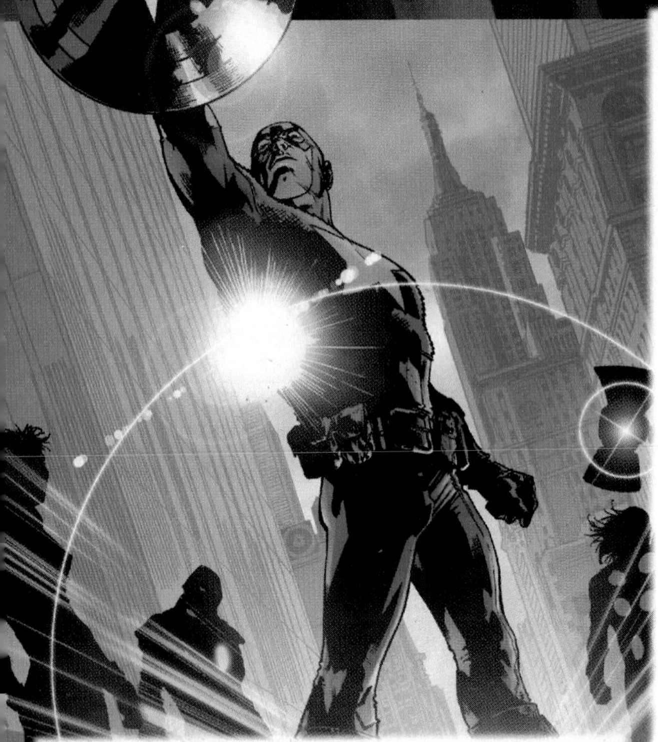

## LIMITED TIME ULTIMATE OFFER

❑ **Yes!** I want both the Ultimates, Ultimate X-Men, and Ultimate Spider-Man for just $56.91!

# A Savings of $24.00!

## Exclusive Subscriber Savings and Services

Your satisfaction guaranteed or your money back on all remaining issues!

**IMPROVED PACKAGING!**

All issues are mailed with cardboard backing in new weather resistant cellophane bags!

## SUBSCRIBE AND SAVE!

**1 Title For $23.97- A savings of $3!**
**2 Titles For $22.97- A savings of $8!**
**3 Or More Titles For $21.97 each- A savings of $15 or more!**

**MARVEL ULTIMATES**

- ❑ ULA — The Ultimates
- ❑ USP — Ultimate Spider-Man
- ❑ UXM — Ultimate X-Men

**X-MEN**

- ❑ CAB — Soldier X (Cable)
- ❑ DDP — Agent X (Deadpool)
- ❑ EXL — Exiles
- ❑ XME — Uncanny X-Men
- ❑ WOL — Wolverine
- ❑ XFO — X-Statix (X-Force)
- ❑ MEN — New X-Men
- ❑ XTR — X-Treme X-Men

**MARVEL KNIGHTS**

- ❑ DDV — Daredevil
- ❑ ELK — Elektra (Mature Readers)
- ❑ PUN — Punisher (Mature Readers)

**MARVEL HEROES**

- ❑ AVE — Avengers
- ❑ BPR — Black Panther
- ❑ CAM — Captain America
- ❑ CMV — Captain Marvel
- ❑ FAN — Fantastic Four
- ❑ INC — Hulk
- ❑ IRM — Iron Man
- ❑ THO — Thor
- ❑ BLT — Thunderbolts
- ❑ CAL — The Call Of Duty NEW!

**SPIDER-MAN**

- ❑ AMZ — Amazing Spider-Man
- ❑ SPI — Peter Parker, Spider-Man
- ❑ TAW — Spider-Man: Tangled Web
- ❑ SPG — Spider-Girl

## Ordering is fast and easy!

❑ **Yes! Sign me up for home delivery of the comics I've checked. I deserve the most in savings, convenience, service, and selection!**

**My satisfaction is guaranteed!**

Check off the subscriptions you want delivered to your home (12 issues each) and return this page or a copy to:

**MARVEL ENTERTAINMENT GROUP, INC.**
P.O. BOX 32 NEWBURGH, NY 12551.

Please provide credit card information or make your check or money order payable to "Marvel Entertainment Group, Inc."

Or order Toll Free at 800-217-9158.

**OFFER GOOD UNTIL 12/31/2002.**
**YES, YOU CAN PHOTOCOPY THIS AD!**

Please print:

NAME OF READER ____________ DATE OF BIRTH (M/D/Y) ____________

STREET ADDRESS ____________ E-MAIL ____________

CITY ____________ STATE ______ ZIP ______

\# of subscriptions ____________ Amount enclosed: $ ____________

Charge my: ❑ VISA ❑ MasterCard

CREDIT CARD # ____________ EXPIRATION DATE ____________

NAME OF CREDIT CARD HOLDER (IF DIFFERENT FROM NAME ABOVE) ____________

SIGNATURE FOR CREDIT CARD ORDERS ____________

Canada, add $10.00 per title (in U.S. funds only, includes GST#R127032852). Foreign, add $12 per title in U.S. funds only. Allow 6 to 10 weeks for delivery of your first issue. 

**H26MD1**